CAMBRIDGE TEXTBOOKS IN LINGUISTICS

General Editors: B. COMRIE, C. J. FILLMORE, R. LASS, R. B. LE PAGE,
J. LYONS, P. H. MATTHEWS, F. R. PALMER, R. POSNER, S. ROMAINE,
N. V. SMITH, J. L. M. TRIM, A. ZWICKY

STATISTICS IN LANGUAGE STUDIES

In this series:

P. H. MATTHEWS *Morphology*
B. COMRIE *Aspect*
R. M. KEMPSON *Semantic Theory*
T. BYNON *Historical Linguistics*
J. ALLWOOD, L.-G. ANDERSSON, Ö. DAHL *Logic in Linguistics*
D. B. FRY *The Physics of Speech*
R. A. HUDSON *Sociolinguistics*
J. K. CHAMBERS and P. TRUDGILL *Dialectology*
A. J. ELLIOT *Child Language*
P. H. MATTHEWS *Syntax*
A. RADFORD *Transformational Syntax*
L. BAUER *English Word-formation*
S. C. LEVINSON *Pragmatics*
G. BROWN and G. YULE *Discourse Analysis*
R. LASS *Phonology*
R. HUDDLESTON *Introduction to the Grammar of English*
B. COMRIE *Tense*
W. KLEIN *Second Language Acquisition*
A. CRUTTENDEN *Intonation*
A. WOODS, P. FLETCHER, A. HUGHES *Statistics in Language Studies*

STATISTICS IN LANGUAGE STUDIES

ANTHONY WOODS
PAUL FLETCHER
ARTHUR HUGHES

UNIVERSITY OF READING

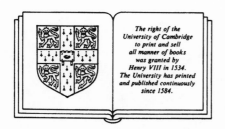

The right of the
University of Cambridge
to print and sell
all manner of books
was granted by
Henry VIII in 1534.
The University has printed
and published continuously
since 1584.

CAMBRIDGE UNIVERSITY PRESS
CAMBRIDGE
LONDON   NEW YORK   NEW ROCHELLE
MELBOURNE   SYDNEY

Published by the Press Syndicate of the University of Cambridge
The Pitt Building, Trumpington Street, Cambridge CB2 1RP
32 East 57th Street, New York, NY 10022, USA
10 Stamford Road, Oakleigh, Melbourne 3166, Australia

First published 1986

British Library cataloguing in publication data

Woods, Anthony
Statistics in language studies. –
(Cambridge textbooks in linguistics)
1. Linguistics – Research – Statistical methods
I. Title   II. Fletcher, Paul   III. Hughes, Arthur,
410'.72   P138.5

Library of Congress cataloguing in publication data

Woods, Anthony.
Statistics in language studies.
(Cambridge textbooks in linguistics)
Bibliography: p.
Includes index.
1. Linguistics – Statistical methods.   I. Fletcher,
Paul.   II. Hughes, Arthur.   III. Title.   IV. Series.
P138.5.w66 1985   519.5   85–24270

ISBN 0 521 25326 8 hard covers
ISBN 0 521 27312 9 paperback

Transferred to digital printing 2003

CONTENTS

Contents

Contents

PREFACE

This book began with initial contacts between linguists (Hughes and Fletcher) and a statistician (Woods) over specific research problems in first and second language learning, and testing. These contacts led to an increasing awareness of the relevance of statistics for other areas in linguistics and applied linguistics, and of the responsibility of those working in such areas to subject their quantitative data to the same kind of statistical scrutiny as other researchers in the social sciences. In time, students in linguistics made increasing use of the Advisory Service provided by the Department of Applied Statistics at Reading. It soon became clear that the dialogue between statistician and student linguist, if it was to be maximally useful, required an awareness of basic statistical concepts on the student's part. The next step, then, was the setting up of a course in statistics for linguistics students (taught by Woods). This is essentially the book of the course, and reflects our joint views on what linguistics students who want to use statistics with their data need to know.

There are two main differences between this and other introductory textbooks in statistics for linguists. First, the portion of the book devoted to probability and statistical inference is considerable. In order to elucidate the sample–population relationship, we consider in some detail basic notions of probability, of statistical modelling, and (using the normal distribution as an example of a statistical model) of the problem of estimating population values from sample estimates. While these chapters (4–8) may on initial reading seem difficult, we strongly advise readers who wish fully to understand what they are doing, when they use the techniques elaborated later in the book, to persevere with them.

The second difference concerns the range of statistical methods we deal with. From the second half of chapter 13 on, a number of multivariate techniques are examined in relation to linguistic data. Multiple regression, cluster analysis, discriminant function analysis, and principal component and factor analysis have been applied in recent years to a range of linguistic problems and the results published. One of the major aims of a textbook directed at students of linguistics is to enable them to evaluate the research literature appropriately. This alone, then, would be sufficient reason for including the multivariate methods. The other reason, of course, is to make the students or researchers aware of such methods so that they can recognise the potential application to their own work, and to supply them with the information necessary to engage in efficient discussion with a statistician.

It is perhaps worth emphasising that no mathematical knowledge other than elementary arithmetic is required to understand the computations which appear in the text. As we have already indicated, grasping the concepts may require effort and some of the symbols used may take a little getting used to. It is largely for this reason that we have supplied exercises: working through these should clarify the concepts and make the symbols more familiar. Extensive mathematical expertise is not required.

We have had advice and data from colleagues and students too numerous to list, and we are grateful to all of them. We owe a special debt of thanks to Lynne Rogers, who has typed innumerable drafts with care and considerable patience.

ANTHONY WOODS

PAUL FLETCHER

ARTHUR HUGHES

July 1985
University of Reading

I

Why do linguists need statistics?

Linguists may wonder why they need statistics. The dominant theoretical framework in the field, that of generative grammar, has as its primary data-source judgements about the well-formedness of sentences. These judgements usually come from linguists themselves, are either–or decisions, and relate to the language ability of an ideal native speaker in a homogeneous speech community. The data simply do not call for, or lend themselves to, the assignment of numerical values which need to be summarised or from which inferences may be drawn. There appears to be no place here for statistics.

Generative grammar, however, despite its great contribution to linguistic knowledge over the past 25 years, is not the sole topic of linguistic study. There are other areas of the subject where the observed data positively demand statistical treatment. In this book we will scrutinise studies from a number of these areas and show, we hope, the necessity for statistics in each. In this brief introduction we will use a few of these studies to illustrate the major issues with which we shall be faced.

As we will demonstrate throughout the book, statistics allows us to summarise complex numerical data and then, if desired, to draw inferences from them. Indeed, a distinction is sometimes made between descriptive statistics on the one hand and inferential statistics on the other. The need to summarise and infer comes from the fact that there is *variation* in the numerical values associated with the data (i.e. the values over a set of measurements are not identical). If there were no variation, there would be no need for statistics.

Let us imagine that a phonetician, interested in the way that voiced–voiceless distinctions are maintained by speakers of English, begins by taking measurements of voice onset times (VOT), i.e. the time between the release of the stop and the onset of voicing, in initial stops. The first set of data consists of ten repetitions from each of 20 speakers of ten /p/-initial words. Now if there were no difference in VOT time, either between words or between speakers, there would be no need here for statistics; the single VOT value would simply be recorded. In fact, of course, very few, if any, of the values will be identical. The group of speakers may produce VOT values that are all distinct on, for example, their first pronunciation of a particular word. Alternatively, the VOT values of an individual speaker may be different from word to word or, indeed, between repetitions of the same word. Thus the phonetician could have as many as 2,000 different values. The first contribution of statistics will be to provide the means of summarising the results in a meaningful and readily understandable way. One common approach is to provide a single 'typical' value to represent all of the VOT times, together with a measure of the way in which the VOT times vary around this value (the mean and the standard deviation – see chapter 3). In this way, a large number of values is reduced to just two.

We shall return to the phonetician's data, but let us now look at another example. In this case a psycholinguist is interested in the nature of aptitude for learning foreign languages. As part of this study 100 subjects are given a language aptitude test and later, after a period of language instruction, an achievement test in that language. One of the things the psycholinguist will wish to know is the form of the relationship between scores on the aptitude test and scores on the achievement test. Looking at the two sets of scores may give some clues: someone who scored exceptionally high on the aptitude test, for instance, may also have done extremely well on the achievement test. But the psycholinguist is not going to be able to assimilate all the information conveyed by the 200 scores simply by looking at each pair of scores separately. Although the kind of summary measures used by the phonetician will be useful, they will not tell the psycholinguist directly about the relationship between the two sets of scores. However, there is a straightforward statistical technique available which will allow the strength of the relationship to be represented in a single value (the correlation – see chapter 10). Once again, statistics serves the purpose of reducing complex data to manageable proportions.

The two examples given have concerned data summary, the reduction of complex data. In both cases they have concerned the performance of a sample of subjects. Of course, the ultimate interest of linguistic investigators is not in the performance only of **samples**. They usually wish to generalise to the performance of larger groups. The phonetician with the sample of 20 speakers may wish to be able to say something about *all* speakers of a particular accentual variety of English, or indeed about speakers of English in general. Similarly, he or she is interested in *all*

/p/-initial words, not just those in the sample. Here again statistics can help. There are techniques which allow investigators to assess how closely the 'typical' scores offered in a sample of a particular size are likely to approximate to those of the group of whom they wish to make the generalisation (chapter 7), provided the sample meets certain conditions (see §§4.4 and 5.5).

Let us take the example of the phonetician further. At the same time as the /p/-initial data were being collected, the ten subjects were also asked to pronounce 20 /b/-initial words. Again, the phonetician could reduce these data to two summary measures: the average VOT time for the group and the standard deviation. Let us consider for the moment only one of these – the **average**, or typical value. The phonetician would then observe that there is a difference between the typical VOT value for /p/-initial words and that for /b/-initial words. The typical VOT value for /p/-initial words would be larger. The question then arises as to whether the difference between the two values is likely to be one which represents a real difference in VOT times in the larger group for which a generalisation will be made, or whether it is one that has come about by chance. (If you think about it, if the measurement is precise there is almost certain to be *some* difference in the sample values.) There are statistical techniques which allow the phonetician to give the probability that the sample difference is indeed the manifestation of a 'real' difference in the larger group. In the example we have given (VOT times), the difference is in fact quite well established in the phonetic literature (see e.g. Fry 1979: 135–7), but it should be clear that there are potentially many claims of a similar nature which would be open to – and would demand – similar treatment.

These two examples hint at the kind of contribution statistics can and should make to linguistic studies, in summarising data, and in making inferences from them. The range of studies for which statistics is applicable is vast – in applied linguistics, language acquisition, language variation and linguistics proper. Rather than survey each of these fields briefly at this point, let us look at one acquisition study in detail, to try to achieve a better understanding of the problems faced by the investigator and the statistical issues involved. What are the problems which investigators want to solve, what measures of linguistic behaviour do they adopt, what is the appropriate statistical treatment for these measures, and how reliable are their results?

We address these issues by returning to voice onset time, now with reference to language acquisition. What precisely are the stages children go through in acquiring, in production, the distinction between voiced and voiceless initial stops in English? (This discussion draws heavily on Macken & Barton 1980a; for similar studies concerning the acquisition of voicing contrasts in other languages the reader is referred to Macken & Barton 1980b for Spanish, Allen 1985 for French, and Viana 1985 for Portuguese.) The inquiry begins from the observation that transcriptions of children's early pronunciations of stops often show no /p/–/b/ distinctions; generally both /p/-targets (adult words beginning with /p/) and /b/-targets (adult words beginning with /b/) are pronounced with initial [b], or at least this is how auditory impressionistic transcriptions represent them. Is it possible, though, that young children are making distinctions which adult transcribers are unable to hear? VOT is established as a crucial perceptual cue to the voiced–voiceless distinction for initial stops; for English there is a 'short-lag' VOT range for voiced stops (from 0 to +30 ms for labials and apicals, 0 to +40 ms for velars) and a 'long-lag' range for voiceless stops (+60 to +100 ms). English speakers perceive stops with a VOT of less than +30 ms (for labials and apicals, +50 ms for velars) as voiced; any value above these figures tends to lead to the perception of the item in question as voiceless. Children's productions will tend to be assigned by adult transcribers to the phonemic categories defined by short- and long-lag VOT. So if at some stage of development children are making a consistent contrast using VOT, but *within* an adult phonemic category, it is quite possible that adult transcribers, because of their perceptual habits, will miss it. How is this possibility investigated? It should be apparent that such a study involves a number of issues for those carrying it out.

(a) We require a group of children, of an appropriate age, to generate the data. For a developmental study like this we have to decide whether the data will be collected longitudinally (from the same children at successive times separated by a suitable interval) or cross-sectionally (from different groups of children, where each group is of a particular age, and the different groups span the age-range that is of interest for us). Longitudinal data have the disadvantage that they take as long to collect as the child takes to develop, whereas cross-sectional data can be gathered within a brief time span. With longitudinal data, however, we can be sure that we are charting the course of growth within individuals and make reliable comparison between time A and time B. With cross-sectional comparisons this is not so clear. Once we have decided on the kind of data we want, decisions as to the *size* of the sample and the selection of its elements have to be addressed. It is on the decisions made here that our ability to generalise the results of a study will depend. The Macken & Barton study was a longitudinal one, using four children who 'were monolingual speakers of English with no siblings of school age ... were producing at least some initial stop words ... showed evidence of normal language development ... and appeared to be co-operative' (1980a: 42–3). In addition, both parents of each child were native speakers of English, and all the children had normal learning. The reasons for aspects of this subject description are transparent; general issues relating to sample size and structure are discussed below (§§4.4 and 7.5).

(b)   A second issue which is common in linguistic studies is the size of the data sample from each individual. The number of subjects in the study we are considering is four, but the number of tokens of /p t k/- and /b d g/-initial adult targets is potentially very large. (An immediate question that might be asked is whether it is better to have relatively few subjects, with relatively many instances of the behaviour in which we are interested from each subject, or many subjects and fewer tokens – see §7.5 for some discussion.) In the VOT acquisition study the investigators also had to decide on the related issue of frequency of sampling and the number of tokens within each of the six categories of initial stop target. As it happens, they chose a fortnightly sampling interval and the number of tokens in a session ranged from a low of 25 to a high of 214. (The goal was to obtain at least 15 tokens for each stop consonant, but this was not always achieved in the early sessions.)

(c)   Once the data are collected and the measurements made on each token from each individual for each session, the information provided needs to be presented in an acceptable and comprehensible form. Macken & Barton restrict themselves, for the instrumental measurements they make, to 15 tokens of each stop type per session. It may well be that each of the 15 tokens within a category has a different VOT value, and for evaluation we therefore need summary values and/or graphic displays of the data. Macken & Barton use both tabular, numerical summaries and graphic representations (see chapters 2 and 3 for a general discussion of methods for data summaries).

(d)   The descriptive summaries of the child VOT data suggest some interesting conclusions concerning one stage of the development of initial stop contrasts in some children. Recall that it is generally held that the perceptual boundary between voiced and voiceless labial or alveolar stops is +30 ms. At an early point in the development of alveolars by one subject, Tessa, the average value for /d/-initial targets is +2.4 ms while the average for /t/-initial targets is +20.50. Both of these values are *within* the adult voiced category, and so the adult is likely to perceive them as voiced.

5

But the values are rather different. Is this observed difference between the two averages a *significant* difference, statistically speaking? Or, restating the question in the terms of the investigation, is the child making a consistent distinction in VOT for /d/-initial and /t/-initial targets, but one which, because it is inside an adult phonemic category, is unlikely to be perceived? The particular statistical test that is relevant to this issue is dealt with in chapter 10, but chapters 3–8 provide a crucial preparation for understanding it.

(e)   We have referred to *one* potentially significant difference for *one* child. As investigators we are usually interested in how far we are justified, on the basis of the sample data we have analysed, in extending our findings to a larger group of subjects than actually took part in our study. The answer to this question depends in large measure on how we handled the issues raised in (b) and (d) above, and is discussed again in chapter 4.

Much of the discussion so far has centred on phonetics – not because we believe that is the only linguistic area in which these issues arise, but because VOT is a readily comprehensible measure and studies employing it lend themselves to a straightforward illustration of concerns that are common to many areas of language study. We return to them continually in the pages that follow with reference to a wide variety of studies.

While the use made of the information in the rest of the book will reflect the reader's own purposes and requirements, we envisage that there will be two major reasons for using the book.

First, readers will want to evaluate literature which employs statistical techniques. The conclusions papers reach are of dubious worth if the measurements are suspect, if the statistical technique is inappropriate, or if the assumptions of the technique employed are not met. By discussing a number of techniques and the assumptions they make, the book will assist critical evaluation of the literature.

Second, many readers will be interested in planning their own research. The range of techniques introduced by the book will assist this aim, partly by way of examples from other people's work in similar areas. We should emphasise that for research planning the book will not solve all problems. In particular, it does not address in detail measurement (in the sense of what and how to measure in a particular field), nor, directly, experimental design; but it should go some of the way to assisting readers to select an appropriate statistical framework, and will certainly enable problems to be discussed in an informed way with a statistician.

Each chapter in the book contains some exemplification in a relevant field of the techniques it explains. The chapter is then followed by extensive exercises which must be worked through, to accustom the reader to the applications of the techniques, and their empirical implications. While the book is obviously not intended to be read through from cover to cover, since different readers will be interested in different techniques, we recommend that *all* users of the book read chapters 2–8 inclusive, since these are central to understanding. It is here that summary measures, probability and inference from samples to populations are dealt with. Many readers will find chapters 4–8 difficult. This is not because they require special knowledge or skills for their understanding. They do not, for example, contain any mathematics beyond simple algebra and the use of a common notation which is explained in earlier chapters. However, they do contain arguments which introduce and explain the logic and philosophy of statistical inference. It is possible to use in a superficial, 'cookbook' fashion the techniques described in later chapters without understanding the material in chapters 4–8, but a true grasp of the meaning and limitations of those techniques will not then be possible.

The second part of the book – from chapter 9 onwards – deals with a variety of techniques, details of which can be found in the contents list at the beginning of the book.

2
Tables and graphs

When a linguistic study is carried out the investigator will be faced with the prospect of understanding, and then explaining to others, the meaning of the data which have been collected. An essential first step in this process is to look for ways of summarising the results which bring out their most obvious features. Indeed if this is done imaginatively and the trends in the data are clear enough, there may be no need for sophisticated analysis. In this chapter we describe the types of table and diagram most commonly employed for data summary.

Let us begin by looking at typical examples of the kind of data which might be collected in language studies. We will consider how, by means of tables, diagrams and a few simple calculations, the data may be summarised so that their important features can be displayed concisely. The procedure is analogous to writing a précis of an article or essay and has similar attractions and drawbacks. The aim is to reduce detail to a minimum while retaining sufficient information to communicate the essential characteristics of the original. Remember always that the use of data ought to enrich and elucidate the linguistic argument, and this can often be done quite well by means of a simple table or diagram.

2.1 Categorical data

It quite commonly arises that we wish to classify a group of people or responses or linguistic elements, putting each unit into one of a set of mutually exclusive classes. The data can then be summarised by giving the **frequency** with which each class was observed. Such data are often called **categorical** since each element or individual of the group being studied can be classified as belonging to one or a (usually small) number of different categories. For example, in table 2.1(a) we have presented the kind of data one might expect on taking a random sample of 364 males with diagnosed speech and language difficulties in the USA (see e.g. Healey *et al.* 1981). We have put these subjects into four different categories of impairment.

8

Table 2.1

(a) *Frequencies of disorders in a sample of 364 language-impaired males in USA*

Stuttering	Phonological disability	Specific language disorder	Impaired hearing	Total
57	209	47	51	364

(b) *Relative frequencies of disorders in a sample of 364 language-impaired males in USA*

Stuttering	Phonological disability	Specific language disorder	Impaired hearing	Total
0.157	0.574	0.129	0.140	1.000

(c) *Frequencies of disorders in a sample of 364 language-impaired males in USA (figures in brackets give relative frequencies as percentages)*

Stuttering	Phonological disability	Specific language disorder	Impaired hearing	Total
57 (16)	209 (57)	47 (13)	51 (14)	364 (100)

Table 2.1(a) itself already comprises a neat and intelligible summary of the data, displaying the number of times that each category was observed out of 364 instances. This number is usually called the **frequency** or **observed frequency** of the category. However, it may be more revealing to display the **proportions** of subjects falling into the different classes, and these can be calculated simply by dividing each frequency by the total frequency, 364. The proportions or **relative frequencies** obtained in this way are displayed in table 2.1(b). Note that no more than three figures are given, though most pocket calculators will give eight or ten. This is deliberate. Very high accuracy is rarely required in such results, and the ease of assimilation of a table decreases rapidly with the number of figures used for each value. Do remember, however, that when you truncate a number you may have to alter the last figure which you wish to include. For example, written to three decimal places, 0.64371 becomes 0.644, while 0.31716 would be 0.317. The rule should be obvious.

A table of relative frequencies is not really informative (and can be downright misleading) unless we are given the total number of observations on which it is based. It should be obvious that the claim that 50% of native English speakers display a certain linguistic behaviour is better supported by the behaviour in question being observed in 500 of 1,000 subjects than in just two of a total of four. (This point is discussed in detail in chapter 9.) It is best to give both frequencies and relative frequencies, as in table 2.1(c). Note here that the relative frequencies have been rounded

9

Tables and graphs

Table 2.2

(a) *Frequencies of disorders in a sample of 560 language-impaired individuals in the USA, cross-classified by sex (frequencies relative to row totals are given in brackets as percentages)*

	Stuttering	Phonological disability	Specific language disorder	Impaired hearing	Total
Male	57 (16)	209 (57)	47 (13)	51 (14)	364 (100)
Female	27 (14)	118 (60)	31 (16)	20 (10)	196 (100)
Total	84 (15)	327 (58)	78 (14)	71 (13)	560 (100)

(b) *Frequencies of disorders in a sample of 560 language-impaired individuals in the USA, cross-classified by sex (frequencies relative to column totals are given in brackets as percentages)*

	Stuttering	Phonological disability	Specific language disorder	Impaired hearing	Total
Male	57 (68)	209 (64)	47 (60)	51 (72)	364 (65)
Female	27 (32)	118 (36)	31 (40)	20 (38)	196 (35)
Total	84 (100)	327 (100)	78 (100)	71 (100)	560 (100)

(c) *Frequencies of disorders in a sample of 560 language-impaired individuals in the USA, cross-classified by sex (frequencies relative to the total sample size are given in brackets as percentages)*

	Stuttering	Phonological disability	Specific language disorder	Impaired hearing	Total
Male	57 (10)	209 (37)	47 (8)	51 (9)	364 (65)
Female	27 (5)	118 (21)	31 (6)	20 (4)	196 (35)
Total	84 (15)	327 (58)	78 (14)	71 (13)	560 (100)

further to only two figures and quoted as percentages (to change any decimal fraction to a percentage it is necessary only to move the decimal point two places to the right).

It often happens that we wish to compare the way in which the frequencies of the categories are distributed over two groups. We can present this by means of **two-way** tables as in table 2.2 where the sample has been extended to include 196 language-impaired females from the same background as the males in table 2.1. In table 2.2(a), the first row is exactly as table 2.1(c); the second row displays the relative frequencies of females *across* disorder categories, and the third row displays relative frequencies for the two groups combined. Table 2.2(b), however, displays the relative frequency of males to females *within* categories. So, for example, of the total number of stutterers (84), 68% are male while 32% are female. In table 2.2(c) the frequencies in parenthesis in each cell are relative to the total number of individuals (560), and we can see, for instance,

Table 2.3

(a) *Frequencies of disorders in a sample of 560 language-impaired individuals in the USA (figures in brackets are percentages)*

Stuttering	Phonological disability	Specific language disorder	Impaired hearing	Total
84 (15)	327 (58)	78 (14)	71 (13)	560 (100)

(b) *Frequencies of disorders in a sample of 560 language-impaired individuals in the USA, cross-classified by sex (percentages in brackets give relative frequencies of sexes within disorders)*

	Stuttering	Phonological disability	Specific language disorder	Impaired hearing	Total
Male	57 (68)	209 (64)	47 (60)	51 (72)	364 (65)
Female	27 (32)	118 (36)	31 (40)	20 (28)	196 (35)

(c) *Frequencies of disorders in a sample of 560 language-impaired individuals in the USA, cross-classified by sex (percentages in brackets give relative frequencies of disorders within sex)*

	Stuttering	Phonological disability	Specific language disorder	Impaired hearing
Male	57 (10)	209 (37)	47 (8)	51 (9)
Female	27 (5)	118 (21)	31 (6)	20 (4)
Total	84 (15)	327 (58)	78 (14)	71 (13)

that the proportion of the total who are male *and* hearing-impaired is approximately 9% (51/560).

These tables have been constructed in a form that would be suitable if only one of them were to be presented. The choice would of course depend on the features of the data which we wanted to discuss. If, on the other hand, more than one of the tables were required it would be neither necessary nor desirable to repeat all the total frequencies in each table. It would be preferable to present a sequence of simpler, less cluttered tables as in table 2.3.

The tables we have introduced so far can be used as a basis for constructing graphs or diagrams to represent the data. Such diagrams will frequently bring out in a striking way the main features of the data. Consider figure 2.1(a) which is based on table 2.1. This type of graph is often called a **bar chart** and allows an 'at a glance' comparison of the frequencies of the classes. Figure 2.1(b) is the same chart constructed from the relative frequencies. Note that its appearance is identical to figure 2.1(a); the only alteration required is a change of the scale of the vertical axis. Since the categories have no inherent ordering, we have chosen to present them in the chart in decreasing order of frequency, but this is a matter of taste.

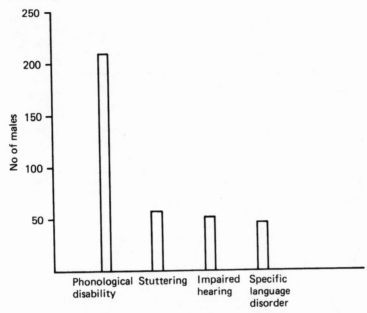

Figure 2.1(a). Bar chart of frequencies of disorders in a sample of 364 language-impaired males in the USA (based on table 2.1).

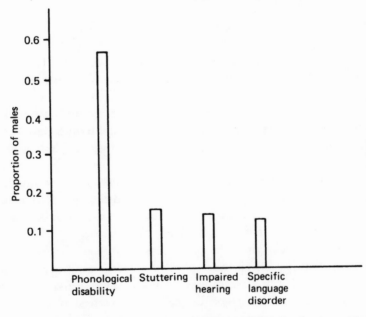

Figure 2.1(b). Bar chart of relative frequencies of disorders in sample of 364 language-impaired males (based on table 2.1).

Figure 2.2 shows how similar diagrams can be used to display the data of table 2.2. Note that in constructing figure 2.2 we have used the proportions relative to the total frequency: that is, we have divided the original frequencies by 560. Whether or not this is the appropriate procedure will depend on the point you wish to make and on how the data were collected.

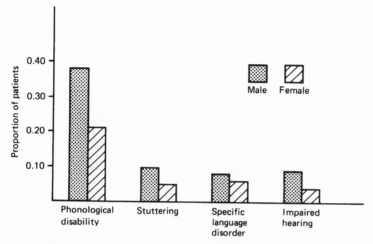

Figure 2.2. Relative frequencies of disorders in a sample of 560 language-impaired individuals, further classified by sex (based on table 2.2c).

If the whole sample were collected without previously dividing the subjects into male and female, figure 2.2 based on table 2.2(c) would correctly give the proportions of a sample of individual patients who fall into different categories, determined both by their sex and by the type of defect they suffer. This would not be true if, say, males and females were recorded on different registers which were sampled separately, since the numbers of each sex in the sample would not then necessarily bear any relation to their relative numbers overall. Figure 2.3 based on table 2.2(a), showing the proportion of males who suffer a particular defect and, separately, the proportion of females suffering the same defect, would be correct. This would *always* be the more appropriate diagram for comparing the distribution of various defects *within* the different sexes.

2.2 Numerical data

The variables considered in the previous section were all classes or categories, and the numbers we depicted arose by counting how often a particular category occurred. It often happens that the variable we are observing takes numerical values, for example, the number of letters in

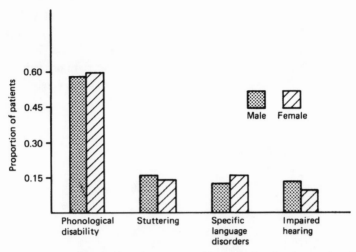

Figure 2.3. Relative frequencies of language disorders in samples of language-impaired individuals, within sexes (based on table 2.3a).

a word or morphemes in an utterance, a student's score in a vocabulary test, or the length of time between the release of a stop and the onset of voicing (VOT), and so on.

If the number of different observed values of the variable is small, then we can present it using the display methods of the previous section. In table 2.4(a) are given the lengths, in morphemes, of 100 utterances observed when an adult was speaking to a child aged 3 years. These have been converted into a **frequency table** in table 2.4(b) and the corresponding bar chart can be seen in figure 2.4. A major difference between this data and the categorical data of the previous section is that the data have a natural order and spacing. All the values between the minimum and maximum actually observed are possible and provision must be made for all

Table 2.4(a). *Lengths of 100 utterances (in morphemes) of an adult addressing a child aged 3 years*

2	7	10	5	6	5	7	9	7	7
11	3	3	7	10	4	3	2	2	9
2	6	2	2	3	7	4	2	3	8
10	2	5	8	4	12	8	4	2	3
7	5	10	3	9	7	4	10	8	4
9	17	5	14	2	6	4	12	3	8
6	6	6	15	10	8	3	6	12	9
10	8	7	2	7	7	10	5	3	7
4	5	10	4	2	3	8	10	7	9
3	2	14	9	5	5	6	9	6	4

Table 2.4(b). *Frequency table of the lengths of 100 utterances (in morphemes) of an adult addressing a child aged 3 years*

Length of utterance	Number of utterances
1	0
2	13
3	12
4	10
5	9
6	9
7	13
8	8
9	8
10	10
11	1
12	3
13	0
14	2
15	1
16	0
17	1

of them on the bar chart, including any which do not actually appear in the data set.

If the number of different values appearing in a data set is large, there will be some difficulty in fitting them all onto a bar chart without crushing them up and reducing the clarity of the diagram. Besides, unless the number of observations is very large, many possible values will not appear

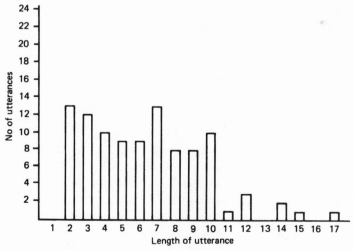

Figure 2.4. Bar chart for data in table 2.4(b). Lengths of 100 utterances (in morphemes) of an adult addressing a child aged 3 years.

Table 2.5(a). *Scores of 108 students in the June 1980 Cambridge Proficiency Examination*

194	184	135	161	186	198	150	240	147	174	197
176	183	117	161	185	186	208	200	157	212	191
174	192	145	162	186	148	241	184	201	208	177
135	229	179	208	209	203	145	201	204	192	179
224	209	179	223	192	221	239	238	199	174	145
226	214	211	215	176	238	184	221	198	196	184
192	164	209	142	196	160	165	166	224	229	184
171	163	207	179	197	120	255	150	233	188	175
225	156	211	190	204	222	219	186	160	189	
218	149	160	188	224	140	220	149	170	197	

Table 2.5(b). *Frequency table of the scores of 108 students in the 1980 Cambridge Proficiency Examination*

Class interval	Tally	Frequency	Relative frequency	Cumulative frequency	Relative cumulative frequency
110–124	||	2	0.02	2	0.02
125–139	||	2	0.02	4	0.04
140–154	卌 卌 |	11	0.10	15	0.14
155–169	卌 卌 ||	12	0.11	27	0.25
170–184	卌 卌 卌 ||||	19	0.18	46	0.43
185–199	卌 卌 卌 卌 |||	23	0.21	69	0.64
200–214	卌 卌 卌 ||	17	0.16	86	0.80
215–229	卌 卌 卌	15	0.14	101	0.94
230–244	卌 |	6	0.06	107	0.99
245–259	|	1	0.01	108	1.00
		108			

at all, causing frequent gaps in the chart, while other values will appear rather infrequently in the data. Table 2.5(a) lists the total score of each of 108 students taking the Cambridge Proficiency Examination (CPE) of June 1980 at a European centre. The marks range from a low of 117 to a maximum of 255 giving a **range** of 255 − 117 = 138. The most frequent score, 184, appears only five times and clearly it would be inappropriate to attempt to construct a bar chart using the individual scores.

The first step in summarising this data is to group the scores into around ten classes (between eight and 15 is usually convenient and practical). The first column of table 2.5(b) shows the classes decided on. The first will contain all those marks in the interval 110–124, the second those lying in the range 125–139, and so on.

Now we count the number of scores belonging to each class. The most efficient, and accurate, method of doing so is to work through the list of scores, crossing out each one in turn and noting it by a **tally mark** opposite the corresponding **class interval**. Tallies are usually counted in blocks of five, the fifth tally stroke being made diagonally to complete a block, as in column 2 of the table. The number of tally marks is noted for each class in column 3. These frequencies are then used to construct what is referred to as a **histogram** of the data (figure 2.5). No gaps are

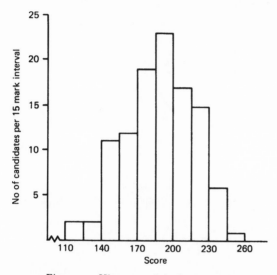

Figure 2.5. Histogram of the frequency data in table 2.5(b).

left between the rectangles, it being assumed by convention that each class will contain all those scores greater than, or equal to, the lower bound of the interval but less than the value of the lower bound of the next interval. So, for example, a score of 125 will go into the tally for the class 125–139, as will a score of 139. *Provided the class intervals are equal*, the height of each rectangle corresponds to the frequency of each class. As in the case of the bar chart, relative frequencies may be used to construct the histogram, this entailing only a change of scale on the vertical axis. Great care has to be taken not to draw a misleading diagram when the class intervals are not all of the same size – a good reason for choosing them to be equal. However, in unusual cases it may *not* be appropriate to have equal width intervals, or one may wish to draw a histogram based on data already grouped into classes of unequal width (see exercise 2.4 and figure 5.2).

The fifth column of table 2.5(b) contains the **cumulative frequencies** for the scores of the 108 students. These cumulative frequencies can be interpreted as follows: two students scored less than 125 marks, 27 scored less than 170 marks and so on. The relative cumulative frequencies of column 6, obtained by dividing each cumulative frequency in column 5 by the total frequency, 108, are usually more convenient, being easily translated into statements such as 25% of the students scored less than 170 marks, while 20% scored at least 215 marks, and so on.

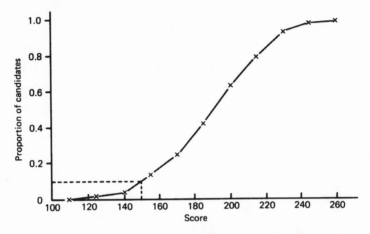

Figure 2.6. Relative cumulative frequency curve for data in table 2.5(b).

We can also make use of this table to answer questions such as 'What is the mark that cuts off the lowest (or highest) scoring 10% of students from the remainder?' Probably the easiest way to do this is via the **relative cumulative frequency curve** of figure 2.6. To draw this curve we plot each relative cumulative frequency against the value at the beginning of the *next* class interval, i.e. plot 0.02 vertically above 125, 0.43 vertically above 185, and so on. Then join up the points with a series of short, *straight* lines connecting successive points. If we now find the position on the vertical axis corresponding to 10% (0.1), draw a horizontal line till it reaches the curve and then drops vertically onto the X-axis, the corresponding score, 151, is an *estimate* (see chapter 7) of the score which 10% of students fail to reach. This score is called the **tenth percentile score**. Any other percentile can be obtained in the same way.

Certain percentiles have a historical importance and special names. The 25th and 75th percentiles are known respectively as the **first quartile** and the **third quartile** (being one-quarter and three-quarters of the way up through the scores) while the 50th percentile, 'halfway' through the data, is called the **median score**. These values are discussed further in the next chapter. In this example, the median is about 190.

2.3 Multi-way tables

It is not uncommon for each observation in a linguistic study to be cross-classified by several factors. Until now we have looked only at one-way classification (e.g. table 2.1) and two-way classification (e.g.

Table 2.6. *44 Indian subjects cross-classified by sex, age and class*

					Sex				
	Male					Female			
	Class					Class			
Age	LM	UM	U	Total	Age	LM	UM	U	Total
16–30	4	4	2	10	16–30	4	4	2	10
31–45	2	2	2	6	31–45	2	2	2	6
Over 45	4	4	4	12	Over 45	—	—	—	—
Total	10	10	8	28	Total	6	6	4	16

table 2.2 – in this latter table the two classifying factors are sex on the one hand and type of language disorder on the other). When subjects, or any other kind of experimental units, are classified in several different ways it is still possible, and helpful, to tabulate the data.

Khan (forthcoming) carried out a study of a number of phonological variables in the spoken English of 44 subjects in Aligarh city in North India. The subjects were classified by sex, age and social class. There were three age groups (16–30, 31–45, over 45) and three social classes (LM – Lower middle, UM – Upper middle, and U – Upper). Table 2.6, an example of a **three-way** table, shows the distribution of the sample of subjects over these categories.

Khan studied several phonological variables relevant to Indian English, including subjects' pronunciation of /d/. The subjects' speech was recorded in four different situations and Khan recognised three different variants of /d/ in her subjects' speech: d-1, an alveolar variant very similar to English pronunciation of /d/; d-2, a post-alveolar variant of /d/; and d-3, a retroflex variant which is perceived as corresponding to a 'heavy Indian accent'. This type of study produces rather complex data since there were 12 scores for each subject: a score for each of the three variants in each of the four situations. One way to deal with this (others are sug-

Table 2.7. *Phonological indices for /d/ of 44 Indian speakers of English*

		Sex						
	Male				Female			
		Class					Class	
Age	LM	UM	U	Age		LM	UM	U
16–30	47.8	50.0	45.9	16–30		56.9	54.8	57.1
	49.4	48.4	51.6			43.1	48.7	52.8
	48.5	49.3				53.3	47.2	
	48.9	52.0				46.7	44.8	
31–45	57.8	50.9	66.7	31–45		51.2	46.5	49.4
	59.4	57.8	51.6			62.1	47.9	43.3
Over 45	51.6	56.4	58.6	Over 45			No data	
	44.0	61.3	61.3					
	59.6	57.1	59.4					
	52.1	51.6	64.7					

Table 2.8. *Average phonological index for /d/ of 44 Indian speakers of English cross-classified by sex and social class*

		Sex	
Class	Male	Female	Both sexes
Lower middle	51.9 (10)	52.2 (6)	52.0 (16)
Upper middle	53.5 (10)	48.3 (6)	51.6 (16)
Upper	57.5 (8)	50.7 (4)	55.2 (12)
All classes	54.1 (28)	50.4 (16)	52.7 (44)

Note: The figures in brackets give the number of subjects whose scores contributed to the corresponding average score.

gested in chapters 14 and 15) is to convert the three frequencies into a single score, which in this case would be an index of how 'Indian-like', on average, a subject's pronunciations of /d/ are. A method suggested by Labov (1966) is used to produce the data presented in table 2.7 (details of the method, which need not concern us here, are to be found in §15.1). Table 2.8 gives the average phonological indices for each sex by class combination.

2.4 Special cases

Although it will usually be possible to display data using one of the basic procedures described above, you should remain always alive to the possibility that rather special situations may arise where you may need to modify or extend one of those methods. You may feel that unusual types of data require a rather special form of presentation. Remember always that the major purpose of the table or graph is to communicate the data more easily without distorting its general import.

Hughes (1979) tape-recorded all the English spoken to and by an adult Spanish learner of English over a period of six months from the time that she began to learn the language solely through conversation with the investigator. Hughes studied the frequency and accuracy with which the learner produced a number of features of English, one of which was the possessor–possessed ordering in structures like *Marta's book*, which is different from that of its equivalent in Spanish, *el libro de Marta*. The learner produced both sequences with English order, like *Marta book*, *Marta's book*, and sequences which seemed to reflect possessor–possessed order in Spanish like *book Marta*. The frequency of such structures during the first 45 hours of learning, and their accuracy, is displayed in figure 2.7, reproduced from the original. The figure contains information about both *spontaneous phrases*, initiated by the learner, and *imitations*. How was it constructed? First, the number of relevant items per hour is indicated by the vertical scale at the right and represented by empty bars (imitations) and solid bars (spontaneous phrases). Second, the percentage of possessor–possessed noun phrases correct, over time, is read from the vertical scale at the left of the graph and represented by a continuous line (spontaneous phrases) and a dotted line (imitations – they were all correct in this example). It is clear that the learner is successful with imitations from the beginning, but much slower in achieving the accurate order in her spontaneous speech. It should be clear from earlier examples how the bars representing frequency are constructed. But how was accuracy defined and represented on this graph?

Hughes first scored all attempts, in order of occurrence, as correct (O) or incorrect (X) in terms of the order of the two elements (imitations and non-imitations being scored separately).

Response no.	1	2	3	4	5	6	7	8	9	10	11	12
	X	X	X	X	X	X	X	O	O	O	X	O

In order not to lose the benefit of the completeness of the record, the data were treated as a series of **overlapping** samples. Percentages of successful attempts at possessor–possessed noun phrases in every set of ten successive examples were calculated. From examples 1–12 the following percentages are derived:

$$\text{Correct in responses} \quad \begin{aligned} 1\text{--}10 &= 30\% \\ 2\text{--}11 &= 30\% \\ 3\text{--}12 &= 40\% \end{aligned}$$

Each percentage was then assigned to the mid-point of the series of responses to which they referred. Thus 30% was considered as the level of accuracy in the period between responses numbered 5 and 6, still 30% in the period between responses 6 and 7, and so on. The average level of accuracy for each hour was then calculated (this kind of average is usually called a **moving average**, since the sample on which it is based 'moves' through time), and this is what is shown in figure 2.7, the points

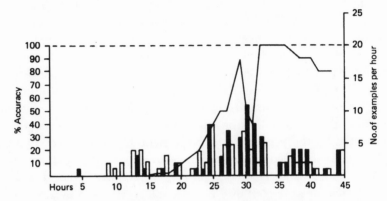

Figure 2.7. Possessor–possessed noun phrases in the speech of a Spanish learner of English (Hughes 1979).

joined by an unbroken line for non-imitations, and by a broken line for imitations. These lines give an indication of the way in which the ability of the speaker to express the possessor–possessed ordering correctly was progressing through time.

We have certainly not exhausted the possibilities for tabular and graphical presentation of data in this short chapter, though you should find that one of the options proposed here will suffice for many data sets. It is worth reiterating that the purpose of such simple summaries is to promote a rapid understanding of the main features of the data, and it goes without saying that no summary method should be used if it obscures the argument or covers serious deficiencies in the data.

SUMMARY

This chapter has shown a number of ways in which data can be summarised in tables and diagrams.

(1) A distinction was made between **categorical** and **numerical** data.

(2) The notion of **relative frequency**, in terms of **proportions** or **percentages**, was introduced.

(3) Advice was given on the construction of:
   (a)   tables: **one-way**, **two-way**, and **multi-way**
   (b)   diagrams: **bar charts**, **histograms**, and **cumulative frequency curves**

(4) **Percentiles, quartiles** and **median scores** were introduced.

(5) It was pointed out that there may be occasions when unusual data will necessitate modification of the basic procedures.

(6) It was emphasised that the function of tables and diagrams is to present information in a readily assimilable form and without distortion. In particular, it was urged that proportions and percentages should always be accompanied by an indication of original frequencies.

EXERCISES

(1) In the Quirk Report (Quirk 1972) the following figures are given as estimates of the number of children in different categories who might require speech therapy. Construct a table of relative frequencies for these categories.

   (i)   Pre-school age children with speech and language problems   60 000
   (ii)   Children in ordinary schools with speech and language problems   180 000
   (iii)   Physically- and/or mentally-handicapped children   42 800
   (iv)   Special groups (language disorders, autism, etc.)   5 000

(2) Assume that the male/female split in the categories above is as follows:
   (i)   40 000/20 000
   (ii)   100 000/80 000
   (iii)   25 000/17 800
   (iv)   3 500/1 500

   (a)   Construct a two-way table of frequencies and relative frequencies, cross-classified by sex (cf. table 2.2(c)).
   (b)   Draw a bar chart of the frequencies in each category.
   (c)   Draw a bar chart of the relative frequencies for each category.

(3) The table below gives the scores of 93 students in a test of English proficiency.

233	159	183	206	149	150	164	162	226	189
205	200	146	190	236	180	155	203	188	166
165	237	172	152	180	141	140	181	194	208
180	173	225	185	191	168	167	209	205	166
165	165	168	156	191	204	161	173	179	174
144	265	186	187	126	133	197	162	254	170
133	171	177	193	132	167	152	121	114	206
156	149	187	178	136	181	156	173	198	149
135	181	129	223	159	153	168	207	205	198
				208	211	222			

Tables and graphs

    (a) Provide a frequency table (cf. table 2.5(b)).

    (b) Provide a histogram of the frequency data in the table.

    (c) Provide a relative cumulative frequency curve for the data.

    (d) What are the scores corresponding to the tenth percentile, the first quartile, and the third quartile?

(4) Suppose that the scores of 165 subjects in a language test are reported in the form of the following frequency table. Construct the corresponding histogram (note that the class intervals are not all the same size).

Class interval of scores	50–79	80–89	90–94	95–99	100–104	105–109	110–119	120–139
Number of subjects	16	20	19	26	28	22	23	11

3
Summary measures

We have seen that diagrams can be helpful as a means for the presentation of a summary version of a collection of data. Often, however, we will find it convenient to be able to talk succinctly about a set of numbers, and the message carried by a graph may be difficult to put into words. Moreover, we may wish to compare various sets of data, to look for important similarities or differences. Graphs may or may not be helpful in this respect; it depends on the specific question we want to answer and on how clearly the answer displays itself in the data. For example, if we compare figure 3.1 (derived from data in table 3.1) with figure 2.4 we can see immediately that the lengths of the utterances of a mother speaking to an 18-month-old child tend to be rather shorter than those in the speech of the same woman speaking to a child aged 3 years.

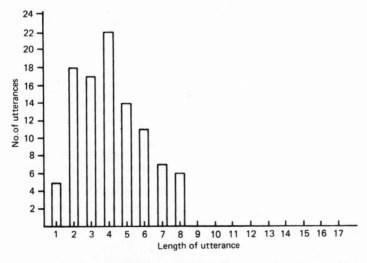

Figure 3.1. Bar chart of lengths of 100 utterances of a mother speaking to a child aged 18 months (data in table 3.1).

Table 3.1. *Frequency table of the lengths of 100 utterances (in morphemes) of an adult addressing a child aged 18 months*

Length of utterance	Number of utterances
1	5
2	18
3	17
4	22
5	14
6	11
7	7
8	6
9	0
10	0
11	0
12	0
13	0
14	0
15	0
16	0
17	0

However, it is quite rare for the situation to be so clear. In figure 3.2(a) we have drawn the histogram of the data of exercise 2.2 (reproduced in table 3.2), which consists of the total scores of 93 students at a Latin

Table 3.2. *Scores, ranked in ascending order, obtained by 93 candidates at a Latin American centre in the Cambridge Proficiency Examination*

114	121	126	129	132	133	133	135	136	140
141	144	146	149	149	149	150	152	152	153
155	156	156	156	159	159	161	162	162	164
165	165	165	166	166	167	167	168	168	168
170	171	172	173	173	173	(174)	177	178	179
180	180	180	181	181	181	183	185	186	187
187	188	189	190	191	191	193	194	197	198
198	200	203	204	205	205	205	206	206	207
208	208	209	211	222	223	225	226	233	236
				237	254	265			

American centre in the June 1980 Cambridge Proficiency in English Examination. In figure 3.2(b) we have repeated the histogram of the scores of the European students already discussed in the previous chapter. The two histograms are rather alike but there are some dissimilarities. Can we make any precise statements about such dissimilarities in the *overall* level of performance of the two groups of students?

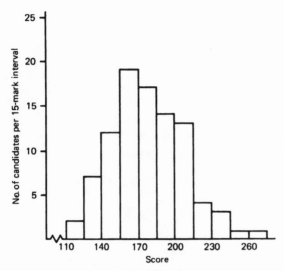

Figure 3.2(a). Histogram of CPE scores of 93 Latin American candidates (data in exercise 2.2).

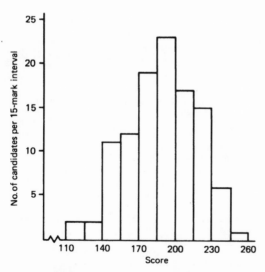

Figure 3.2(b). Histogram of CPE scores of 108 European candidates (data in table 2.5).

3.1 **The median**

We have drawn the cumulative relative frequency curve for the Latin American group in figure 3.3(a) and again repeated that for the European students in figure 3.3(b). In both diagrams we have marked in the **median**, or 50th percentile, introduced in chapter 2. Remember that this is the score which divides each set of scores into two nearly equal subgroups; one of these contains all the scores less than the median, the other all those greater than the median. We see that the median score for the Latin American students, about 174, is somewhat lower than that for the Europeans, about 190, and we might use this as the basis for a statement that, in June 1980, a Latin American student at the centre of the ability range for his group scored a little less well than the corresponding European. It is clear from the histograms that there are many students

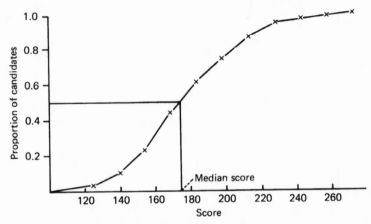

Figure 3.3(a). Relative cumulative frequency curve for CPE scores of 93 Latin American subjects (data in exercise 2.2).

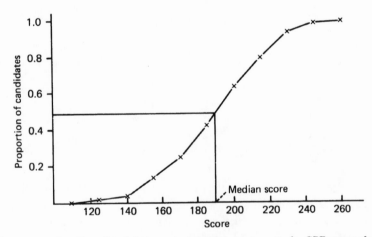

Figure 3.3(b). Relative cumulative frequency curve for CPE scores of 108 European subjects (data in table 2.5).

in both sets who obtained scores close to the relevant median. This, together with the central position of each median in its own data set, gives rise to the idea of a representative score for the group, expressed in phrases such as 'a *typical* student' or 'utterances of *average* length'.

The median provides a way to specify a 'typical' or 'average' value which can be used as a descriptor for a whole group. Although some Latin Americans scored much higher marks than many Europeans (indeed the highest score from the two groups was from a Latin American), we nevertheless can feel that we know something meaningful about the relative performance of each group as a whole when we have obtained the two median values.

3.2 The arithmetic mean

The median is only one type of average and there are several others which can be extracted from any set of numbers. Perhaps the most familiar and widely used of these – many of us have learned to call it *the* average – is the **arithmetic mean**, or just **mean**, which is calculated for any set of numerical values simply by adding them together and dividing by the number of values in the set. The mean score for the Latin American students (from table 3.2) is given by:

$$(114 + 121 + \ldots + 265) = 16517$$
$$16517 \div 93 = 177.6$$

The mean length of the utterances (in morphemes) of a mother speaking to a child aged 3 years (from table 2.4(a)) is:

$$(2 + 7 + \ldots + 4) = 635$$
$$635 \div 100 = 6.35$$

This is a convenient point for an introduction to the kind of simple algebraic notation which we will use throughout the book. Although we will require little knowledge of mathematics other than simple arithmetic, the use of some basic mathematical notation is, in the end, an aid to clear argument and results in a great saving in space.

When we wish to refer to a general data set, without specifying particular numerical values, we will designate each number in the set by means of a letter and a suffix. For example, X_{26} will just mean the 26th value in some set of data. The suffixes do not imply an ordering in the values of the numbers; it will not be assumed that X_1 is greater (or smaller) than X_{100}, but only that X_1 is the first and X_{100} the 100th in some list of numbers. For example, in table 2.4(a) the first utterance length recorded is 2 morphemes while the last utterance length recorded is 4 morphemes: thus $X_1 = 2$, $X_{100} = 4$.

If we wish to refer to different data sets in the same context we use different letters. For instance, X_1, X_2, ..., X_{28} and Y_1, Y_2, ..., Y_{28} would be labels for two different lists each containing 28 numbers. More generally we write X_1, X_2, ..., X_n to mean a list of an indefinite number (n) of numerical values, and we write X_i to refer to an unspecified member of the set.

The arithmetic mean of the data set X_1, X_2, ..., X_n is usually designated as $\bar{X}$ and defined as:

$$\bar{X} = \text{(sum of the values)} \div \text{(number of values)}$$

$$= (X_1 + X_2 + \ldots + X_n) \div n$$

$$= \frac{1}{n}(X_1 + X_2 + \ldots + X_n)$$

$$= \frac{1}{n}\sum_i X_i$$

where the symbol $\sum_i$ means 'add up all the Xs indicated by different values of the suffix i'. This may be simplified further and written:

$$\bar{X} = \frac{1}{n}\Sigma X$$

3.3 The mean and the median compared

We now have two possible measures of 'average' or 'typical', the mean and the median. They need not have the same value. For example, the 93 Latin American students have a mean score of 177.6, while the median extracted from figure 3.3(a) has a value of 174. Moreover, although the median score for the group of Latin American students happens to be similar to the mean score, this need not be the case – as we discuss below. Why should there be more than one average, and how can we reconcile differences between their values?

In order to be able to discuss the different properties of the median and the mean, we need to know how the former can be calculated rather than obtained from the cumulative frequency curve, although the graphical method is usually quite accurate enough for most purposes. In table 3.2 we have written the scores of the 93 Latin American students in ascending order, from the lowest to the highest mark. The 47th mark in this ranked

Table 3.3. *Lengths of utterances, ranked in ascending order, of adult speaking to child aged 3 years*

2	2	2	2	2	2	2	2	2	2
2	2	2	3	3	3	3	3	3	3
3	3	3	3	3	4	4	4	4	4
4	4	4	4	4	5	5	5	5	5
5	5	5	5	6	6	6	6	6	6
6	6	6	7	7	7	7	7	7	7
7	7	7	7	7	7	8	8	8	8
8	8	8	8	9	9	9	9	9	9
9	9	10	10	10	10	10	10	10	10
10	10	11	12	12	12	14	14	15	17

list, 174, has been circled; 46 students scored less than this and 46 scored more. Hence 174 is the median score of the group. You may like to try the same procedure for the European students. There are 108 of these and you should find that when ranked in ascending order the 54th score is 189 and the 55th 190. Thus there is no mark which exactly divides the group into two equal halves. Conventionally, in such a case, we take the average of the middle pair, so that here we would say that the median score is 189.5. The same convention is adopted even when the middle pair have the same value. The utterance lengths of table 2.4(a) are written in rank order in table 3.3. Of the 100 lengths, the 50th and 51st, the middle pair, both have the value 6, and the median will therefore be: $1/2 (6 + 6) = 6$.

Although the mean and the median are both measures for locating the 'centre' of a data set, they can sometimes give rather different values. It is helpful to investigate what features of the data might cause this, to help us decide when one of the values, mean or median, might be more appropriate than the other as an indicator of a typical value for the data. This is best done by means of a very simple example. Consider the set of five numbers 3, 7, 8, 9, 13. The median value is 8 and the mean is 8 ($\bar{X} = 1/5 (3 + 7 + 8 + 9 + 13) = 8$). In this case the two measures give exactly the same result. Note that the numbers are distributed exactly symmetrically about this central value: 3 and 13 are both the same distance from 8, as are 7 and 9; the mean and the median will always have the same value when the data has this kind of symmetry. If we do the same for the values 3, 7, 8, 9, 83, we find that the median is still 8, but the mean is now 22. In other words, the presence of one extreme value has increased the mean dramatically, causing it to be rather different in value from the more typical group of small values (3, 7, 8, 9), falling between them and the very large extreme value. The median, on the other hand, is quite unaffected by the presence of a single, unusually large number and retains the value it had previously. One would say that the median is a **robust** indicator of the more typical values of the data, being unaffected by the occasional atypical value which might occur at one or other extreme.

When a set of data contains one or more observations which seem to have quite different values from the great bulk of the observations it may be worthwhile treating them separately by excluding the unusual value(s) before calculating the mean. For example, in this very simple case we could say that the data consists of four observations with mean 6.75 (3, 7, 8, 9) together with one very large value, 83. This is not misleading provided that the complete picture is honestly reported. Indeed, it may be a preferable way to report if there is some indication, other than just its value, that the observation is somehow unusual.

When the data values are symmetrically distributed, as in the previous example, then the mean and median will be equal. On the other hand, the difference in value between the mean and median will be quite marked if there is substantial **skewness** or lack of symmetry in a set of data; see figures 3.4(a) and 3.4(b). A data set is said to be skewed if the highest point of its histogram, or bar chart, is not in the centre, hence causing one of the 'tails' of the diagram to be longer than the other. The skewness is defined to be in the direction of the longer tail, so that 3.4(a) shows a histogram 'skewed to the right' and 3.4(b) is a picture of a data set which is 'skewed to the left'.

We have seen that the median has the property of robustness in the presence of an unusually extreme value and the mean does not. Nevertheless, the mean is the more commonly used for the 'centre' of a set of data? Why is this? The more important reasons will become apparent in later chapters, but we can see already that the mean can claim an advantage on grounds of convenience or ease of calculation for straightforward sets of data. In order to calculate the median we have to rank the data. At the very least we will need to group them to draw a cumulative frequency curve to use the graphical method. This can be very tedious indeed for a large data set. For the mean we need only add up the values, in whatever order. Of course, if the data are to be processed by computer both measures can be obtained easily.

However, there are situations when both the mean and the median can be quite misleading, and these are indicated by the diagrams in figures 3.5(a) and 3.5(b). In case (a) it is clear that the data are dominated by one particular value, easily the most typical value of the set. The most frequent value is called the **modal value** or **mode**. The median (3) is equal to the mode, while the mean (3.42) is larger. More typically, unless the mode is in the centre of the chart, the mean and the median will both be different from the mode, and from each other, but the median

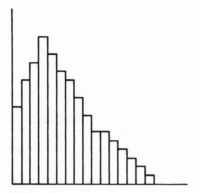

Figure 3.4(a). Histogram skewed to the right.

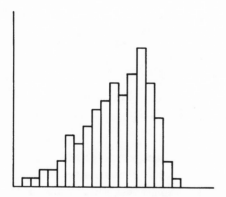

Figure 3.4(b). Histogram skewed to the left.

will be closer to the mode than the mean will be. We might feel that the mode is the best indicator of the typical value for this kind of data. Figure 3.5(b) shows a rather different case. Because the histogram is symmetrical, the mean and median are equal, but either is a silly choice as a 'typical value'. However, neither is there a single mode in this case.

These last two examples stand as a warning. For reasons which will soon become clear, it becomes a habit to assume that, unless otherwise indicated, a data set is roughly symmetrical and bell-shaped. Important departures from this should always be clearly indicated, either by means of a histogram or similar graph or by a specific descriptive label such as 'U-shaped', 'J-shaped', 'bi-modal', 'highly skewed', and so on.

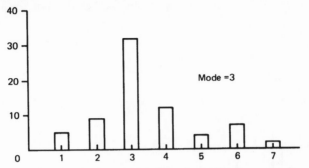

Figure 3.5(a). A hypothetical bar chart with a pronounced mode.

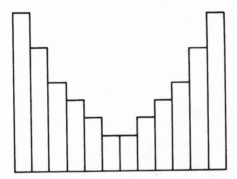

Figure 3.5(b). A symmetrical U-shaped histogram.

3.4 Means of proportions and percentages

It happens frequently that data are presented as percentages or proportions. For example, suppose that the problem of interest were the distribution of a linguistic variable in relation to some external variable such as social class. To simplify matters we will consider the distribution of the variable (say, the proportion of times [n] is used word-finally in words like *winning, running*, as opposed to [ŋ]) in one social group, which we will call Middle working class (MWC). Let us suppose that we have two conditions for collecting the data: (a) a standard interview, and (b) a wordlist of 200 items. Ten different subjects are examined under each condition, and table 3.4 shows the number of times a verb with progressive ending was pronounced with final [n], expressed as a fraction of the total number of verbs with progressive endings used by the subject in the interview. If we calculate for each subject a percentage of [n]-final forms in

Table 3.4. *Pronunciation of words ending '-ing' by 10 Middle working class speakers*

	(a) Interview			(b) Wordlist		
Subject	Number of [n] endings	Number of tokens	%	Number of [n] endings	Number of tokens	%
1	10	44	22.7	36	200	18.0
2	87	193	45.1	48	200	24.0
3	111	216	51.4	64	200	32.0
4	55	103	53.4	56	200	28.0
5	145	241	60.2	70	200	35.0
6	116	183	63.4	61	200	30.5
7	77	194	39.7	62	200	31.0
8	126	218	57.8	53	200	26.5
9	109	223	48.9	77	200	38.5
10	6	32	18.8	42	200	21.0
Total	842	1647		569	2000	

the interview condition, we obtain the values in the fourth column of the table. If we take the mean of the percentages in that column, we obtain a value of 46.14%. However, on looking at the data we can see that the eight subjects who provide the great bulk of the data (1571 tokens) have percentages which are close to or much higher than 46.14. The two subjects whose percentages are low are responsible for only 76 tokens, yet their inclusion in the sample mean as calculated above greatly reduces its numerical value. It is generally good practice to avoid, as far as possible, collecting data in such a way that we have less information about some subjects in the study than we have about others. It will not always be possible to achieve this – certainly not where the experimental material consists of segments of spontaneous speech or writing. The use of wordlists can remove the problem, since then each subject will provide a similar number of tokens. However, it is noteworthy that the two experimental conditions have given quite different results for many of the subjects; some of them give only half the proportion of [n] endings in the wordlist that they express in spontaneous speech.

At this point we should note that it may sometimes be inappropriate to take simple averages of percentages and proportions. Suppose that the data of table 3.4 for the interview condition (a) were not observed on ten different subjects but rather were the result of analysing ten different speech samples from a single individual for whom we wish to measure the percentage of [n] endings. Over the complete experiment this subject would have provided a total of 1,647 tokens, of which 842 were pronounced

[n]. This gives a percentage of $(842/1647) \times 100 = 51.12\%$. By adding all the tokens in this way we have reduced the effect of the two situations in which both the number of tokens and the proportion of [n] endings were untypically low. It will not always be obvious whether this is a 'better' answer than the value obtained by averaging the ten individual percentages. You should think carefully about the meaning of the data and have a clear understanding of what it is you are trying to measure. Of course, if the base number of tokens is constant it will not matter which method of calculation is used; both methods give the same answer. For the wordlist condition (b) of table 3.4, the average of the ten percentages is 28.45% and 569 is exactly 28.45% of 2,000.

Suppose an examination consists of two parts, one oral scored out of 10 by an observer, the other a written, multiple choice paper with 50 items. The examination score for each subject will consist of one mark out of 50 and another out of 10. For example, a subject may score 20/50, (40%) in the written paper and 8/10 (80%) in the oral test. How should his overall percentage be calculated? The crux of the matter here is the weight that the examiner wishes to give to each part of the test. If the oral is to have equal weight with the written test then the overall score would be $1/2 (40\% + 80\%) = 60\%$. However, if the scoring system has been chosen to reflect directly the importance of each test in the complete examination, the written paper should be five times as important as the oral. The tester might calculate the overall score by the second method above:

$$\frac{20 + 8}{50 + 10} = \frac{28}{60} = 46.7\%$$

This latter score is frequently referred to as a **weighted mean score** since the scores for the individual parts of the examination are no longer given equal weights. It may be calculated thus:

$$46.7\% = \frac{50 \times 40\% + 10 \times 80\%}{60}$$

where each percentage is multiplied by the required 'weight'. If the scores for the individual parts were given equal weights the mean score would be 60%, as above. It is important to be clear about the meaning of the two methods and to understand that they will often lead to different results.

It sometimes occurs that published data are presented only as proportions or percentages without the original values being given. This is a serious error in presentation since, as we will see in later chapters, it often prevents analysis of the data by another researcher. It may be difficult to interpret a percentage or a 'mean' percentage when it is not clear what was the base quantity (i.e. total number of observations) over which the original proportion was measured, especially when the raw (i.e. original) values on which the percentages were based are not quoted.

3.5 Variability or dispersion

We introduced the mean and the median as measures which would be useful for the comparison of data sets, and it is certainly true that if we calculate the means (or medians) of two sets of scores, say, and find them to be very different, then we will have made a significant discovery. If, on the other hand, the two means are similar in value, or the medians are, this will not usually be sufficient evidence for the statement that the complete sets of scores have a similar overall shape or structure. Consider the following extreme, but artificial, example. Suppose one group of 50 subjects have all scored exactly the same mark, 35 out of 50 say, in some test, while in another group of the same size, 25 score 50 and 25 score 20. In each case the mean and median mark would be 35. However, there is a clear difference between the groups. The first is very homogeneous, containing people all of an equal, reasonably high level of ability, while the second consists of one subgroup of extremely high-scoring and another of rather low-scoring subjects. The situation will rarely be as obvious as this, but the example makes it clear that in order to make meaningful comparisons between groups it will be necessary to have some measure of how the scores in each group relate to their 'typical value' as determined by the mean or median or some other average value. It is therefore usual to measure (and report) the degree to which a group lacks homogeneity, i.e. the variability, or **dispersion**, of the scores about the average value.

Furthermore, we have argued in the opening chapter that it is variability between subjects or between linguistic tokens from the same subject which makes it necessary to use statistical techniques in the analysis of language data. The extent of variability, or heterogeneity if you like, in a population is the main determinant of how well we can generalise to that population the characteristics we observe in a sample. The more variability, the greater will be the sample size required to obtain a given quality of information (see chapter 7). It is essential to have some way of measuring variability.

3.6 Central intervals

We would not expect to find in practice either of the outcomes described in the previous section. For example, when we administer a

Table 3.5. *Frequency tables of marks for two groups of 200 subjects*

Class intervals (marks)	Group 1			Group 2		
	Frequency	Cumulative frequency	Relative cumulative frequency	Frequency	Cumulative frequency	Relative cumulative frequency
0–4				4	4	0.02
5–9				4	8	0.04
10–14	1	1	0.01	6	14	0.07
15–19	1	2	0.01	8	22	0.11
20–24	6	8	0.04	6	28	0.14
25–29	10	18	0.09	12	40	0.20
30–34	14	32	0.16	17	57	0.29
35–39	36	68	0.34	21	78	0.39
40–44	62	130	0.65	43	121	0.61
45–49	38	168	0.84	23	144	0.72
50–54	17	185	0.93	16	160	0.80
55–59	8	193	0.97	9	169	0.85
60–64	5	198	0.99	8	177	0.89
65–69	2	200	1.00	4	181	0.91
70–74				6	187	0.94
75–79				4	191	0.96
80–84				4	195	0.98
85–89				3	198	0.99
90–94				2	200	1.00
95–99						

test to a group of subjects we usually expect their marks to vary over a more or less wide range. Table 3.5 gives two plausible frequency tables of marks for two different groups of 200 subjects. The corresponding histograms and cumulative frequency curves are given in figures 3.6 and 3.7. We can see from the histograms that the marks of the second group are more 'spread out' and from the cumulative frequency curves that the median mark is the same for both groups (i.e. 42).

How can we indicate numerically the difference in the spread of marks? One way is by means of intervals centred on the median value and containing a stated percentage of the observed data values. For example, q_1 and q_3, the first and third quartiles, have been marked on both cumulative frequency curves.[1] This means that generally half of all the observed values will lie between q_1 and q_3. We write (q_1, q_3) to represent *all* the possible values between q_1 and q_3 and we would say that (q_1, q_3) is a **50% central interval**; 'central' because it is centred on the median, which itself is the centre point of the data set, and '50%' because it contains 50% of the values in the data set. The length of the interval, q_3 minus q_1, is

---

[1] These were defined in §2.2. One-quarter of the observed values are smaller than the first quartile, while three-quarters are smaller than the third quartile. The first quartile, q_1, is often referred to as the 25th percentile, P_{25}, because 25% of the data have a value smaller than q_1. Similarly, q_3 may be called the 75th percentile, P_{75}.

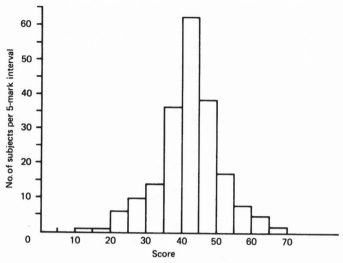

Figure 3.6(a). Histogram for data of Group 1 from table 3.5.

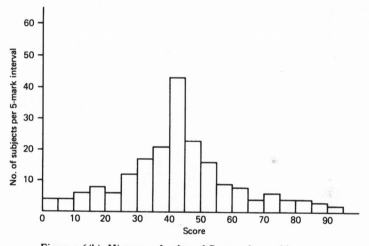

Figure 3.6(b). Histogram for data of Group 2 from table 3.5.

called the **interquartile distance** (sometimes, the **interquartile range**). In the example above, figure 3.7(a) shows a 50% central interval (37.5, 47.5) while for figure 3.7(b) the interval is (32.5, 51.5). The interquartile distance gives a measure of how widely dispersed are the data. If at least half the values are very close to the median, the quartiles will be close together; if the data do not group closely around the median, the quartiles will be further apart. For the two cases shown in figures 3.7(a) and 3.7(b), the interquartile distances are 10 and 19 respectively, reflecting the wider

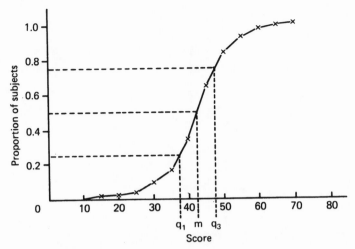

Figure 3.7(a). Relative cumulative frequency curve for data of Group 1 from table 3.5.

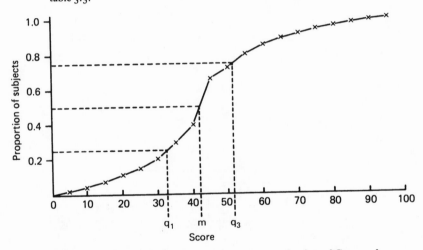

Figure 3.7(b). Relative cumulative frequency curve for data of Group 2 from table 3.5.

dispersion of the values in Group 2. The quartiles do not have any special claim to exclusive use for defining a central interval. Indeed, as we shall see in later chapters, central intervals containing a higher proportion of the possible values are much more commonly used.

3.7 **The variance and the standard deviation**

Before the use of computers to manage experimental data it was common to reject the use of the interquartile distance as a measure of dispersion because of the need to rank the data values to obtain the median and quartiles. With the advent of easy-to-use computer packages like MINITAB (see Appendix B) this is no longer a constraint, and the quartiles and percentiles can provide a useful, descriptive measure of variability. However, classical statistical theory is not based on percentiles, and other measures of dispersion have been developed whose theoretical properties are better known and more convenient. The first of these that we will discuss is the **variance**.

Suppose we have a data set X_1, X_2, ... X_n with arithmetic mean, $\bar{X}$. We could calculate the difference between each value and the mean value, as follows: $d_1 = X_1 - \bar{X}$, $d_2 = X_2 - \bar{X}$, etc. It might seem that the average of these differences would give some measure of how closely the data values cluster around the mean, $\bar{X}$. In table 3.6 we have carried out this calculation for the number of words per sentence in a short reading text. Notice that some values of the difference (second column) are positive, some are negative. and that when added together they cancel out to zero. This will happen with any set of data. However, it is still appealing to use the difference between each value and the mean value as a measure of dispersion. There is a method of doing this which will not give the

Table 3.6. *Calculation of the variance of number of words per sentence in a short reading text.*

Number of words per sentence	$d_i (= X_i - \bar{X})$	d_i^2
3	−6.75	45.56
7	−2.75	7.56
4	−5.75	33.06
9	−0.75	0.56
12	2.25	5.06
2	−7.75	60.06
14	4.25	18.06
14	4.25	18.06
6	−3.75	14.06
9	−0.75	0.56
11	1.25	1.56
17	7.25	52.56
18	8.25	68.06
12	2.25	5.06
10	0.25	0.06
8	−1.75	3.06

$\Sigma X = 156 \qquad \Sigma d_i = 0 \qquad \Sigma d_i^2 = 332.96$

$\bar{X} = 9.75$

$$V = \frac{332.96}{n-1} = \frac{332.96}{15} = 22.20$$

same answer (i.e. zero) for every data set and which has other useful mathematical properties. After calculating the differences d_i, we square each to get the **squared deviations** about the mean, d_i^2 (third column). We next total these squared deviations ($\Sigma d_i^2 = 332.96$). Finally, we divide this total by $(n-1)$ (the number of values minus 1). The result of this calculation is the **variance** (V):

$$\frac{\overset{\Sigma}{\underset{1}{d_i^2}}}{n-1} \quad or \quad \frac{1}{n-1}\underset{1}{\Sigma}d_i^2$$

This would be the arithmetic mean of the square deviations if the divisor were the sample size n. The reason for dividing by $(n-1)$ instead is technical and will not be explained here. Of course, if n is quite large, it will hardly make any difference to the result whether we divide by n or by $(n-1)$, and it is convenient, and in no way misleading, to think of the variance as the average of the squared deviations.

One inconvenient aspect of the variance is the units in which it is measured. In table 3.6 we calculated the variance of the number of words per sentence in a short reading text. Each X_i is a number of words and $\bar{X}$ is therefore the mean number of words per utterance. But what are the units of d_i^2? If we multiply five words by five words what kind of object do we have? Twenty-five what? The variance, V, will have the same units as each d_i^2, i.e. 'square words'. This concept is unhelpful from the point of view of empirical interpretation. However, if we take the square root of the variance, this will again have the unit 'words'. This measure, which is referred to as the **standard deviation**, referred to by the symbol s, has many other useful properties and, as a result, the standard deviation is the most frequently quoted measure of variability. Note, in passing, that $s = \sqrt{V}$; thus $s^2 = V$, and the variance is frequently referred to by the symbol s^2.

Before electronic calculators were cheap and readily available it was the custom at this point in statistical textbooks to introduce a number of formulae to simplify the process of calculating s or (equivalently) s^2. However, on a relatively inexpensive calculator the mean, $\bar{X}$, and the standard deviation, s, of any data set can be obtained simultaneously by entering the data values into the calculator in a prescribed fashion.[2]

[2] Many calculators will give two possible values of the standard deviation. One of these, designated s_{n-1} or σ_{n-1} is the value calculated according to our formula and we recommend its use on all occasions. The other, s_n or σ_n, has been calculated by replacing $(n-1)$ by n in our formula, and its use is best avoided. As noted above, when n is reasonably large there will be very little difference between the two values.

The standard deviation is one of the most important statistical measures. It indicates the typical amount by which values in the data set differ from the mean, $\bar{X}$, and no data summary is complete until all relevant standard deviations have been calculated.

3.8 Standardising test scores

A major application of the standard deviation is in the process known as **standardising**, which can be carried out on any set of ordered, numerical data. One important use of standardising in language studies is to facilitate the comparison of test scores, and an example of this will be used to demonstrate the method.

Suppose that two individuals, A and B, have been tested (each by a different test) on their language proficiency and have achieved scores of 41 and 53 respectively. Naively, one might say without further ado that B has scored 'higher' or 'better' than A. However, they have been examined by different methods and questions must be asked about the comparability of the two tests. Let us suppose that both tests were taken by large numbers of subjects at the same time as they were taken by the two individuals that interest us, and that we have no reason to believe that, overall, the subjects taking the two tests differed in any systematic way. Suppose also that the mean score on the first test was 44 and that on the second test the mean was 49. We note immediately that A has scored below the average in one test while B has scored above the average in the other, so that there is an obvious sense in which B has done better than A. The comparison will not always be so obvious.

Let us assume, as before, scores of 41 and 53 for A and B in their respective tests, but that now the mean scores for the two tests are, respectively, 49 and 58. Both individuals now have lower than average scores. A has scored 8 marks below the mean, while B has just 5 marks less than the mean for this test. Does this imply that B has achieved a relatively higher score? Not necessarily. It depends how 'spread out' the scores are for the two tests. It is just conceivable that B's mark of 53 is the lowest achieved by anyone for the test while, say 40% of the candidates on the other test scored less than A. In that case, B could be right at the bottom of the ability range while A would be somewhere near the middle. The comparison can properly be made only by taking into account the standard deviations of the test scores as well as their means. Suppose, for example, that the two tests had standard deviations of 8 marks and 5 marks respectively. Then the distance of A's score of 41 from the mean of his test is exactly the value of the standard deviation $(49 - 8 = 41)$.

The same is true for B. The distance of *his* score of 53 from the mean is exactly the value of the standard deviation on the test that *he* took ($58 - 5 = 53$). Both scores can be said to be one standard deviation less than their respective means and, taking into account in this way the different dispersion of scores in the two tests, there is a sense in which both A and B have achieved the same scores relative to the other candidates who took the tests at the same time.

If the complete sets of scores for the two above tests had had exactly the same mean *and* exactly the same standard deviation, any mark on one test would have been directly comparable with the same mark on the other. But of course this is not usually the case. Standardising test scores facilitates comparisons between scores on different tests. To illustrate, suppose now that we have the scores X_1, X_2, ..., etc. of a set of subjects for some test and that the mean and standard deviation of these scores are $\bar{X}$ and s respectively. Begin by changing each score, X_i, to a new score, Y_i, by subtracting the mean:

$$Y_i = X_i - \bar{X}$$

Now change each of the scores, Y_i, into a further new score, Z_i, by dividing each Y by s, the standard deviation of the original X scores:

$$Z_i = Y_i \div s$$

In table 3.7 this procedure has been applied to a small set of hypothetical scores to demonstrate the outcome. The original scores of the first column have a mean of $\bar{X} = 53$ and a standard deviation of $s_X = 15.12$. The mean, $\bar{X}$, is subtracted from each of the original scores to give a new value, Y, in the second column. The mean of these new values is $\bar{Y} = 0$ but the standard deviation is $s_Y = 15.12$, the same value as before. Finally, each value in the second column is changed into a standardised value, Z, by dividing by 15.12. The five values in column 3 now have a mean of zero and a standard deviation of 1.

By these two steps we have changed a set of scores, X_1, X_2, etc. with mean $\bar{X}$ and standard deviation s, into a new set of scores Z_1, Z_2, etc., with mean zero and standard deviation 1. The Z scores are the **standardised X scores**. The process of standardising can be described by the single formula:

$$Z = \frac{X - \bar{X}}{s}$$

Suppose two different language proficiency tests which purport to measure the same ability are administered to all available high school students

Table 3.7. *An example of the*
standardising procedure on a
hypothetical data set

$X \to$ subtract $\bar{X} \to$	$Y \to$ divide by $s_X \to Z$ $s_X \to$	
73	20	1.32
42	−11	−0.73
36	−17	−1.12
51	−2	−0.13
63	10	0.66
$\bar{X} = 53$	$\bar{Y} = 0$	$\bar{Z} = 0$
$s_X = 15.12$	$s_Y = s_X = 15.12$	$s^Z = 1$

in a certain area, each test on a different day. Their scores on the first
test have a mean of 92 and a standard deviation of 14, and on the second
test a mean of 143 and a standard deviation of 21. Student A, who for
some reason or other is prevented from taking the second test, scores
121 on the first. Student B misses the first test but scores 177 on the
second. If we wanted to compare the performance of these two students
we could standardise their scores. The standardised score for Subject A
is:

$$Z_A = \frac{121 - 92}{14} = 2.07$$

and for Subject B is:

$$Z_B = \frac{177 - 143}{21} = 1.62$$

Since Z_A is greater than Z_B we would say that Subject A has scored higher
than Subject B on a standardised scale. It will be seen in chapters 6–8
that quite precise statements can often be made about such comparisons
and that standardised values play an important role in statistical theory.

SUMMARY

This chapter introduces and explains various numerical quantities or
measures which can be used to summarise sets of data in just a few numbers.

(1) The **median** and the **mean** (or **arithmetic mean**) were defined as measures
of the 'typical value' of a set of data.

(2) The properties of the mean and median were discussed and the median was
shown to be more **robust** than the mean in the presence of one or two unusually
extreme values.

(3) It was pointed out that there were two common ways (the ordinary mean

45

or the **weighted mean**) of calculating the mean proportion of a set of proportions and the motivation and result of each type of mean were discussed.

(4) The **variance**, the **standard deviation** and the **interquartile distance** were presented as measures of variability or **dispersion**; the concept of the **central interval** was introduced.

(5) **Standardised scores** were explained and shown to be an appropriate tool for comparing the scores of different subjects on different tests.

EXERCISES

(1) (a) Work out the mean, median and mode for the data in table 2.4. What conclusions can you reach about the most suitable measure of central tendency to apply to these data?

(b) Follow the same procedures for the data of table 3.1.

(2) The following table gives data from the June 1980 application of the CPE to a group of Asian students. For this data, construct a table of frequencies within appropriate class intervals, cumulative frequencies and relative cumulative frequencies. Draw the corresponding histogram and the relative cumulative frequency curve. Estimate the median and the interquartile distance.

123	132	154	136	121	220	106	92	127	134
127	70	121	116	70	131	136	170	74	114
65	112	81	193	172	134	221	217	138	138
51	113	136	108	97	146	75	188	123	92
191	195	74	173	167	159	149	115	147	85
88	96	255	93	171	219	84	118	90	111
128	78	213	149	110	156	156	172	129	110

(3) Calculate mean and standard deviation scores for the mean length of utterance data in tables 2.4 and 3.1.

(4) An institute which offers intensive courses in oriental languages assigns beginning students to classes on the basis of their language aptitude test scores. Some students will have taken Aptitude Test A, which has a mean of 120 and a standard deviation of 12; the remainder will have taken Test B, which has a mean of 100 and a standard deviation of 15. (The means and standard deviations for both tests were obtained from large administrations to comparable groups of students.)

Student	Test A	Test B
P	132	—
Q	124	—
R	—	122
S	81	—
T	—	75
U	—	91

(a) Calculate the standardised score for each of the students listed in the table and rank the students according to their apparent ability, putting the best first.

(b) The institute groups students into classes C, D, E or F according to their score on Test A as follows: those scoring at least 140 are assigned to Class C; those with at least 120 but less than 140 are Class D; those with at least 105 but less than 120 are Class E. The remainder are assigned to Class F. In which classes would you place students R, T and U?

4
Statistical inference

4.1 The problem

Until now we have been considering how to describe or summarise a set of data considered simply as an object in its own right. Very often we want to do more than this: we wish to use a collection of observed values to make inferences about a larger set of potential values; we would like to consider a particular set of data we have obtained as representing a larger class. It turns out that to accomplish this is by no means straightforward. What is more, an exhaustive treatment of the difficulties involved is beyond the scope of this book. In this chapter we can only provide the reader with a general outline of the problem of making inferences from observed values. A full understanding of this exposition will depend to some degree on familiarity with the content of later chapters. For this reason we suggest that this chapter is first read to obtain a general grasp of the problem, and returned to later for re-reading in the light of subsequent chapters.

We will illustrate the problem of **inference** by introducing some of the cases which we will analyse in greater detail in the chapters to come. One, for example, in chapter 8, concerns the size of the comprehension vocabulary of British children between 6 and 7 years of age. It is obviously not possible, for practical reasons, to test all British children of this age. We simply will not have the resources. We can only test a sample of children. We have learned, in chapters 2 and 3, how to make an adequate description of an observed group, by, for example, constructing a histogram or calculating the mean and standard deviation of the vocabulary sizes of the subset of children selected. But our interest is often broader than this; we would like to know the mean and standard deviation which *would* have been obtained by testing all children of the relevant age. How close would these have been to the mean and standard deviation actually observed? This will depend on the relationship we expect to hold between the group we have selected to measure and the larger group of children from which it has been selected. How far can we assume the characteristics of this latter group to be similar to those of the smaller group which has been observed? This is the classical problem of statistical inference: how to infer from the properties of a part the likely properties of the whole. It will turn up repeatedly from now on. It is worth emphasising at the outset that because of the way in which samples are selected in many studies in linguistics and applied linguistics, it is often simply not possible to generalise beyond the samples. We will return to this difficulty.

4.2 **Populations**

A **population** is the largest class to which we can generalise the results of an investigation based on a subclass. The population of interest (or **target population**) will vary in type and magnitude depending on the aims and circumstances of each different study or investigation. Within the limits set by the study in question, the population, in statistical terms, will always be considered as the set of *all possible* values of a variable. We have already referred to one study which is concerned with the vocabulary of 6–7-year-olds. The variable here is scores on a test for comprehension vocabulary size; the population of interest is the set of all possible values of this variable which could be derived from all 6–7-year-old children in the country. There are two points which should be apparent here. First, although as investigators our primary interest is in the individuals whose behaviour we are measuring, a **statistical population** is to be thought of as a set of values; a mean vocabulary size calculated from a sample of observed values is, as we shall see in chapter 7, an estimate of the mean vocabulary size that would be obtained from the complete set of values which form the target population. The second point that should be apparent is that it is often not straightforward in language studies to define the target population. After all, the set of '6–7-year-old children in Britain', if we take this to refer to the period between the sixth and seventh birthdays, is changing daily; so for us to put some limit on our statistical population (the set of values which would be available from these children) we have to set some kind of constraint. We return to this kind of problem below when we consider **sampling frames**. For the moment let us consider further the notion of 'target' or 'intended' population in relation to some of the other examples used later in the book.

Utterance length. If we are interested in the change in utterance length over time in children's speech, and collect data which sample utterance length, the statistical population in this case is composed of the *length values* of the individual utterances, not the utterances themselves. Indeed, we could use the utterances of the children to derive values for many different variables and hence to construct many different statistical populations. If instead of measuring the length of each utterance we gave each one a score representing the number of third person pronouns it contained, the population of interest would then be 'third person pronoun per utterance scores'.

Voice onset time (VOT). In the study first referred to in chapter 1, Macken & Barton (1980a) investigated the development of children's acquisition of initial stop contrasts in English by measuring VOTs for plosives the children produced which were attempts at adult voiced and voiceless stop contrasts. The statistical population here is the VOT measurements for /p, b, t, d, k and g/targets, not the phonological items themselves. Note once again that it is not at all easy to conceptualise the target population. If we do not set any limit, the population (the values of all VOTs for word-initial plosives pronounced by English children) is infinite. It is highly likely, however, that the target population will necessarily be more limited than this as a result of the circumstances of the investigation from which the sample values are derived. Deliberate constraints (for example a sample taken only from children of a certain age) or accidental ones (non-random sampling – see below) will either constrain the population of interest or make *any* generalisation difficult or even impossible.

Tense marking. In the two examples we have just looked at, the population values can vary over a wide range. For other studies we can envisage large populations in which the individual elements can have one of only a few, or even two, distinct values. In the Fletcher & Peters (1984) study (discussed in chapter 7) one of the characteristics of the language of children in which the investigators were interested was their marking of lexical verbs with the various auxiliaries and/or suffixes used for tense, aspect and mood in English. They examined frequencies of a variety of individual verb forms (modal, past, present, *do*-support, etc.). However, it would be possible to consider, for example, just past tense marking and to ask, for children of a particular age, which verbs that referred to past events were overtly marked for past tense, and which were not. So if we looked at the utterances of a sample of children of 2;6, we could assign the value 1 to each verb marked for past tense, and zero to unmarked verbs. The statistical population of interest (the values of the children's past referring verbs) would similarly be envisaged as consisting of a large collection of elements, each of which could only have one or the other of these two values.

A population then, for statistical purposes, is a set of **values**. We have emphasised that in linguistic studies of the kind represented in this book it is not always easy to conceptualise the population of interest. Let us assume for the moment, however, that by various means we succeed in defining our target population, and return to the problem of statistical inference from another direction. While we may be ultimately interested in populations, the values we observe will be from samples. How can we ensure that we have reasonable grounds for claiming that the values from our sample are accurate estimates of the values in the population? In other words, is it possible to construct our sample in such a way that we can legitimately make the inference from its values to those of the population we have determined as being of interest? This is not a question to which we can respond in any detail here. Sampling theory is itself the subject of many books. But we can illustrate some of the difficulties that are likely to arise in making generalisations in the kinds of studies that are used for exemplification in this book, which we believe are not untypical of the field as a whole.

Common sense would suggest that a sample should be representative of the population, that is, it should not, by overt or covert bias, have a structure which is too different from the target population. But more technically (remembering that the statistical population is a set of values), we need to be sure that the values that constitute the sample somehow reflect the target statistical population. So, for example, if the possible range of values for length of utterance for 3-year-olds is 1 to 11 morphemes, with larger utterances possible but very unusual, we need to ensure that we do not introduce bias into the sample by only collecting data from a conversational setting in which an excessive number of *yes–no* questions are addressed to the child by the interlocutor. Such questions would tend to increase the probability of utterance lengths which are very short – minor utterances like *yes*, *no*, or short sentences like *I don't know*. The difficulty is that this is only one kind of bias that might be introduced into our sample. Suppose that the interlocutor always asked open-ended questions, like *What happened*? This might increase the probability of longer utterances by a child or children in the sample. And there must be sources of bias that we do not even contemplate, and cannot control for (even assuming that we can control for the ones we *can* contemplate).[1]

---

[1] We have passed over here an issue which we have to postpone for the moment, but which is of considerable importance for much of the research done in language studies. Imagine the case where the population of interest is utterance lengths of British English-speaking pre-school children. We have to consider whether it is better to construct a sample which consists of many utterances from a few children, or one which consists of a small number of utterances from each of many children. We will return to this question, and the general issue of sample size, in chapter 7.

Fortunately there is a method of sampling, known as **random sampling** that can overcome problems of overt or covert bias. What this term means will become clearer once we know more about probability. But it is important to understand from the outset that 'random' here does not mean that the events in a sample are haphazard or completely lacking in order, but rather that they have been constructed by a procedure that allows every element in the population a known probability of being selected in the sample.

While we can never be entirely sure that a sample is representative (that it has roughly the characteristics of the population relevant to our investigation), our best defence against the introduction of experimenter bias is to follow a procedure that ensures random samples (one such procedure will be described in chapter 5). This can give us reasonable confidence that our inferences from sample values to population values are valid. Conversely, if our sample is not constructed according to a random procedure we *cannot* be confident that our estimates from it are likely to be close to the population values in which we are interested, and any generalisation will be of a dubious nature.

How are the samples constructed in the studies we consider in this book? Is generalisation possible from them to a target population?

4.3 The theoretical solution

It will perhaps help us to answer these questions if we introduce the notion of a **sampling frame** by way of a non-linguistic example. This will incidentally clarify some of the difficulties we saw earlier in attempts to specify populations.

Suppose researchers are interested in the birth weights of children born in Britain in 1984 (with a view ultimately to comparing birth weights in that year with those of 1934). As is usual with any investigation, their resources will only allow them to collect a subset of these measurements – but a fairly large subset. They have to decide where and how this subset of values is to be collected. The first decision they have to make concerns the sources of their information. Maternity hospital records are the most obvious choice, but this leaves out babies born at home. Let us assume that health visitors (who are required to visit all new-born children and their mothers) have accessible records which can be used. What is now required is some well-motivated limits on these records, to constitute a sampling frame within which a random sample of birth weights can be constructed.

The most common type of sampling frame is a list (actual or notional) of all the subjects in the group to which generalisation is intended. Here, for example, we could extract a list of all the babies with birth-dates in the relevant year from the records of all health visitors in Great Britain. We could then choose a simple random sample (chapter 5) of n of these babies and note the birth weights in their record. If n is large, the mean weight of the sample should be very similar (chapter 7) to the mean for all the babies born in that year. At the very least we will be able to say how big the discrepancy is likely to be (in terms of what is known as a 'confidence interval' – see chapter 7).

The problem with this solution is that the construction of the sampling frame would be extremely time-consuming and costly. Other options are available. For example, a sampling frame could be constructed in two or more stages. The country (Britain) could be divided into large regions, Scotland, Wales, North-East, West Midlands, etc., and a few regions chosen from this **first stage sampling frame**. For each of the selected regions a list of Health Districts can be drawn up (**second stage**) and a few Health Districts chosen, at random, from each region. Then it may be possible to look at the records of all the health visitors in each of the chosen Districts or perhaps a sample of visitors can be chosen from the list (**third stage**) of all health visitors in each district.[2]

The major constraint is of course resources – the time and money available for data collection and analysis. In the light of this, sensible decisions have to be made about, for example, the number of Health Districts in Britain to be included in the frame; or it may be necessary to limit the inquiry to children born in four months in the year instead of a complete year. In this example, the sampling frame mediates between the population of interest (which is the birth weights of all children born in Britain in 1984) and the sample, and allows us to generalise from the sample values to those in the population of interest.

If we now return to an earlier linguistic example, we can see how the sampling frame would enable us to link our sample with a population of interest. Take word-initial VOTs. Our interest will always be in the individuals of a relatively large group and in the measurements we derive from their behaviour. In the present case we are likely to be concerned with English children between 1;6 and 2;6, because this seems to be the time when they are learning to differentiate voiceless from voiced initial stops using VOT as a crucial phonetic dimension. Our resources will be

[2] The analysis of the data gathered by such complex sampling schemes can become quite complicated and we will not deal with it in this book. Interested readers should see texts on sampling theory or survey design or consult an experienced survey statistician.

limited. We should, however, at least have a sampling frame which sets time limits (for instance, we could choose for the lower limit of our age-range children who are 1;6 in a particular week in 1984); we would like it to be geographically well-distributed (we might again use Health Districts); within the sampling frame we must select a random sample of a reasonable size.[3]

That is how we might go about selecting children for such a study. But how are language samples to be selected from a child? Changing the example, consider the problem of selecting utterances from a young child to measure his mean length of utterance (mlu – see chapter 13). Again it is possible to devise a sampling frame. One method would be to attach a radio microphone to the child, which would transmit and record every single utterance he makes over some period of time to a tape-recorder. Let us say we record all his utterances over a three-month period. We could then attach a unique number to each utterance and choose a simple random sample (chapter 5) of utterances. This is clearly neither sensible nor feasible – it would require an unrealistic expenditure of resources. Alternatively, and more reasonably, we could divide each month into days and each day into hours, select a few days at random and a few hours within each day and record all the utterances made during the selected hours. (See Wells 1985: chapter 1, for a study of this kind.) If this method of selection were to be used it would be better to assume that that child is active only between, say, 7 a.m. and 8 p.m. and select hours from that time period.

In a similar way, it will always be possible to imagine how a sampling frame could be drawn up for any finite population if time and other resources were unlimited. The theory which underlies all the usual statistical methods assumes that, if the results obtained from a sample are to be generalised to a wider population, a suitable sampling frame has been established and the sample chosen randomly from the frame. In practice, however, it is frequently impossible to draw up an acceptable sampling frame – so what, then, can be done?

4.4 The pragmatic solution

In any year a large number of linguistic studies of an empirical nature are carried out by many researchers in many different locations.

---

[3] The issues raised in the first footnote crop up again here; measurements on linguistic variables are more complex than birth weights. We could again ask whether we should collect many word-initial plosives from few children, or few plosives from many children (see chapter 7). A similar problem arises with the sample chosen by several stages. Is it better to choose many regions and a few Health Districts in each region or vice versa?

The great majority of these studies will be exploratory in nature; they will be designed to test a new hypothesis which has occurred to the investigator or to look at a modification of some idea already studied and reported on by other researchers. Most investigators have very limited resources and, in any case, it would be extravagant to carry out a large and expensive study unless it was expected to confirm and give more detailed information on a hypothesis which was likely to be true and whose implications had deep scientific, social or economic significance. Of necessity, each investigator will have to make use of the experimental material (including human subjects) to which he can gain access easily. This will almost always preclude the setting up of sampling frames and the random selection of subjects.

At first sight it may look as if there is an unbridgeable gap here. Statistical theory requires that sampling should be done in a special way before generalisation can be made formally from a sample to a population. Most studies do not involve samples selected in the required fashion. Does this mean that statistical techniques will be inapplicable to these studies? Before addressing this question directly, let us step back for a moment and ask what it is, in the most general sense, that the discipline of statistics offers to linguistics if its techniques are applicable.

What the techniques of statistics offer is a common ground, a common measuring stick by which experimenters can measure and compare the strength of evidence for one hypothesis or another that can be obtained from a sample of subjects, language tokens, etc. This is worth striving after. Different studies will measure quantities which are more or less variable and will include different numbers of subjects and language tokens. Language researchers may find several different directions from which to tackle the same issue. Unless a common ground can be established on which the results of different investigations can be compared using a common yardstick it would be almost impossible to assess the quality of the evidence contained in different studies or to judge how much weight to give to conflicting claims.

Returning to the question of applicability, we would suggest that a sensible way to proceed is to accept the results of each study, in the first place, as though any sampling had been carried out in a theoretically 'correct' fashion. If these results are interesting – suggesting some new hypothesis or contradicting a previously accepted one, for example – then is time enough to question how the sample was obtained and *whether this is likely to have a bearing on the validity of the conclusions reached*. Let us look at an example.

In chapter 11 we discuss a study by Hughes & Lascaratou (1981) on the gravity of errors in written English as perceived by two different groups: native English-speaking teachers of English and Greek teachers of English. We conclude that there seems to be a difference in the way that the two groups judge errors, the Greek teachers tending to be more severe in their judgements. How much does this tell us about possible differences between the complete population of native-speaking English teachers and Greek teachers of English? The results of the experiment would carry over to those populations – in the sense to be explained in the following four chapters – if the samples had been selected carefully from complete sampling frames. This was certainly not done. Hughes and Lascaratou had to gain the co-operation of those teachers to whom they had ready access. The formally correct alternative would have been prohibitively expensive. However, both samples of teachers at least contained individuals from different institutions. If all the English teachers had come from a single English institution and all the Greek teachers from a single Greek school of languages then it could be argued that the difference in error gravity scores could be due to the attitudes of the *institutions* rather than the nationality of the teachers. On the other hand, all but one of the Greek teachers worked in Athens (the English teachers came from a wider selection of backgrounds) and we might query whether their attitudes to errors might be different from those of their colleagues in different parts of Greece. Without testing this argument it is impossible to refute it, but on common sense grounds (i.e. the 'common sense' of a researcher in the teaching of second languages) it seems unlikely.

This then seems a reasonable way to proceed. Judge the results *as though* they were based on random samples and then look at the possibility that they may be distorted by the way the sample was, in fact, obtained. However, this imposes on researchers the inescapable duty of describing carefully how their experimental material – including subjects – was actually obtained. It is also good practice to attempt to foresee some of the objections that might be made about the quality of that material and either attempt to forestall criticism or admit openly to any serious defects.

When the subjects themselves determine to which experimental group they belong, whether deliberately or accidentally, the sampling needs to be done rather more carefully. An important objective of the Fletcher & Peters (1984) study mentioned earlier was to compare the speech of language-normal with that of language-impaired children. In this case the investigators could not randomly assign children to one of these groups – they had already been classified before they were selected. It is important in this kind of study to try to avoid choosing either of the samples such that they belong obviously to some special subgroup.

There is one type of investigation for which proper random sampling is *absolutely essential*. If a reference test of some kind is to be established, perhaps to detect lack of adequate language development in young children, then the test must be applicable to the whole target population and not just to a particular sample. Inaccuracies in determining cut-off levels for detecting children who should be given special assistance have economic implications (e.g. too great a demand on resources) and social implications (language-impaired children not being detected). For studies of this nature, a statistician should be recruited before *any* data is collected and before a sampling frame has been established.

With this brief introduction to some of the problems of the relation between sample and population, we now turn in chapter 5 to the concept of probability as a crucial notion in providing a link between the properties of a sample and the structure of its parent population. In the final section of that chapter we outline a procedure for random sampling. Chapter 6 deals with the modelling of statistical populations, and introduces the normal distribution, an important model for our purposes in characterising the relation between sample and population.

SUMMARY

In this chapter the basic problem of the **sample–population** relationship has been discussed.

(1) A **statistical population** was defined as a set of all the values which might ever be included in a particular study. The **target population** is the set to which generalisation is intended from a study based on a sample.

(2) Generalisation from a sample to a population can be made formally only if the sample is collected **randomly** from a **sampling frame** which allows each element of the population a known chance of being selected.

(3) The point was made that, for the majority of linguistic investigations, resource constraints prohibit the collection of data in this way. It was argued that statistical theory and methodology still have an important role to play in the planning and analysis of language studies.

EXERCISES

(1) In chapter 9 we refer to a study by Ferris & Politzer (1981) in which children with bilingual backgrounds are tested on their English ability via compositions in response to a short film. Read the brief account of the study (pp. 139ff),

find out what measures were used, and decide what would constitute the elements of the relevant statistical population.

(2) See if you can do the same for Brasington's (1978) study of Rennellese loan words, also explained in chapter 9 (pp. 142–4).

(3) Review the Macken & Barton (1980a) study, detailed in chapter 1. In considering the 'intended population' for this study, what factors do we have to take into account?

(4) In a well-known experiment, Newport, Gleitman & Gleitman (1977) collected conversational data from 15 mother–child pairs, when the children were aged between 15 and 27 months and again six months later. One of the variables of interest was the number of *yes/no* interrogatives used by mothers at the first recording. If we simply consider this variable, what can we say is the intended population? Is it infinite?

5
Probability

The link between the properties of a sample and the structure of its parent population is provided through the concept of **probability**. The concept of probability is best introduced by means of straightforward non-linguistic examples. We will return to linguistic exemplification once the ideas are established. The essentials can be illustrated by means of a simple game.

5.1 **Probability**

Suppose we have a box containing ten plastic discs, of identical shape, of which three are red, the remainder white. The discs are numbered 1 to 10, the red discs being those numbered 1, 2 and 3. The game consists of shaking the box, drawing a disc, without looking inside, and noting both its number and its colour. The disc is returned to the box and the game repeated indefinitely. What proportion of the draws do you think will result in disc number 4 being drawn from the box? One draw in three? One draw in five? One draw in ten?

Surely we would all agree that the last is the most reasonable. There are ten discs. Each is as likely to be drawn as the others every time the game is played. Since there are ten discs with different numbers, we should expect that each number will be drawn about one-tenth of the time in a large number of draws, or **trials** as they are often called. We would say that the probability of drawing the disc numbered 4 on any one occasion is one in ten, and we will write:

$$P(\text{disc number 4}) = \frac{1}{10} = 0.1$$

Instead of determining the probability of disc 4 being drawn in the game, we could ask another question, perhaps, 'What is the probability on any occasion that the disc drawn is red?' Since three out of the ten discs are of this colour, that is three-tenths of the discs in the box are red, then:

$$P(\text{red disc}) = \frac{3}{10} = 0.3$$

In the same way we can ask questions about the probabilities of many other outcomes. For example:

(i) the probability of drawing an even-numbered disc, since there are five of them, is:

$$P(\text{even-numbered disc}) = \frac{5}{10} = 0.5$$

(ii) the probability of drawing a disc which is both red and odd numbered, since there are two of them (1 and 3), is:

$$P(\text{red, odd-numbered disc}) = \frac{2}{10} = 0.2$$

and so on.

It is helpful to play such games to gain some insight into the relation between the relative frequency of particular outcomes in a series of trials and your *a priori* expectations based on your knowledge of the contents of the box. You could repeat the game 100 times and see what is the actual proportion of red discs which is drawn. It is even better if a number of people play the game simultaneously and compare results. Table 5.1 shows what happened on one occasion when 42 students each played the game 100 times. Although the proportion of red discs drawn by individual students varied from 0.20 to 0.39, the mean proportion of red discs drawn over the whole group was 0.2995, very close to the value one would expect, i.e. 0.3.

It should be clear that the actual *number* of red discs is not the important quantity here. The properties of the game depend only on the *proportion* of discs of that colour. For example, if the box contained 10,000 discs of which 3,000 were red it would continue to be true that P(red disc) = 0.3. This has some practical relevance. Suppose that a village contained 10,000 people of whom 30% were male, though this fact was unknown to us. If we wished to try to establish this proportion without having to identify the sex of every person in the village, we could play the above game, but this time with people instead of discs. We would repeatedly choose a person at random (a detailed method for random selection will be given in the final section of this chapter) and note whether the person chosen was male or female. If we repeated the process n times, we could use the proportion of males among these n people as an *estimate* of the proportion or **expected relative frequency** of males in the population. We saw from table 5.1 that it was possible to assess the properties of a sampling

Table 5.1. *Number of times a red disc was drawn from a box*
containing 3 red and 7 white discs in 100 trials by 42 students

20	21	22	24	24	25	26	26	26	26	27	27	28	28	28
29	29	29	29	29	30	30	30	30	31	31	31	32	32	33
33	33	33	34	34	35	36	36	37	37	38	39			

Number of red discs	Frequency
20–22	3
23–25	3
26–28	9
29–31	12
32–34	8
35–37	5
38–40	2

Mean of results of the 42 students is 29.952 per 100 draws

Mean proportion is therefore 0.29952

game empirically, when the proportions of different types are known. It is also possible to study the properties of sampling games theoretically. In establishing the proportion of males in the village, for instance, it is possible to find out how many persons should be sampled in order to give a reasonably accurate estimate, by using methods that are explained in chapter 7 (see especially §7.6). As we shall see, if we take a sample of 400 persons we can expect with reasonable confidence (a 5% probability of error) that the proportion of males in the sample is between 28% and 32%, and we can be almost sure (a 1% probability of error) that the proportion of males in the sample would not be less than 25% or greater than 35%. (Compare these figures to the actual proportion of 30%.)

We should point out that, in practice, it is not common to use the sampling procedure we have employed in the game where each disc/person is replaced in the box/village after its type has been noted. It is more common to take out a whole group of discs/people simultaneously and note the type of every element in the sample. This is equivalent to choosing the discs/people one at a time and then *not* replacing those already chosen before selecting the next. Provided only a small proportion of the total (say less than 10%) of the total is sampled it will not make much difference whether the sampling is done with or without replacement.

5.2 Statistical independence and conditional probability

Table 5.2 displays the numbers of individuals of either sex in two different hypothetical populations classed as monolingual or bilingual. Each population contains the same number of individuals, 10,000,

Table 5.2. *Numbers of monolingual or bilingual adults in two hypothetical populations cross-tabulated by sex*

Population A			
	Male	Female	Total
Bilingual	2 080	1 920	4 000
Monolingual	3 120	2 880	6 000
	5 200	4 800	10 000
Population B			
Bilingual	2 500	1 500	4 000
Monolingual	2 700	3 300	6 000
	5 200	4 800	10 000

of whom 5,200 are male and 4,800 are monolingual. However, in population A the proportion of males who are bilingual is 2080/5200 = 0.4, the same as the proportion of bilingual females (1920/4800). In population B, on the other hand, 2500/5200 males, i.e. 0.48, are bilingual while the proportion of bilingual females is only 0.31. This kind of imbalance may be observed in practice, for example, among the Totonac population of Central Mexico, where the men are more accustomed to trade with outsiders and are more likely to speak Spanish than the more isolated women. A similar effect may be encountered in first-generation immigrant communities where the men learn the tongue of their adopted country quickly at their place of employment while the women spend much more time at home, either isolated or mingling with others of their own ethnic and linguistic group.

Suppose that we were to label every member of such a population with a different number and then write each number on a different plastic disc. All the discs are to be of identical shape, but if the number corresponds to a male it is written on a white disc, if female it is written on a red. The discs are placed in a large box and well shaken. Then one is chosen without looking in the box. Clearly this is one way of choosing objectively a single person, i.e. a sample of size one, from the whole population, and you should see immediately that the following probability statements can be made about such a person chosen from either of the two populations, A or B.

The probability of a male being chosen:

$$P(male) = \frac{5200}{10\,000} = 0.52$$

The probability of a female:

$$P(female) = 0.48$$

The probability of a monolingual:
$$P(\text{monolingual}) = 0.6$$

The probability of a bilingual:
$$P(\text{bilingual}) = 0.4$$

(Notice that when the population is partitioned in such a way that each individual belongs to one and only one category, e.g. male–female or monolingual–bilingual, the total probability over all the categories of the partition is always 1.0; $0.52 + 0.48 = 1.0$ and $0.4 + 0.6 = 1.0$, for either population.)

Although the two populations have identical proportions of male–female and of monolingual–bilingual individuals, they have otherwise different structures. We see this when we look at finer detail:

For population A:

$$P(\text{male and bilingual}) \qquad = \frac{2080}{10\,000} = 0.208$$

$$P(\text{female and bilingual}) \qquad = \frac{1920}{10\,000} = 0.192$$

$$P(\text{male and monolingual}) \quad = \frac{3120}{10\,000} = 0.312$$

$$P(\text{female and monolingual}) = \frac{2880}{10\,000} = 0.288$$

$$\text{Total} \quad \underline{1.000}$$

For population B:

$$P(\text{male and bilingual}) \qquad = \frac{2500}{10\,000} = 0.25$$

$$P(\text{female and bilingual}) \qquad = \frac{1500}{10\,000} = 0.15$$

$$P(\text{male and monolingual}) \quad = \frac{2700}{10\,000} = 0.27$$

$$P(\text{female and monolingual}) = \frac{3300}{10\,000} = 0.33$$

$$\text{Total} \quad \underline{1.00}.$$

Probability

Suppose that, for either population, we continue drawing discs until the very first white disc appears, that is, until the first male person is chosen. What is the probability that this first male is bilingual? Notice that this is not the same as asking for the probability that the first person chosen is male and bilingual. We keep going until we choose the first male and this deliberately excludes the females from consideration. In fact, we are restricting our attention to the subpopulation of males and then asking about the probability of an event which could occur when we impose that restriction or condition. For this reason, such probability is called a **conditional probability**.

To signal the restriction that we will consider only males, we will use a standard notation, P(bilingual|male), where the vertical line indicates that a restriction is being imposed, and we say that we require the 'probability that a chosen person is bilingual *given that* the person is male'. Since, in population A, there are a total of 5,200 males of whom 2,080 are bilingual, the value of the conditional probability is:

$$P(\text{bilingual} | \text{male}) = \frac{2080}{5200} = 0.4$$

Note that this is *exactly* the same as the probability that a person chosen, *irrespective* of sex, will be bilingual, i.e.

$$P(\text{bilingual} | \text{male}) = P(\text{bilingual}) = 0.4$$

We can calculate the probability in a similar fashion for the likelihood that a chosen person is bilingual, given that she is female:

$$P(\text{bilingual} | \text{female}) = \frac{1920}{4800} = 0.4$$

Note that this is again the same as the probability for bilinguals, irrespective of sex:

$$P(\text{bilingual}) = \frac{4000}{10\,000} = 0.4$$

If we wish to determine the probability that a chosen person is male, given that the person is bilingual, the calculation is as follows:

$$P(\text{male} | \text{bilingual}) = \frac{2080}{4000} = 0.52$$

Note that this is the same probability as:

$$P(\text{male} | \text{monolingual}) = \frac{3120}{6000} = 0.52$$

and

$$P(\text{male}) = \frac{5200}{10\,000} = 0.52$$

From these examples we can see that, in population A, whichever restriction as to sex is imposed on selection (or indeed if there is no restriction at all), the probability of bilingualism/monolingualism remains unchanged. Similarly, whichever restriction as to language category we impose (or if there is no restriction at all), the probability of male/female remains the same.

In a population with these characteristics, the variables 'sex' and 'language category' are said to be **statistically independent**. In practice, this means that knowing the value of one gives no information about the other.

Population B exhibits rather different properties. We know already that $P(\text{bilingual}) = 0.4$, but we can see:

$$P(\text{bilingual}\,|\,\text{male}) = \frac{2500}{5200} = 0.48 \neq 0.4$$

and

$$P(\text{bilingual}\,|\,\text{female}) = \frac{1500}{4800} = 0.31 \neq 0.4$$

(Both these conditional probabilities have been rounded to two decimal places.) It is clear that in this case a person's language category will be dependent on that person's sex. That is to say, if a male is selected, then we know there is a higher chance that this person is bilingual than if a female had been chosen. In general, $P(X\,|\,Y)$, the probability that event X occurs, given that the event Y has already occurred, can be calculated by the rule:

$$P(X\,|\,Y) = \frac{P(X \text{ and } Y)}{P(Y)}$$

For example, in population B:

$$P(\text{bilingual}\,|\,\text{male}) = \frac{P(\text{bilingual and male})}{P(\text{male})}$$

$$= \frac{0.25}{0.52} = 0.48$$

Probability

There is one important property of population A which results from the independence of the two variables. Consider the probability that the first person chosen is both male and bilingual. It turns out that:

$$P(\text{male } and \text{ bilingual}) = \frac{2080}{10\,000} = 0.208$$

$$P(\text{male}) \qquad = \frac{5200}{10\,000} = 0.52$$

$$P(\text{bilingual}) \qquad = \frac{4000}{10\,000} = 0.4$$

Now, $0.208 = 0.4 \times 0.52$, so that we can see that the probability of a person being chosen who is both male *and* bilingual can be calculated as follows:

$$P(\text{male } and \text{ bilingual}) = P(\text{male}) \times P(\text{bilingual})$$

This result holds *only* because the two variables of sex and linguistic type are independent.

In population B, on the other hand, we have P(male and bilingual) = 0.25, while, for the same population, P(male) = 0.52 and P(bilingual) = 0.4, so that:

$$P(\text{male and bilingual} \neq P(\text{male}) \times P(\text{bilingual})$$

This indicates the lack of independence between the two variables in this population. However, the relation:

$$P(\text{male and bilingual}) = P(\text{male}\,|\,\text{bilingual}) \times P(\text{bilingual})$$

does hold, since:

$$P(\text{male}\,|\,\text{bilingual}) = 2500/4000 = 0.625$$
$$P(\text{bilingual}) = 0.4$$
$$0.4 \times 0.625 = 0.25$$

In general, for any two possible outcomes, X and Y, of a sampling experiment:

$$P(\text{X and Y occur together}) = P(\text{X}\,|\,\text{Y}) \times P(\text{Y}) = P(\text{Y}\,|\,\text{X}) \times P(\text{X})$$

5.3 **Probability and discrete numerical random variables**

The examples we have seen so far have been concerned with rather simple categorical variables such as sex or linguistic category. However, the situation is very similar when we consider discrete numerical variables, the only difference being that the extended range of values in

Table 5.3. *Hypothetical family size distribution of 1,000 families*

No. of children (X)	No. of families	Proportion
0	121	0.121
1	179	0.179
2	263	0.263
3	217	0.217
4	99	0.099
5	61	0.061
6 or more	60	0.060
Total	1000	

such variables allows us to introduce a richer variety of outcomes whose probability we might want to consider.

Suppose that 1,000 families have given rise to the population of family sizes (i.e. number of children) summarised in table 5.3. In this population, let us choose one family at random. What is the probability that X, the number of children in this family, is 3?

$$\text{Answer: } P(X = 3) = 0.217$$

since that is the proportion of the family sizes which take the value 3. Similarly,[1]

$$P(X = 5) \quad = 0.061$$
$$P(X \leqslant 2) \quad = P(X = 0) + P(X = 1) + P(X = 2)$$
$$= 0.121 + 0.179 + 0.263 = 0.563$$
$$P(0 < X \leqslant 3) = P(X = 1 \text{ or } 2 \text{ or } 3) = 0.659$$

Table 5.3 is an example of a **probability distribution** of a **random variable**. A random variable can be thought of as any variable whose value, which cannot be predicted with certainty, is ascertained as the outcome of an experiment, usually a sampling experiment, or game of some kind. For example, if we decide to choose a family at random from the hypothetical 1,000 families, we do not know for certain what the size of that family will be until after the sampling has been done. The distribution of such a random variable is simply the list of probabilities of the different values that the variable can take. If the different possible values of the variable can be enumerated or listed, as in this case, it is called a **discrete** random variable. Discrete variables may be numerical, like 'family size' or categorical like 'sex' or 'colour'. (In the previous section we saw an example of the categorical variable 'colour' which took the

[1] The symbol < means 'is less than', while ⩽ means 'is less than or equal to'. Similarly, the symbol > means 'is greater than', while ⩾ means 'is greater than or equal to'.

two values 'red' and 'white' with probabilities 0.3 and 0.7 respectively.)
The distribution of a discrete random variable can be represented by a
bar chart: figure 5.1, for example, gives the bar chart corresponding to
table 5.3. We have already seen similar diagrams in figures 2.1 and 2.3,
and these can be considered as approximations to the bar charts of the
discrete random variables 'types of deficit' and 'length of utterance' based
on samples of values of the corresponding random variables.

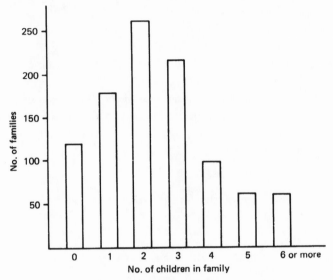

Figure 5.1. Bar chart corresponding to data of table 5.3.

For any discrete, numerical random variable, the probability that a single
random observation has one of a possible range of values is just the sum
of the individual probabilities for the separate values in the range (see
exercise 5.3). Note that the actual size of the population is irrelevant once
the proportion of elements taking a particular value is known.

5.4 Probability and continuous random variables

Suppose that a statistical population is constructed by having
each of a large number of people carry out a simple linguistic task and
noting the reaction time, in seconds, for each person's response. We suppose that the device used to measure the time is extremely accurate and
measures to something like the nearest millionth of a second. In fact,
conceptually at least, there is no limit to the accuracy with which we
could measure a length of time. Ask yourself what is the next largest time
interval greater than 1.643217 seconds. Whatever figure you give it is always

Table 5.4. *Hypothetical distribution of task times*

Time (in seconds) Y		Proportion of times in this range
From	To just less than	
0	20	0.035
20	30	0.031
30	40	0.061
40	50	0.154
50	55	0.202
55	60	0.230
60	70	0.161
70	80	0.071
80	100	0.055

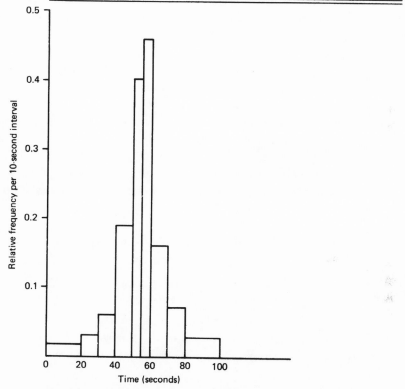

Figure 5.2. Distribution of task times of table 5.3.

possible to suggest one even closer. For example, if 1.6432171 seconds is suggested, that is less close than 1.64321705 which, in turn, is not as close as 1.643217049, and so on. A variable with this property is called **a continuous variable**. Table 5.4 gives a hypothetical relative frequency table for the population of task times and figure 5.2 the corresponding histogram. There are several points worth noting here.

Probability

First, the class intervals are not all of the same width and you should examine how the histogram is adjusted to account for this. In particular, the class interval 0–20 has a higher proportion of the population than its neighbouring class 20–30 and yet the corresponding rectangle in the histogram is less tall; it is the *areas* of the rectangles (i.e. width × height) which correspond to the relative frequencies of the classes. Second, we do not need to state the actual number of elements of the population belonging to each class since, for calculating probabilities, we need only know the relative frequencies. Thirdly, the upper bounds of the class intervals are given as 'less than 20 seconds', 'less than 30 seconds', and so on since, because of the accuracy of our measuring instrument, we are assuming it is possible to get as close to these values as we might wish.

Let us choose, at random, one of these task times and denote it by Y. What is the probability that Y takes the value 25, say? We need to think rather carefully about this. Since we are measuring to the nearest millionth of a second, the range from 0 to 100 contains a possible 100 million different possible values, even more if our instrument for measuring times is even more accurate. The probability of getting a time of any fixed, exact value, say 25.000000 seconds or 31.163217 seconds is very small. To all intents and purposes it is zero. This means that we will have to content ourselves with calculating probabilities for ranges of values of the variable, Y. For example:

$$P(Y < 20) \quad = 0.035$$
$$P(Y < 50) \quad = 0.035 + 0.031 + 0.061 + 0.154 = 0.281$$
$$P(40 \leqslant Y < 55) = 0.154 + 0.202 = 0.356$$

(P($40 \leqslant Y < 55$) is to be interpreted as the probability that Y is equal to or greater than 40 but less than 55.)

In each case we simply identify the required range of values on the histogram and calculate the total area of the histogram encompassed by that range. Note here a very special point which was not true in the previous section:

$$P(Y < 20) = P(Y \leqslant 20)$$

because, since the probability of getting any *exact* value is effectively zero:

$$P(Y \leqslant 20) = P(Y < 20) + P(Y = 20)$$
$$= P(Y < 20) + 0$$

This means that for continuous variables it will not matter whether or not we write < or ≤; the probability does not change.

Now, suppose we try to calculate P($10 < Y < 20$). How can we evaluate

70

this probability? The range does not coincide with the endpoints of class intervals as all the previous examples did. Remember that in the histogram the area defined by a particular range *is* the probability of obtaining a

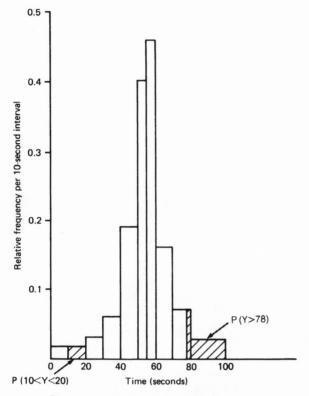

Figure 5.3(a). Estimating probabilities.

value within that range. If we shade, on the histogram, the area corresponding to $10 < Y < 20$ (and refer to table 5.4 for the proportion of times that fall in this range) we see immediately that the required probability $1/2 \times 0.035 = 0.0175$ – see figure 5.3(a). Similarly:

$$P(Y > 78) = \frac{2}{10} \times 0.071 + 0.055$$

and – see figure 5.3(b):

$$P(50 < Y < 87) = 0.202 + 0.230 + 0.161$$

$$+ 0.071 + \left(\frac{7}{20} \times 0.055\right)$$

71

However, these probabilities will be only approximately correct, since the histogram of figure 5.2 is drawn to a rather crude scale on wide class intervals. Its true shape may be something like the smooth curve in figure 6.6. It would then be more difficult to calculate the area corresponding to the interval $10 < Y < 20$, but there are methods which enable it to be done to any required degree of accuracy so that tables can be produced. We will return to this idea in the next chapter.

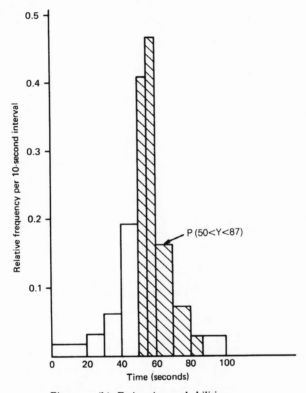

Figure 5.3(b). Estimating probabilities.

5.5 Random sampling and random number tables

We can now return to the issue of random selection and explain in more detail what we mean by a 'random sample'. We have already indicated that 'random' does not mean 'haphazard' or 'without method'. In fact the selection of a truly random sample can be achieved only by closely following well-defined procedures. For illustration, let us suppose that we wish to select a sample of three subjects from a population of eight. (Obviously this situation would never arise in practice, but keeping the sample and population sizes small simplifies the explanation.) **Random sampling** or, in full, **simple random sampling**, is a selection process which in this case will ensure that every sample of three subjects has the same probability of being chosen. Suppose the eight subjects of the population are labelled A, B, C, D, E, F, G, and H. Then there are 56 possible different samples of size 3 which could be selected:

ABC	ABD	ABE	ABF	ABG	ABH	ACD	ACE	ACF	ACG
ACH	ADE	ADF	ADG	ADH	AEF	AEG	AEH	AFG	AFH
AGH	BCD	BCE	BCF	BCG	BCH	BDE	BDF	BDG	BDH
BEF	BEG	BEH	BFG	BFH	BGH	CDE	CDF	CDG	CDH
CEF	CEG	CEH	CFG	CFH	CGH	DEF	DEG	DEH	DFG
		DFH	DGH	EFG	EFH	EGH	FGH		

Now suppose that 56 identical, blank discs are obtained and the three-letter code for a different sample inscribed on each disc. If the discs are now placed in a large drum or hat and well mixed, and then just one is chosen by blind selection, the three subjects corresponding to the chosen letter code would constitute a simple random sample.

The problem with this method is that, for even quite moderate sizes of sample and population, the total number of possible samples (and hence discs) becomes very large. For example, there are around a quarter-of-a-million different samples of size 4 which can be chosen from a population of just 50. It is impossible to contemplate writing each of these on a different disc just to select a sample. Fortunately there is a much quicker method to achieve the same result. Let us return, for the moment, to the example of choosing a sample of three from a population of eight. Take eight discs and write the letter A on the first disc, B on the second, etc, until there is a single disc corresponding to each of the letters A–H. Thoroughly mix the discs and choose one of them blindfold. Mix the remaining seven discs, choose a second, mix the remaining six and choose a third. It can be shown mathematically that this method of selection also gives each of the 56 possible samples exactly the same chance of being chosen. However, this is still not a practicable method. For very large populations it would require a great deal of work to prepare the discs and it may be difficult to ensure that the mixing of them is done efficiently. There is another method available which is both more practicable and more efficient.

Each member of the population is labelled with a number: 1, 2, ..., N, where N is the total population size. Tables of **random numbers** can then be used to select a random sample of n different numbers between

Table 5.5. *Random numbers*

44	59	62	26	82	51	04	19	45	98	03	51	50	14	28	02	12	29	88	87
85	90	22	58	52	90	22	76	95	70	02	84	74	69	06	13	98	86	06	50
44	33	29	88	90	49	07	55	69	50	20	27	59	51	97	53	57	04	22	26
47	57	22	52	75	74	53	11	76	11	21	16	12	44	31	89	16	91	47	75
03	20	54	20	70	56	77	59	95	60	19	75	29	94	11	23	59	30	14	47

I and N. The individuals corresponding to the chosen numbers will constitute the required random sample. A table of random numbers is given in appendix A (table A1). A portion of the table is given in table 5.5 and we will use this to demonstrate the procedure. Suppose we wish to select a random sample of ten subjects from a total population of 7,832. The digits in the table should be read off in non-overlapping groups of four, the same as the number of digits in the total population size. It does not matter whether they are read down columns or across rows – we read across for this example. The first 14 four-digit numbers created in that way are:

4459	6226	8251	0419	4598	0351	5014
2802	1229	8887	8590	2258	5290	2276

and would lead to the inclusion in the sample of the individuals numbered 4459, 6226, 419, 4598, 351, 5014, 2802, 1229, 2258, 2276 and 5290. The numbers 8251, 8887 and 8590 are discarded since they do not correspond to any individual of the population (which contains only 7,832 individuals). If a number is repeated it is ignored after the first time it is drawn. It is not necessary actually to write numbers against the names of *every* individual in the population before obtaining the sample. All that is required is that the individuals of the sample are uniquely identified by the chosen random numbers. For example, the population may be listed on computer output, each page containing 50 names. The random number 4459 then corresponds to the ninth individual on page 90 of the output. Similarly, 25 random words could be chosen from a book of 216 pages in which each page contains 30 lines and no line contains more than 15 words, as follows. Obtain 25 random numbers between 001 and 216 (pages); for each of these obtain one random number between 01 and 30 (lines on a page) and one random number between 01 and 15 (words in the line). This time, if a page number is repeated, that page should be included both (or more) times in the sample. Only if page, line and word number *all* coincide with a previous selection (i.e. the very same word token is repeated) should the choice be rejected.

It is good practice not to enter the random number tables always at the same point but to use some simple rule of your own for determining the entry point, based on the date or the time, or any quantity of this kind which will not always have the same value on every occasion you use the tables. Many calculators have a facility for producing random numbers, which can be useful if tables are not available.

Simple random sampling is not the only acceptable way to obtain samples. Although it does lead to the simplest statistical theory and the most direct interpretation of the data, it may not be easy to see how to obtain a simple random sample of, say, a child's utterances or tokens of a particular phonological variant. This is discussed briefly in chapter 7. However a sample is collected, if the result is to be a simple random sample it must be true that all possible samples of that size have exactly the same chance of being selected.

SUMMARY

This chapter has introduced the concept of **probability** and shown how it can be measured both empirically and, in some situations, theoretically.

(1) The probability of a particular outcome to a sampling experiment was identified with the **expected relative frequency** of the outcome.

(2) The concept of **statistical independence** was discussed; to say that two events, X and Y, are independent is equivalent to the statement that P(X and Y both true) = P(X) × P(Y).

(3) The **conditional probability** of one event given that another has already occurred was defined as P(X|Y) = P(X and Y)/P(Y).

(4) If two events, X and Y, are independent, then P(X|Y) = P(X) and P(Y|X) = P(Y); that is, the conditional probabilities have the same values as the unconditional probabilities.

(5) The concept of a **probability distribution** was introduced. For **discrete** variables, the probability distribution can be presented as a table; for **continuous** variables it takes the form of a histogram and the probability that the variable lies in a certain range can be identified as the area of the corresponding part of the histogram.

(6) It was demonstrated how a **simple random sample** can be selected from a finite population with the help of **random number tables**.

EXERCISES

(1) Replicate yourself the experiment whose results are tabulated in table 5.1. Include the result from your 100 trials to table 5.1, and recalculate the mean.

(2) Using datum 41 as the entry point (you will find it in appendix A, table A1, 6th row, 4th column) and using this book as your data source, list the sample of 25 words suggested by the procedure on page 74.

Probability

(3) Using the probability distribution of family size in table 5.3, calculate the probability that a randomly chosen family has:

    (a)   more than 3 children
    (b)   fewer than 4 children
    (c)   at least 2 but no more than 5 children

(4) Estimate from figure 5.2 the following:

$$P(Y > 23) \qquad P(50 \leqslant Y < 60)$$
$$P(14 \leqslant Y < 92) \quad P(91 \leqslant Y < 96)$$

(5) Calculate from table 5.3 the following:

$$P(X \leqslant 4)$$
$$P(0 < X \leqslant 4)$$

(6) Calculate from the data for population B in table 5.2:

$$P(\text{male} \,|\, \text{bilingual})$$
$$P(\text{female} \,|\, \text{bilingual})$$

6
Modelling statistical populations

We pointed out in chapter 4 that the solution of many of our problems will depend on our ability to infer accurately from samples to populations. In chapter 5 we introduced the basic elements of probability and argued that it is by means of probability statements concerning random variables that we will be able to make inferences from samples to populations. In the present chapter we introduce the notion of a statistical model and describe one very common and important model.

We should say at the outset that the models with which we are concerned here are not of the kind most commonly met in linguistic studies. They are not, for instance, like the morphological models proposed by Hockett (1954); nor do they resemble the psycholinguists' models of speech production and perception. The models discussed in this chapter are statistical models for the description and analysis of random variability. No special mathematical knowledge or aptitude is required in order to understand them.

6.1 A simple statistical model

Statistical models are best introduced by means of an example. In chapter 1 we discussed in detail a study which looked at the voice onset time (VOT) for word-initial plosives in the speech of children in repeated samples over an eight-month period. For our present purpose we will consider only the VOTs for one pair of stop targets, /t/ and /d/, for one child at 1;8. To make our exposition easier, we will also assume that the tokens were in the same environment (in this case preceding /uː/). Look at table 6.1. The fictitious data displayed there are what one would expect to see only if an individual's VOT for a particular element in a certain environment were always precisely the same, i.e. if the population of an individual's VOTs for that element in that environment had a single value. Such VOTs would be like measurement of height or arm length. Provided that the measurement is very accurate, we do not have to measure

Table 6.1. *Hypothetical sample of VOTs in absence of variation*

VOT for /d/	VOT for /t/
14.25	22.3
14.25	22.3
14.25	22.3
14.25	22.3
14.25	22.3
14.25	22.3
14.25	22.3
14.25	22.3
	22.3
	22.3

Table 6.2. *Hypothetical, but realistic, sample of VOTs from a single subject*

VOT for /d/	VOT for /t/
17.05	16.81
11.70	24.32
18.09	20.17
15.78	28.31
13.94	18.27
14.52	21.03
16.74	17.94
16.16	19.37
	23.16

the length of a person's arms over and over again in order to know whether the left arm is longer than the right. In the same way, we would not have to take repeated measures of an individual's VOTs for /d/- and /t/-targets in a specific environment. In the case of the child, on the basis of a single accurate measurement of each, we would be able to say that the population VOT for /d/ (14.25 ms) is shorter than that for /t/ (22.3 ms) in the environment /_uː/. Put another way, it would be clear that the sample /d/ VOT and the sample /t/ VOT do not come from the same statistical population.

But of course VOTs are not like that. The data in table 6.2, though again invented, are much more realistic. This time there is considerable variation amongst /d/ VOTs and amongst /t/ VOTs in the same environment. As a result, it is no longer possible to make a simple comparison between a single /d/ VOT and a single /t/ VOT and come to a straightforward decision as to whether the /d/ VOTs and the /t/ VOTs came from the same population. In order to make this decision we will have to infer the structure of the populations from the structure of the samples.

If it were possible ever to obtain the complete population of /d/ VOTs for this child we could then calculate the mean VOT for the population. Let us designate it by μ. (It is customary for population values to be represented by Greek characters and for sample values to be represented by Roman characters.) Any individual value of VOT could then be understood as the sum of two elements: the mean, μ, of the population plus the difference, ε, between the mean value and the actual, observed VOT. A sample of VOTs, $X_1, X_2, \ldots, X_n$ could then be expressed as:

$$X_1 = \mu + \varepsilon_1$$
$$X_2 = \mu + \varepsilon_2$$
$$\cdot \qquad \cdot$$
$$\cdot \qquad \cdot$$
$$\cdot \qquad \cdot$$
$$X_n = \mu + \varepsilon_n$$

μ is often called the 'true value' and ε_i the 'error in the i-th observation'.[1] Neither the word 'true' nor the word 'error' is meant to imply a value judgement. We suggest a more neutral terminology below.

Any individual (observed) value can then be seen as being made up of two elements: the true value (the mean of the population), and the distance, or **deviation**, of the observed value from the true value. To illustrate this, let us imagine that the mean of the population of the child's /d/ VOTs in the stated environment is 14.95. (Of course, in fact, the population mean can never be known for certain without observing the entire population, something which is impossible since there is no definite limit to the number of tokens of this VOT which the child might express.) So $\mu = 14.95$. If we take the observed /d/ VOTs in table 6.2, these can be restated as follows:

$$14.95 + 2.10$$
$$14.95 - 3.25$$
$$14.95 + 3.14$$
(etc.)

---

[1] This is one of the many examples of statistical terminology appropriate to the context in which a concept or technique was developed being transferred to a wider context in which it is inappropriate or, at least, confusing. Scientists such as Pascal, Laplace and, particularly, Gàuss in the second half of the eighteenth, and first part of the nineteenth, centuries were concerned with the problem of obtaining accurate measurements of physical quantities such as length, weight, density, temperature, etc. The instruments then available were relatively crude and repeated measurements gave noticeably different values. In that context it seemed reasonable to propose that there was a 'true value' and that a specific measurement could be described usefully in terms of its deviation from the true value. Furthermore, it seemed intuitively reasonable that the mean of an indefinitely large number of measurements would be extremely close to the true value provided the measuring device was unbiassed. By analogy, the mean of a population of measurements is often referred to as the 'true' value (cf. the 'true test score' in chapter 13) and any deviation from this mean as an 'error' or 'random error'.

The second element, the error, indicates the position of each observed value relative to the true value or mean. It will be represented by the symbol ε and its value may be either positive or negative. The division into true value and error can be extended to the population as a whole; any possible VOT for a /d/-target which might ever be pronounced by this child in this context can be represented as:

$$\mu + \varepsilon$$

And that is an example of a statistical model. However, this definition of the model is not complete until some way is found to describe the variation in the value of ε from one VOT to another.

Returning to the child's VOTs, we use the model in this case to restate our problem. Is the mean of the population of /d/ VOTs the same as the mean of the population of /t/ VOTs? Does $\mu_{/t/}$ equal $\mu_{/d/}$?[2] If so, we assume that the /d/ VOTs and /t/ VOTs are members of the same population and that the child is not distinguishing between /d/ and /t/ in terms of VOT in the specified environment.

The example we have used in this chapter has concerned one individual providing a number of VOT values. But the model we have presented (population mean plus error) can also be applied in cases where a number of individuals have each provided a single value.

6.2   The sample mean and the importance of sample size

So far we have said that a population may be modelled by considering each of its values expressed as $\mu + \varepsilon$. In the final section of chapter 4 we discussed some of the inferences we might want to make from a sample to a population. We may often wish to extract information from the sample about the value of the population mean, μ. Suppose now that we have a sample, $X_1, X_2 \ldots, X_n$, of n values from some population. It seems reasonable to imagine that there will be a more or less strong resemblance between the sample mean and the population mean. In particular, it appears to be a common intuition that in a 'very large' sample the sample mean should have a value 'very close' to the population mean, μ. Let us explore this intuition by considering a sample of just five observations:

$X_1 = \mu + \varepsilon_1, X_2 = \mu + \varepsilon_2, X_3 = \mu + \varepsilon_3, X_4 = \mu + \varepsilon_4$, and $X_5 = \mu + \varepsilon_5$.

---

[2] It will be chapter 11 before we finally obtain the answer to this question. In the meantime, the reader is asked to accept that the truth will eventually be revealed and that the argumentation which will cause the delay is necessary to a proper understanding of the statistical methods used in obtaining the answer.

Now, for the sample mean, $\bar{X}$, we have:

$$\bar{X} = \frac{1}{n}\Sigma X_i$$

$$= \frac{1}{5}[X_1 + X_2 + X_3 + X_4 + X_5]$$

$$= \frac{1}{5}[(\mu + \varepsilon_1) + (\mu + \varepsilon_2) + (\mu + \varepsilon_3) + (\mu + \varepsilon_4) + (\mu + \varepsilon_5)]$$

$$= \frac{1}{5}[5\mu + (\varepsilon_1 + \varepsilon_2 + \varepsilon_3 + \varepsilon_4 + \varepsilon_5)]$$

$$= \mu + \bar{\varepsilon} \quad (\bar{\varepsilon} \text{ signifies mean error})$$

Clearly, the value of $\bar{X}$ can also be expressed as a true value plus an error, where the true value is still μ, the population mean of the original Xs and the error is the average value of the original errors. However, the mean of several errors is likely to be smaller in size than single errors, if only because some of the original errors will be negative and some will be positive so that there will be a certain amount of cancelling out. It would seem, then, that the mean of a sample will have the same true value about which we require information and will tend to have a smaller error than the typical single measurement. The larger the sample size, the smaller the error is likely to be. This is such a central concept to the foundations of statistical inference that it is worth studying it in some detail via a simple dice-throwing experiment.

A properly manufactured dice should be in the shape of a cube with each face marked by a different one of the numbers 1, 2, 3, 4, 5 or 6, and be perfectly balanced so that no face is more likely to turn up than any other when the dice is thrown. If we were asked to predict the proportion of occurrences of any one number, say 3, in the entire population of numbers resulting from possible throws of the dice, our best prediction, given that there are six faces, would be one-sixth. We would expect each of the six numbers to occur on one-sixth of the occasions that the dice was thrown. This can be represented in a bar chart (figure 6.1), which would be a model for the population bar chart, i.e. a bar chart derived from all possible throws of a perfect dice. It is possible to calculate what would be the population mean, μ, of all the possible throws of this dice. Suppose the dice is thrown a *very* large number of times, N. Each possible value will also appear a very large number of times. Suppose the value

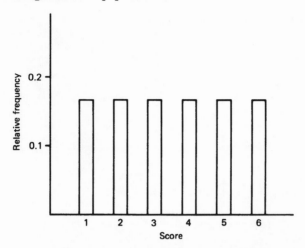

Figure 6.1. Bar chart for population of single throws of an ideal dice.

1 appears N_1 times, 2 appears N_2 times, and so on. The total score achieved by the N throws will then be:

$$N_1 \times 1 + N_2 \times 2 + N_3 \times 3 + N_4 \times 4 + N_5 \times 5 + N_6 \times 6$$

and the mean will be:

$$\mu = \frac{1}{N}(N_1 + 2N_2 + 3N_3 + 4N_4 + 5N_5 + 6N_6)$$

$$= \frac{N_1}{N} + 2\left(\frac{N_2}{N}\right) + 3\left(\frac{N_3}{N}\right) + 4\left(\frac{N_4}{N}\right) + 5\left(\frac{N_5}{N}\right) + 6\left(\frac{N_6}{N}\right)$$

If N is an indefinitely large number, the model of figure 6.1 implies that each possible value appears in one-sixth of throws. In other words:

$$\frac{N_1}{N} = \frac{N_2}{N} = \frac{N_3}{N} = \frac{N_4}{N} = \frac{N_5}{N} = \frac{N_6}{N} = \frac{1}{6}$$

and:

$$\mu = \frac{1}{6} + \left(2 \times \frac{1}{6}\right) + \left(3 \times \frac{1}{6}\right) + \left(4 \times \frac{1}{6}\right) + \left(5 \times \frac{1}{6}\right) + \left(6 \times \frac{1}{6}\right)$$

$$= 3.5$$

With a similar kind of argument it is possible to show that the standard deviation of the population of dice scores is s = 1.71.

A real dice was thrown 1,000 times and the results are shown in figure 6.2. As we might expect from the model shown in figure 6.1, each of

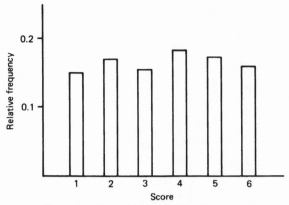

Figure 6.2. Typical histogram for the scores of 1000 single dice throws.

the values occurred with roughly equal frequency. The mean of the 1,000 values is 3.61 and the standard deviation is 1.62. The actual outcome is similar to what would be predicted by the model we constructed for the population of throws of a perfect dice.

Using the model of the previous section we could express the value, X, of any particular throw of the dice as:

$$X = \mu_X + \varepsilon$$

where $\mu_X = 3.5^3$ and ε takes one of the values 2.5 (X = 6), 1.5 (X = 5), 0.5 (X = 4), −0.5 (X = 3), −1.5 (X = 2) and −2.5 (X = 1).

Furthermore, from the physical properties of the dice we would expect that each of the 'errors' is equally likely to occur. This is a particularly simple model for the random error component ε, viz. that all errors are equally likely. The model is adequately expressed by the bar chart of figure 6.3 (which is identical to that in figure 6.1 except that the possible values of ε are marked on the horizontal axis rather than the possible scores), or by the formal statement:

'ε can take the six values 2.5, 1.5, 0.5, −0.5, −1.5, or −2.5'

and, for any particular throw:

$$P(\varepsilon = 2.5) = P(\varepsilon = 1.5) = P(\varepsilon = 0.5) = P(\varepsilon = -0.5) =$$
$$P(\varepsilon = -1.5) = P(\varepsilon = -2.5) = \frac{1}{6}$$

---

[3] We have written μ_X here to indicate that we wish to refer to the population mean of the variable X. We will shortly introduce more variables and, to avoid confusion, it will be necessary to use a different symbol for the population mean of each different variable. Note here how inappropriate is the term 'true value'. Although the mean of the population of dice scores is $\mu_X = 3.5$, it is never possible to achieve such a score on a single throw.

This latter description of the model is another example of a **probability distribution** (see §5.3), the term for a list or a formula which indicates the relative frequency of occurrence of the different values of a random variable.

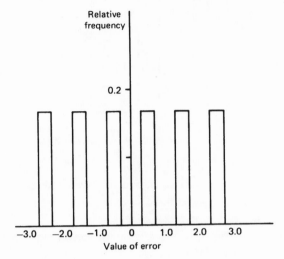

Figure 6.3. Bar chart of population of 'errors' for a single throw of a dice.

It is already obvious that the use of the word 'error' is hard to sustain, and we will from now on usually adopt the more neutral term **residual** which indicates that ε is the value remaining when μ has been subtracted $(\mu + \varepsilon - \mu = \varepsilon)$.

A second experiment was carried out with the dice. This time, after every ten throws the mean was taken of the numbers occurring in these throws. Thus if the first ten throws were 2, 2, 6, 3, 4, 1, 2, 5, 2, 6, a mean score of 3.3 ($33 \div 10$) was noted. In this way, 1,000 numbers, each a mean of ten scores, were obtained: let us call them Y_1, Y_2 ..., Y_{1000}. These numbers are a sample of a population of means – the means that would occur if the procedure were repeated indefinitely. Since there is effectively no limit to the number of times that the procedure could be repeated, the population of mean scores is infinite. The distribution, or histogram, of the population is known as **the sampling distribution of the sample mean**. The histogram of the sample of 1,000 mean scores is shown in figure 6.4.

Note that the histogram is quite symmetrical; it is shaped rather like an inverted bell. Furthermore, the mean of these 1,000 sample means was 3.48 and their standard deviation was 0.62, which is about one-third of the standard deviation of the original population of scores of single throws. Each of the individual mean scores can be written as $Y_i = \mu_Y + \varepsilon_i$ where, as we have shown above, $\mu_Y = \mu_X = 3.5$ (since each Y is the average of a sample of Xs) and the residuals are means of the residuals of single

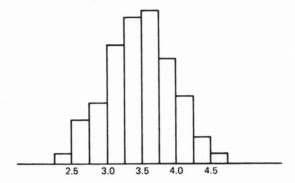

Figure 6.4. Histogram of 1000 means of ten dice throws.

scores and thus will generally be smaller than those for single scores. This seems to be borne out by the smaller value of the standard deviation which indicates that the Y values are less spread out than the X values. The histogram of figure 6.4 shows this feature quite clearly when it is compared with figure 6.2.

The whole experiment was repeated several times, using a different sample size each time. In every experiment 1,000 mean scores were obtained; the means and standard deviations of the 1,000 scores for each sample size are recorded in table 6.3. It can be seen that as the sample size is increased the standard deviation of the sample mean decreases, indicating that the larger the sample size, the closer the sample mean is likely to be to the true value. There is, indeed, a simple relationship which can be demonstrated theoretically between the standard deviation of a population of sample means and the standard deviation of the population of single scores. To obtain the standard deviation for sample means of samples of size n the standard deviation of single scores should be divided by the square root of n. For example, in this case the population standard deviation of single scores is 1.71. For the population of sample means based on samples of size 10, the standard deviation will be $1.71 \div \sqrt{10} = 0.54$. (The *sample* of 1,000 such sample means had a *sample* standard deviation of 0.62.) Other examples appear in table 6.3.

The results of the series of experiments support the intuition that the sample mean should be 'something like' the population mean and that

Table 6.3. *The mean and the standard deviation of the sample mean*

Number of throws averaged for each score	Typical sample of 1000 scores		Population of scores	
	Mean	Standard deviation	Mean (μ)	Standard deviation
1	3.61	1.62	3.5	1.71
10	3.47	0.62	3.5	$\dfrac{1.71}{\sqrt{10}} = 0.54$
25	3.49	0.29	3.5	$\dfrac{1.71}{\sqrt{25}} = 0.34$
100	3.51	0.14	3.5	$\dfrac{1.71}{\sqrt{100}} = 0.17$
400	3.50	0.098	3.5	$\dfrac{1.71}{\sqrt{400}} = 0.086$
1000	3.50	0.059	3.5	$\dfrac{1.71}{\sqrt{1000}} = 0.054$

the bigger the sample, the closer the sample mean will tend to be to the population mean. However, we would like to be more specific than this. For example, we would like to be able to calculate a sample mean from a single sample and then say how close we believe it to be to the true value. Alternatively, it would be useful to know what size of sample we need to attain a particular accuracy. In order to answer such questions we need a model to describe the way that the value of the residual, ε, might vary from one measurement to another.

6.3 A model of random variation: the normal distribution

The model to be presented in this section is one for **random variation**. This term is in general use for those variations in repeated measurements which we seem unable to control. For example, the VOTs in table 6.2 are all different, though they purport to be several measurements of the same quantity all obtained under similar conditions, and they vary according to no recognisable or predictable pattern. It is not easy to define randomness. Its essential quality is lack of predictability. If we think of the child producing tokens of /d/ in the specified environment, there is no way in which we can predict in advance precisely what the VOT of the next token will be. In this sense, the variation in VOTs is random.[4]

Random variation can take many forms. The histogram of a population of measurements could be symmetrical with most of the values close to the mean, or skewed to the right with most values quite small but with a noticeable frequency of larger-than-average values. We have already discussed in chapter 2 the possibility that a histogram could be U-shaped or bi-modal, in which case most values would be either somewhat larger or somewhat smaller than the mean and very few will be close to the mean value. With this range of diversity, is it possible to formulate a general and useful model of random variation?

In figure 6.5 we have superimposed the histograms for several of our dice experiments. As we increase the number of throws whose mean is calculated to give a score, the histogram of the scores becomes more peaked and more bell-shaped. It is a fact that, *even if the histogram of single scores had been skewed, or U-shaped, or whatever, the histograms of the means would still be symmetrical and bell-shaped for large samples*. Furthermore, it can be demonstrated theoretically that, for large samples, the histogram of the sample mean will always have the same mathematical formula irrespective of the pattern of variation in the single measurements that are used to calculate the means. The formula was discovered by Gauss about two centuries ago and the corresponding general histogram (figure 6.6) is still often called the Gaussian curve, especially by engineers and physicists. During the nineteenth century the Gaussian curve was widely used, in the way that we describe below and in succeeding chapters, to analyse statistical data. Towards the end of that century other models were proposed for the analysis of special cases though the Gauss model was still used much more often than the others. Possibly as a result of this it became known as the **normal curve** or **normal distribution** and this is how we will refer to it henceforth.

We have here an example of a very stable and important statistical phenomenon. If samples of size n are repeatedly drawn from any population, and the sample means (i.e. the means of each of the samples) are plotted

---

[4] Even if there were a discernible pattern, attributable perhaps to the effect of fatigue, it would still be impossible to make precise predictions about future VOTs; there would still be a random element. It is simpler at this stage of our exposition to deny ourselves the luxury of introducing a third element, such as fatigue effect, into our model of VOT populations.

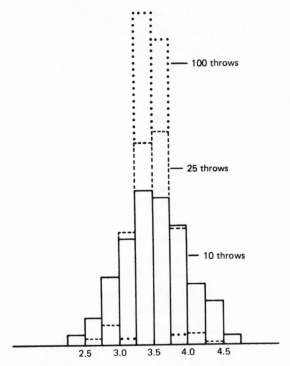

Figure 6.5. Histogram of means of different numbers of dice throws.

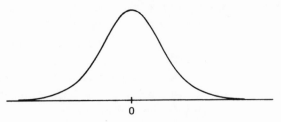

Figure 6.6. The normal, or Gaussian, curve.

in a histogram, we find the following three things happen, provided that n, the sample size, is large: (1) the histogram is symmetrical; (2) the mean of the set of sample means is very close to that of the original population; (3) the standard deviation of the set of sample means will be very close to the original population standard deviation divided by the square root of the sample size, n.

We can go further than this. If the sample size, n, is large enough, then the histogram of the means of the samples of size n can always be very closely described by a single mathematical formula, irrespective of

88

the population from which the samples are drawn. The only differences will be (a) the position of the centre of the histogram will depend on the value of the original population mean, μ; and (b) the degree to which it is peaked or flat depends on σ, the standard deviation of the original population; the larger σ is, the more spread out will be the histogram; the smaller σ is, the higher will be the peak in the centre.

This patterning of sample means allows us to develop a statistical model for the histogram of the population of sample means from any experiment. In order to construct such a model for a particular case we need to know the mean and standard deviation of the population from which each sample is drawn. Each such model histogram, which will exhibit the shared characteristics of the histograms in figure 6.5, will closely approximate the true population histogram of figure 6.6, provided that the sample size is 'large'. (We will have more to say in succeeding chapters about the means of 'large' in this context.)[5]

The normal distribution is basic to a great deal of statistical theory which assumes that it provides a good model for the behaviour of the sample mean. It is this which will allow us to give answers to some of the various problems which we set ourselves in chapter 4. Before we can do this, however, we must learn to use the tables of the normal distribution.

6.4 Using tables of the normal distribution

We said in the previous section that the normal distribution is a good model for the statistical behaviour of the sample mean. We will use it in this way in future chapters. But this is not its only use. It turns out that any variable whose value comes about as the result of summing the values of several independent, or almost independent, components can be modelled successfully as a normal distribution. The size of a plant, for example, is likely to be determined by many factors such as the amount of light, water, nutrients and space, as well as its genetic make-up, etc. And it is indeed true that the distribution of the sizes of a number of plants of the same species grown under similar conditions can be modelled rather well by a normal distribution, i.e. a histogram representing the

---

[5] The discussion in the last few paragraphs can be summarised by what is known as the **Central Limit Theorem**: 'Suppose the population of values of a variable, X, has mean μ and standard deviation σ. Let $\bar{X}(n)$ be the mean of a sample of n values randomly chosen from the population. Then as n gets larger the true histogram of the population of all the possible values of $\bar{X}(n)$ becomes more nearly like the histogram of a normal distribution with mean μ and standard deviation $\sigma/\sqrt{n}$. This result will be true whatever is the form of the original population histogram of the variable, X.'

sizes of plants of a certain species will have the characteristic 'normal' shape. This is true of many biological measurements.[6] It is also often true of scores obtained on educational and psychological tests. Certainly tests can be constructed in such a way that the population of test scores will have a histogram very like that of a normal distribution. We need not bother how such tests are constructed. For the rest of this chapter we will simply assume that we have such a test.

The test we have in mind is a language aptitude test, that is, a test designed to predict individuals' ability to learn foreign languages. The distribution of test scores, over all the subjects we might wish to administer the test to, can be modelled quite closely by a normal distribution with a mean of 50 marks and a standard deviation of 10 marks. Suppose that we know that a score of less than 35 indicates that the test-taker is most unlikely to be successful on one of the intensive foreign language courses. We might wish to estimate the proportion of all test-takers who would score below 35. We can do this very easily using tables of the normal distribution. In the following italicised passage we say something about how the tables are constructed and this will help explain why they can be used in the way that they are, and in particular, why we do not need to have separate tables for every possible combination of mean and standard deviation. The reader may wish to skip this passage in order to see how the tables are used, returning to this point in the text only later.

A normal distribution can have any mean or standard deviation. We therefore cannot give tables of every possible normal distribution – there are simply too many possibilities. Fortunately, one of the exceptional and extremely useful properties of the normal model is that an observation from any normal distribution can be converted to an observation from the **standard normal distribution** *by using the standardisation procedure described in §3.9. The population mean of a standardised variable is always zero and its standard deviation is 1. Let us try to see why this is true.*

Suppose a variable, X, comes from a population with mean μ and standard deviation σ. First we change X into a new variable, Y, by the rule:

$$Y = X - \mu$$

When we subtract a constant quantity from all the elements in a population,

---

[6] Equally, it is *not* true of many variables. The distribution of income or wealth in many societies is usually skewed, with the great bulk of individuals receiving less than the mean income since the mean is inflated by a few very large incomes. A similar effect can often be seen in the distribution of the time required to learn a new task – a few individuals will take *very* much longer than the others to learn a new skill. It ought not to be difficult to think of other examples.

the same value is subtracted from the mean. So the mean value of the new variable, Y, will be equal to the mean value of X minus μ. That is:

$$(mean\ Y) = (mean\ X) - \mu$$
$$= \mu - \mu$$
$$= 0$$

The standard deviation of Y will, however, be exactly the same as that of X. All the values of X have been reduced by the same amount; they will still have the same relative values to one another and to the new mean value. In other words, subtraction of a constant quantity from all the elements of a population will not affect the value of the standard deviation (exercise 6.3). To complete the standardisation we have to change this standard deviation so that it will have the value 1. We can do that by dividing all the Y values by the number σ, the standard deviation of Y (and X). When a variable is divided by some number, the mean is divided by the same number. So if we write $Z = Y/\sigma$ it will be true that:

$$mean\ of\ Z = \frac{(mean\ of\ Y)}{\sigma} = \frac{0}{\sigma} = 0$$

Furthermore (see exercise 6.4):

$$standard\ deviation\ of\ Z = \frac{(standard\ deviation\ of\ Y)}{\sigma} = \frac{\sigma}{\sigma} = 1$$

By these two steps we have changed X, a variable with population mean μ and standard deviation σ, into Z, a variable whose mean is zero and standard deviation is unity, 1. Remember what the two steps are. From each value X we subtract μ, the mean of the population of X values, and then divide the result by the population standard deviation, σ. As before, we can write the complete rule in a single formula:

$$Z = \frac{X - \mu}{\sigma}$$

Z is called a standardised random variable whether or not the distribution of the original scores can be modelled successfully as a normal distribution. However, it is a special property of the normal distribution that if X was normally distributed then Z will also have a normal distribution. We say that Z has the **standard normal distribution**. *We can exploit all this to change questions about any normally distributed random variable into* *equivalent questions about the standard normal variable and then use tables of that variable to answer the question. In other words, we do not need tables for every different normal distribution.*

We want to know the proportion of test-takers we can expect to achieve a score of less than 35. To put this another way, if we choose a test-taker at random and obtain his test score, X, we wish to know the likelihood that the inequality X < 35 will be true. In order to answer this question, we will have to alter it until it becomes an equivalent question about the corresponding standardised score. (This is because, as was explained in the italicised passage, the tables we will use relate to the standard normal distribution.) This can be done as follows:

$$X < 35 \text{ is equivalent to } X - 50 < 35 - 50 \text{ (subtracting the mean)}$$

$$\text{is equivalent to } X - 50 < -15$$

$$\text{is equivalent to } \frac{X - 50}{10} < \frac{-15}{10} \text{ (dividing by the standard deviation)}$$

$$\text{is equivalent to } \frac{X - 50}{10} < -1.5$$

What have we done? We have altered X by subtracting the population mean and dividing by the standard deviation; we have standardised X and changed it into the standard normal variable Z. Thus:

$$X < 35 \text{ is equivalent to } Z < \frac{35 - 50}{10}$$

$$\text{i.e. } Z < -1.5$$

This is another way of saying that a subject whose test score is less than 35 will have a standardised test score less than −1.5. (Note that the minus sign is extremely important.)

Table A2 in appendix A gives the probability that Z < −1.5. Notice that the table consists of several pairs of columns. The left column of each pair gives values of Z. The right column gives the area of the standard normal histogram that lies to the left of the tabulated value of Z. (The relationship between areas in histograms and probabilities was discussed in chapter 5.) The diagram and rubric at the head of the table should be helpful.

For the example we have chosen we find P = 0.0668. Hence we can say that about 7% (6.68%) of scores will be less than 35. The accuracy of this answer will depend on how closely the distribution of the population of test results can, in fact, be described by the normal distribution with the same mean and variance as the population. If the population of test scores has a distribution which cannot be modelled by a normal distribution, it would be inappropriate to use standard scores in this way, since Z would not have a standard normal distribution.

SUMMARY

This chapter has discussed the concept of a **statistical model**.

(1) A model for a single measurement, X, was proposed: $X = \mu + \varepsilon$ where μ is the **'true' value** or **population mean** and ε the **error, deviation from the mean** or **residual**.

(2) It was argued that means of samples of measurements would be less variable than individual measurements.

(3) The **sampling distribution of the sample mean** was introduced: for any random variable X with mean μ and standard deviation σ, the variable $\bar{X}$, calculated from a sample of size n, will have the same mean μ but a smaller standard deviation, $\sigma/\sqrt{n}$. Furthermore, if n is large, $\bar{X}$ will have a **normal distribution**.

(4) It was shown how to use **tables of the standard normal distribution** to answer questions about any normally distributed variable.

EXERCISES

(1) (a) Using the procedure of exercise 5.2, choose a random sample of 100 words and find the mean and standard deviation of the sample of 100 word lengths.

(b) Divide the 100 words into 25 subsamples of 4 words each and calculate the mean word length of each subsample.

(c) Calculate the mean and standard deviation of the 25 subsample means.

(d) Discuss the standard deviations obtained in (a) and (c) above.

(2) Assuming that the 'true' mean VOT for /d/ for the observed child is 14.25, calculate the residuals for the /d/ VOTs of table 6.2.

(3) (a) Calculate the standard deviations of the /d/ VOTs of table 6.2.

(b) Calculate the standard deviation of their residuals (see exercise 6.2). Discuss.

(4) (a) Calculate the standard deviation of the /t/ VOTs of table 6.2.

(b) Divide each VOT by the standard deviation calculated in (a).

(c) Calculate the standard deviation of these modified values and discuss the result.

(5) A score, Y, on a test is normally distributed with mean 120 and standard deviation 20. Find:

(a) $P(Y < 100)$ (b) $P(Y > 140)$

(c) $P(Y < 130)$ (d) $P(Y > 105)$

(e) $P(100 < Y < 130)$ (f) $P(135 < Y < 150)$

(g) the score which will be exceeded by 95% of the population.

(Hint: You may find it helpful to begin by drawing sketches similar to figure 5.3.)

7
Estimating from samples

Chapter 6 introduced the normal distribution and the table associated with it. In the present chapter we will show how to make use of these to assess how well population values might be estimated by samples. We return to the question of measuring the /d/ VOT for a child (1;8) discussed in the previous chapter. We introduced there a model for a specific token, X, of VOT expressed by the child, namely:

$$X = \mu + \varepsilon$$

which says that the value of the token can be considered as a mean (or 'true') value plus a random residual. If the value of μ were known we could use this single value as *the* /d/ VOT for the child and go on perhaps to compare it with *the* /t/ VOT (i.e. the mean of the population of /t/ VOTs) of the same child to decide whether the child is distinguishing between /d/ and /t/. In the present chapter we will consider the extent to which the value of μ can be estimated from a sample of /d/ VOTs. In chapter 11 we will return to the problem of comparing two different populations of VOTs.

7.1 Point estimators for population parameters

It has to be recognised at the outset that the question we have just posed concerns *population* means. Clearly we do not have direct access to the population means; all we can do is estimate them from the sample values available to us. The question is 'how?'

It seems intuitively reasonable to suppose that the mean value, $\bar{X}$, of a sample of /d/ VOTs will be similar to the mean, μ, of the population of VOTs that the child is capable of producing. But how accurate is this intuition? How similar will the two values be? $\bar{X}$ has two mathematical properties which sanction its use as an estimator for μ. First of all, it is **unbiassed**. In other words, in some samples $\bar{X}$ will be smaller than μ, in some it will be larger, but on average the value will be correct;

the mean of an infinitely large number of such sample means would be the mean of the population, the very quantity which we wish to estimate. Second, $\bar{X}$ is a **consistent** estimator. This is the technical term used to describe an estimator which is more likely to be close to the true value of the parameter it is estimating if it is based on a larger sample. We have seen that this is the case for $\bar{X}$ in figure 6.5. The larger the sample size, the more closely the values of $\bar{X}$ will cluster around the population mean, μ.

In fact, it is extremely common to use $\bar{X}$ as an estimator of the population mean, not just for VOTs. The mean of any sample can be used to estimate the mean of the population from which the sample is drawn. A single number calculated from a sample of data and used to estimate a population parameter is usually referred to as a **point estimator** (in opposition to the interval estimators introduced below). There are many instances of a sample value being used as a point estimator of the corresponding population parameter. The proportion, $\hat{p}$, of incorrectly marked past tense verbs in a sample of speech from a 2-year-old child is an unbiassed and consistent estimator of the proportion of such errors in the child's speech as a whole. The variance, s^2, of a sample of values from any population is likewise an unbiassed[1] and consistent estimator of the population variance, σ^2.

7.2 Confidence intervals

Although a point estimator is an indicator of the possible value of the corresponding population parameter, it is of limited usefulness by itself. Its value depends on the characteristics of a single sample; a new sample from the same population will provide a different value. It is therefore preferable to provide estimates which take into account explicitly this sampling variability and state a likely range within which the population value may lie. This is the motivation behind the idea of a confidence interval. We will illustrate the concept by considering again the VOT problem discussed at the beginning of the chapter.

Suppose that we have a sample of 100 /d/-target VOTs from a single child and find that the sample has a mean value of $\bar{X} = 14.88$ ms and a standard deviation $s = 5.00$ ms. Let us suppose further that the *population* of /d/ VOTs which could be produced by the child has mean μ and standard

---

[1] In chapter 3 it was stated that, in the calculation of s^2, the sum of squared deviations is divided not by the sample size, n, but by $(n-1)$. The main reason for this is to ensure that s^2 is an unbiassed estimator of σ^2. If n were used in the denominator the sample variance would, on average, underestimate the population variance, though the discrepancy, or bias, would be negligible in large samples.

deviation σ, though of course we cannot know what these values are. Now we discovered in the previous chapter that, for reasonably large samples of size n, $\bar{X}$ is a random observation taken from a normally distributed population of possible sample means. The mean of that population is also μ but its standard deviation is $\sigma/\sqrt{n}$. Again, we know from the characteristics of the normal distribution discussed in chapter 6 that it follows that 95% of samples from this population will have a mean value, $\bar{X}$, in the interval $\mu \pm 1.96\, \sigma/\sqrt{n}$ (i.e. within 1.96 standard deviations of the true mean value). If σ is small or n is very large, or both, the interval will be narrow, and $\bar{X}$ will then usually be 'rather close' to the population value, μ. What we must do now is see just how close we can expect a sample mean of 14.88 to be to the population mean, given a sample size of 100 and an estimated σ of 5. You may wish to skip the italicised argumentation that follows, returning to it only when you have appreciated the practical outcome.

We can first calculate the standard deviation of $\bar{X}$, the sample mean:

$$s_{\bar{X}} = \frac{\sigma}{\sqrt{n}} = \frac{5}{\sqrt{100}} = \frac{5}{10} = 0.5$$

Using the same argument as in §6.4 we know that:

$$\frac{\bar{X} - \mu}{0.5} = Z$$

has a standard normal distribution and that[2], from table A3:

$$P(-1.96 < Z < 1.96) = 0.95$$

In other words: $\qquad P(-1.96 < \dfrac{\bar{X} - \mu}{0.5} < 1.96) = 0.95$

But the inequality: $\qquad \dfrac{\bar{X} - \mu}{0.5} < 1.96$

is the same as: $\qquad \bar{X} - \mu < (1.96 \times 0.5)$

---

[2] Strictly speaking we have shown this to be true only if the population standard deviation is known, whereas here the sample standard deviation, usually called the standard error, has been used. However, it can be shown that the argument still holds, even when the sample value is used, provided the sample size is large: n = 100 ought to be large enough. Questions about sample size are discussed further in §7.5.

Estimating from samples

Similarly, the inequality: · $-1.96 < \dfrac{\bar{X} - \mu}{0.5}$

is the same as: $\mu < \bar{X} + (1.96 \times 0.5)$

Therefore, in place of: $P(-1.96 < Z < 1.96) = 0.95$

we can write:

$$P\{(\bar{X} - 1.96 \times 0.5) < \mu < (\bar{X} + 1.96 \times 0.5)\} = 0.95$$

Now, the value of μ is some fixed but unknown quantity. The value of $\bar{X}$ varies from one sample to another. The statement:

$$P\{(\bar{X} - 1.96 \times 0.5) < \mu < (\bar{X} + 1.96 \times 0.5)\} = 0.95$$

means that if samples of size 100 are repeatedly chosen at random from a population with $\sigma = 5$ then for 95% of those samples the inequality will be true. In other words, the interval $\bar{X} \pm (1.96 \times 0.5)$ will contain the value μ about 95% of the time. This interval is called a 95% **confidence interval** for the value of μ.

In the present example, the value 0.5 is just the standard deviation of $\bar{X}$ which we know to have the value $\sigma/\sqrt{n}$ in general. So (in general) we can say that:

$$\bar{X} \pm 1.96\left(\frac{\sigma}{\sqrt{n}}\right)$$

is a 95% confidence interval for μ, the population mean. If you like, you may interpret this by saying that you are '95% certain' that μ lies inside the interval derived from a particular sample. In large samples (see §7.5) the sample standard deviation, s, can be used in place of σ and the interval $\bar{X} \pm 1.96\,(s/\sqrt{n})$ will still be a 95% confidence interval for μ.

In the case we have used to exemplify the procedure, we have $\bar{X} = 14.88$ and the interval is $14.88 \pm (1.96 \times 0.5)$. Thus we are '95% sure' that the mean /d/ VOT of the child in his speech as a whole lies in the interval (13.90, 15.86) milliseconds. The sample standard deviation of the sample mean is called the **standard error** of the sample mean, and the 95% confidence interval is often written as: $\bar{X} \pm 1.96$ (standard error of $\bar{x}$).

The term standard error is generally used to refer to the *sample* standard deviation of any estimated quantity.

7.3 Estimating a proportion

Another question raised in chapter 4 which we will deal with here concerned the estimating of proportions. How can we estimate from a sample of a child's speech (at a particular period in its development) the proportion of the population of tokens of correct irregular past tenses as opposed to (correct and incorrect) inflectionally marked past tenses, e.g. *ran, brought*, as opposed to *runned, bringed, danced*. In a sample of an English child's conversations during her third year, the following totals were observed:

> Correct irregular past tense: 987
> Inflectionally marked past tense: 372
> Total: 1359

The proportion (p̂) of inflectionally marked past tenses in this sample is $372/1359 = 0.2737$. Within what range would we expect the population proportion (p) to be? Just as with the mean (μ) in the previous section, it will be possible to say that we can be 95% sure that the population proportion is within a certain range of values. Indeed, the question about proportions can be seen as one about means. Suppose that a score, Y, is provided for each verb where:

> $Y_i = 1$ if the i-th verb is inflectionally marked
> $Y_i = 0$ if the i-th verb is not inflectionally marked

The mean of Y is $\bar{Y} = \Sigma Y_i/n$ and this is just the proportion of verb tokens which are inflectionally marked.

Thus p̂ is in fact a sample mean and we know, therefore, from the Central Limit Theorem, that the population of values of p̂ will have a normal distribution for large samples. In order to calculate confidence intervals for the p as we did in the previous section for μ, we need to know the standard deviation of the population of sample proportions. As it turns out, there is a straightforward way of calculating this. At the same time, however, for a technical reason, the confidence limits for p are not calculated in quite the same way as for μ. The reader may wish to avoid the explicit discussion of these complicating factors and go directly to the formula for determining confidence limits for p, which is immediately after the italicised passage.

We noted in the preceding paragraph that we need to know the standard deviation of the population of sample proportions. We could estimate the

Estimating from samples

sample variance of the sample of Y values, s_Y^2, and then use $s_Y/\sqrt{n}$ as the standard deviation of $\hat{p}$. We would then, for large n, have as a 95% confidence interval for the true value p, the interval $\hat{p} \pm 1.96 \, s_Y/\sqrt{n}$.

In fact this procedure will do perfectly well for large values of n. On the other hand, it is the case that the value of s_Y^2 is always very close to $\hat{p}(1-\hat{p})$. (It can be shown algebraically that:

$$s_Y^2 = \frac{n}{n-1}\hat{p}(1-\hat{p})$$

and for large n the factor $n/n-1$ is almost exactly equal to 1 and can be ignored.) This means that we can avoid calculating s_Y^2 and that, as soon as we have calculated $\hat{p}$ we can write immediately that $s_Y^2 = \hat{p}(1-\hat{p})$, so that $s_Y = \sqrt{\hat{p}(1-\hat{p})}$ and $\bar{Y} = \hat{p}$. Thus a 95% confidence interval for p is:

$$\hat{p} \pm \left\{ 1.96 \sqrt{\frac{\hat{p}(1-p)}{n}} \right\}$$

For our example:

$$\Sigma Y = 372$$

$$\bar{Y} = \frac{372}{1359} = 0.274 = \hat{p}$$

$$s_Y^2 = \hat{p}(1-\hat{p}) = \frac{372}{1359} \times \frac{987}{1359} = 0.1988$$

Hence, a 95% confidence interval for the true proportion of inflectionally marked past tenses in the speech of this child during this period is $0.2737 \pm \sqrt{(0.1988 \div 1359)} = 0.2737 \pm 0.0121$, i.e. $(0.2616, 0.2858)$.

Unfortunately, for a technical reason which we will not explain here (see Fleiss 1981), this will give an interval which is a little too narrow. In other words, the probability that the true value of p lies inside the confidence interval will actually be a bit less than 95%. A minor correction ought to be used to adjust the interval to allow for this.

The formula to give the correct 95% confidence interval is:

$$\hat{p} \pm \left\{ 1.96 \sqrt{\frac{\hat{p}(1-\hat{p})}{n}} + \frac{1}{2n} \right\}$$

In the present case this means:

$$0.2737 \pm \left(0.0121 + \frac{1}{2718} \right)$$

i.e. (0.2612, 0.2862). This is now a more accurate 95% confidence interval for the true proportion. The correction has not made much difference here because the sample size was rather large. It would be more important in smaller samples.

7.4 Confidence intervals based on small samples

The second issue which we will deal with in this chapter concerns the estimates of population values on the basis of small samples. In chapter 4 mention was made of a study of syntactic and lexical differences between normal and language-impaired children in which Fletcher & Peters (1984) isolated a small group of children (aged 3–6 years) who failed the Stephens Oral Screening Test and who were also at least six months delayed on the Reynell Developmental Language Scales: Receptive. The children had hearing and intelligence within normal limits, were intelligible, and had not previously had speech therapy. Two hundred utterances were collected from each child in conversations under standard conditions and these were subjected to syntactic and lexical analysis. The purpose of the study was to make a preliminary identification of grammatical and lexical categories which might distinguish language-impaired children from normal. There were a number of categories examined in the study which discriminated the groups; for the purposes of this section we will consider only one, 'verb expansion'. This is a measure of the occurrence of auxiliary plus verb sequences in the set of utterances by a subject. The data for 'verb expansion' in the language-impaired group are shown in table 7.1. Given a sample mean here of 0.254, how close would we expect this to be to the mean score of the *population* from which the sample was drawn? How does the small sample size affect the way we go about establishing a confidence interval?

Because of the small sample size we cannot rely on the Central Limit Theorem, nor can we assume that the sample variance is very close to the true population variance (which is unknown). We can proceed from

Table 7.1. *Verb expansion scores of eight children*

Child 1	.235
2	.270
3	.265
4	.300
5	.320
6	.275
7	.105
8	.260

this point *only if we are willing to assume that the population distribution can be modelled by a normal distribution*, i.e. that verb expansion scores over all the children of the target population would have a histogram close to that of a normal distribution. The validity of the procedure which follows depends on this basic assumption. Fortunately, many studies have shown that the procedure is quite robust to some degree of failure in the assumption. However, we should always remember that if the distribution of the original population were to turn out to be decidedly non-normal the method we explain here might not be applicable. In the present example there is no real problem. The score for each child is the proportion of auxiliary plus verb sequences found in a sample of 200 utterances. As we have argued above, a sample proportion is a special type of sample mean and the Central Limit Theorem allows us to feel secure that a sample mean based on 200 observations will be normally distributed. Hence the verb expansion scores will meet the criterion of normality.

The method of calculating confidence intervals for small samples is, in fact, essentially the same as for larger samples. The difference stems from the fact that for smaller samples the quantity $(\bar{X} - \mu)/(s/\sqrt{n})$ does not have a standard normal distribution because s^2 is not a sufficiently accurate estimator of σ^2 in small samples even when, as here, we are assuming that the population is normally distributed. This means that we cannot establish a confidence interval by the argument used above. Fortunately, the distribution of $(\bar{X} - \mu)/(s/\sqrt{n})$ is known, provided the individual X values are normally distributed, and is referred to as the **t-distribution**. The t-distribution has a symmetric histogram like the normal distribution, but is somewhat flatter. For large samples it is virtually indistinguishable from the standard normal distribution. In small samples, however, the t-distribution has a somewhat larger variance than the standard normal distribution.

In order to calculate the 95% confidence interval we make use of the formula $\bar{X} \pm ts/\sqrt{n}$, in which t is the appropriate 5% value taken from the tables of the t-distribution (table A4). This t-value varies according to sample size. You will see that on the left of the tables there is a column of figures headed **degrees of freedom** which run consecutively, 1, 2, 3, etc. This is a technical term from mathematics which we shall not attempt to explain here (but see chapter 9). It is important to enter the tables at the correct point in this column, i.e. with the correct number of degrees of freedom. The appropriate number is $(n - 1)$ (one less than the number of observations in the sample). Thus, even without understanding the concept of degrees of freedom, you can see that by doing this we take into account the size of the sample and hence the shape of the distribution for that sample size. Since in the present case there are eight observations, the t-value will be based on 7 df. We enter the table at 7 df and move to the right along that row until we find the value in the column headed '5%'. The value found there (2.36) is the **5% t-value** corresponding to 7 df and may be entered into the formula presented above.

So the 95% confidence interval is:

$$0.254 \pm \left(\frac{0.0653}{\sqrt{8}} \times 2.36\right) = 0.254 \pm 0.054$$

i.e. from 0.200 to 0.308; we are 95% confident that the true mean verb expansion score for the population from which the eight subjects were drawn lies between 0.196 and 0.312. Note that if we had constructed the confidence interval, incorrectly, using the standard normal tables we would have calculated the 95% confidence interval to be (0.206, 0.302), thus overstating the precision of the estimate. The smaller the sample, the greater would be this overstatement.

7.5 Sample size

At various points in the book we have already referred to 'large' and 'small' samples and will continue to do so in the remaining chapters. What do we mean by a large sample? As in any other context, 'large' is a relative term and depends on the criteria used to make the judgement. Let us consider the most important cases.

7.5.1 *Central Limit Theorem*

In the discussion of the theorem in chapter 6 we pointed out on several occasions that it is only in 'large' samples that we can feel secure that the sample mean will be normally distributed. The size of sample required depends on the distribution of the individual values of the variable being studied and frequently not much will be known about that. If the variable itself happens to be normally distributed then the mean of *any* size of sample, however small, will have a normal distribution. If the variable is not normal but has a population histogram which has a single mode and is roughly symmetrical, i.e. is no more than slightly skewed, then samples of 20 or so will probably be large enough to ensure the normality of the sample mean. Only when the variable in question is highly skewed or has a markedly bi-modal histogram will much larger samples be required. Even then, a sample of, say, 100 observations ought to be large enough.

7.5.2 *When the data are not independent*

The above comments on sample size are relevant where the observations in the sample are independent of one another, an assertion impossible to sustain for certain types of linguistic data.

For example, suppose we wish to estimate, for a single child, the proportion of verbs marked for the present perfect in his speech. If we analyse a single, long conversational extract of the subject's speech it is perfectly possible that, following a question from his interlocutor like 'What have you been doing?', he will respond with a series of utterances that contain verbs marked for present perfect. Thus, if he produces, say, five consecutive verbs marked for present perfect, it may be argued that he has made only one choice and not five. There is a sense in which he has provided a single instance of the verb form in which we are interested, not five. If, on the other hand, we admit for analysis only every twentieth verb that the subject produces, we might more reasonably hold that each tense or aspect choice appearing in the samples is independent of the others, and could consider that the tokens we have selected constitute a random sample. What implications does this view of independence have for research in applied linguistics and the efficient collection and analysis of language data, particularly when they comprise natural speech?

Information is a commodity which has to be paid for like any other; and resources (money or time) available to purchase it will always be limited. A data set consisting of n related values of a variable always contains less information for the estimation of population means and proportions than does a sample of n independent observations of the same variable. (The extent of the loss of information will depend on how *correlated* – see chapter 10 – the observed values are.) Thus, if it is possible to obtain n independent values *at the same cost* as n interdependent values it will be more efficient to do so. In particular, if the values are not independent much bigger samples than usual will be needed to assume that the sample means are normally distributed. Suppose we have decided to transcribe and analyse 100 utterances. (For simplicity, assume that each utterance contains only one main verb. The message will still be the same even if this is not true, but the argument is more complex.) We might: (a) record and transcribe the first 100 utterances; (b) record a total of 500 utterances and transcribe every fifth utterance. The transcription costs will be roughly equal in both cases but strategy (b) will require a recording period five times as long as (a). However, if it is still possible to carry out the recording in a single session the real difference in cost may not be very large. Even if this is not possible, the extra inconvenience of needing

Table 7.2. *Standard errors from different sampling rules (sample size 50)*

Spacing between verbs	Standard error (%)
Consecutive	2.17
Every second	1.41
Every third	1.12
Every fourth	1.05
Every fifth	0.99
Every tenth	0.84
Every twentieth	0.71

two or three sessions may well be repaid by data which are more informative in the sense that the standard errors of estimated quantities are smaller – i.e. confidence intervals are narrower and hypothesis tests more sensitive.[3]

Suppose, for the sake of illustration, that the subject, throughout his speech as a whole, puts 50% of his verbs in the present perfect. The probability that a randomly chosen verb in a segment of his speech is present perfect will then be 0.5. However, if the first verb in the segment is marked in this way then the probability that the next verb he utters is also present perfect will be greater than 0.5 (because of a 'persistence effect'). The fifth or tenth verb in a sequence is much less likely to be influenced by the first than is the immediate successor. Again to illustrate, let us suppose that the probability that the next verb is the same type as its immediate predecessor is 0.9. Now suppose that 100 verbs are sampled to estimate the proportion of present perfects uttered by the subject. We could choose 100 consecutive verbs, every other verb, every fifth verb, etc. Table 7.2 shows how the standard error of the estimated proportion decreases as a bigger gap is left between the sampled verbs. (There is no simple formula available to calculate these standard errors. They have been obtained by a computer simulation of the sampling process.)

7.5.3 *Confidence intervals*

There are two criteria involved here in the definition of 'large'. One is, as before, the question of how close to normal is the distribution of the variable being studied. The second is the amount of knowledge available about the *population* variance. Usually the only information about this comes from the sample itself via the value of the sample variance.

---

[3] Of course there will be many occasions when an investigator may be interested in a sequence of consecutive utterances. We simply wish to point out that information on some variables may be collected rather inefficiently in that case.

If the variable in question has a normal distribution, a confidence interval can be obtained for any sample size using the t-tables and the methods of the previous section. For samples of more than 50 or so the t-distribution is virtually indistinguishable from the standard normal and the confidence interval of §7.2 would be appropriate. If, on the other hand, there is some doubt about the normality of the variable, then it will not be possible to calculate a reliable interval for small samples. Biological measurements of most kinds can be expected to be approximately normally distributed. So can test scores, if the test is constructed so that the score is the sum of a number of items or components more or less independent of one another. Apart from that, certain types of variable are known from repeated study to have approximately the correct shape of distribution. If you are studying a variable about which there is some doubt, you should always begin by constructing a histogram of the sample if the sample size makes that feasible; gross deviations from the normal distribution ought to show up then (see also chapter 9). With smaller samples and a relatively unknown type of variable only faith will suffice, though it must be remembered that the accuracy of any conclusions we make *may* be seriously affected if the variable has an unusual distribution. However, whatever the form of the data it should be safe to rely on a confidence interval based on a sample of 100 or more observations and calculated as in §7.2.

7.5.4 *More than one level of sampling*

In many cases a study will require sampling at two different levels. In the verb expansion study discussed above a sample of children was first chosen and then a sample of utterances taken from each child. How should the experimenter's effort be distributed in such cases? Is it better to take a large number of utterances from a small number of children, or vice versa? Does it matter?

There is no single or simple answer to this question. Reduction in the value of data caused by lack of independence also occurs when the data are obtained from several subjects. Consider an example. In chapter 11 we discuss the relationship between age and mean length of utterances (MLU) in young children. Suppose we wished to estimate the MLU for children aged 2;6. We might look at many utterances from a few children or a few utterances from many children – will it matter? Clearly, repeated observations of the same child are likely to be related. A child may have a tendency to make utterances which are rather shorter or rather longer than average for his peer group. It is quite easy to demonstrate that if n utterances are to be used to estimate MLU for the whole age group then the most precise answer would be obtained by sampling one utterance from each of n children of that age. However, this will also be the most expensive sampling scheme. It will inevitably be cheaper to take more utterances from fewer children. Furthermore, by reducing the number of children it will almost certainly be possible to increase the *total* number of utterances. We may be able to use the same resources to analyse, say, 20 utterances from each of 25 children (500 utterances in total) or 75 utterances from each of 10 children (750 utterances in total) and it may be far from obvious which option would give the best results. It depends, in part, on the question being addressed: whether interest lies principally in variations between children, in variability in the speech of individuals, or in estimating the distribution of some linguistic variable over the population as a whole.

There is no room here to give a fuller discussion of this problem whose solution, in any case, requires a fair degree of technical knowledge. Reference and text books on sampling problems tend to be difficult for the layman largely because of the considerable variety of notation and terminology they employ and the level of technical detail they include. You should consult an experienced survey statistician before collecting large quantities of observational data of this kind.

7.5.5 *Sample size to obtain a required precision*

Let us return to the example of §7.2. Suppose we decide that we want to estimate the true average VOT for the child and that we want to be 95% sure that our estimate differs from the population value by no more than one millisecond. What size of sample ought we to take?

Another way of stating this requirement is that the 95% confidence interval for the true mean should be of the form $\bar{X} \pm 1$. On the other hand, when we obtained the 95% confidence interval in §7.2 it was $\bar{X} \pm (1.96(\sigma/\sqrt{n}))$. Hence we require that $1.96(\sigma/\sqrt{n}) = 1$. In this example we have estimated that $\sigma = 5$, so we have $(1.96 \times 5)/(\sqrt{n}) = 1$, or:

$$\sqrt{n} = 1.96 \times 5 = 9.8$$
$$n = (9.8)^2 = 96.04$$

So, to meet the tolerance that we have insisted on we should need to obtain the test scores of 96 or 97 randomly sampled /d/ VOTs – we would probably round up to n = 100.

We can obtain a general formula for the sample size in exactly the same way. Suppose that, with a certain confidence, we wish to estimate a population mean with an error no greater than d. Then we have to choose the sample size n to satisfy:

$$1.96 \frac{\sigma}{\sqrt{n}} = d$$

(corresponds to $\dfrac{1.96\sigma}{\sqrt{n}} = 1$ in the last example)

or

$$1.96\sigma = d\sqrt{n}$$

or

$$\frac{1.96\sigma}{d} = \sqrt{n}$$

Thus the formula to choose the appropriate sample size to estimate a population mean with 95% confidence is:

$$n = \left(\frac{1.96\sigma}{d}\right)^2$$

where d indicates the required precision. The value obtained from this formula will rarely be a whole number and we would choose the next largest convenient number as we did in the example.

We notice that n will be large if (a) the value of d is small – we are insisting on a high degree of accuracy; and (b) σ^2, the population variance, is large – we then have to overcome the inherent variability of the population. The value of d is chosen by the experimenter. However, σ is a problem. Usually its value will not be known. One way round this is to take a fairly small sample, say 20 or 30, and calculate directly the sample variance s^2. We can then use s in place of σ in the formula for the appropriate sample size, in the study proper.

Thus the formula to choose the appropriate sample size to estimate a population mean with 95% confidence in ignorance of the population variance is:

$$n = \left(\frac{1.96s}{d}\right)^2$$

The problem is that our estimate of the population variance based on a rather small sample might be quite inaccurate, but this is usually the best we can do.

If we are estimating a proportion, p, a different kind of solution is available. First, let us begin by writing the simplest form for the confidence interval for p, i.e.

$$\hat{p} \pm 1.96\sqrt{\frac{p(1-p)}{n}}$$

leaving out the special correction. We then have:

$$d = 1.96\sqrt{\frac{p(1-p)}{n}}$$

or

$$d^2 = 1.96^2\frac{\{p(1-p)\}}{n}$$

or

$$n = \frac{1.96^2}{d^2}\{p(1-p)\}$$

This formula seems to suffer from a difficulty similar to the previous one. We will not know the population value of p. Even if we decide to use $\hat{p}$, the estimate of p, in the expression for the standard deviation as we did previously, we will not know the value of $\hat{p}$ until after the sample is taken. However, it should not take you long to convince yourself that if p is a number between zero and 1, then $p(1-p)$ cannot be larger than 0.25 and this will happen when $p = 0.5$. We can then obtain a value of n which will never be too small by using $p(1-p) = 0.25$. Thus the formula to choose a conservatively large sample size to estimate a population proportion with 95% confidence is:

$$n = 0.25\frac{1.96^2}{d^2}$$

where d indicates the required precision.

Suppose, for example, that we wish to estimate what percentage of the population has a given characteristic and that, with 95% confidence, we wish to get the answer correct to 1% either way. That is the same as saying that we want a 95% confidence interval for the proportion, p, of the form $\hat{p} \pm 0.01$ (remember that a percentage is just 100 times a proportion); so we need:

$$n = 0.25\frac{(1.96)^2}{(0.01)^2}$$

$$= 9604 \text{ (a large sample!)}$$

If we require the answer only within 10% either way, then:

$$n = 0.25 \frac{(1.96)^2}{(0.1)^2} = 96$$

If the true value of p is small (<0.2) or large (>0.8) then this procedure may greatly exaggerate the sample size required. If you suspect that this may be the case and sampling is expensive or difficult, then you should consult a statistician.

7.6 Different confidence levels

There is nothing sacred about the value of 95% which we have used throughout this chapter to introduce and discuss the concept of confidence intervals, though it is very commonly used. However, one experimenter may wish to quote a range of values within which he is '99% sure' that the true population mean will lie. Another may be content to be '90% confident' of including the true value. What will be the consequence of changing the **confidence level** in this way?

When the idea of a 95% confidence interval was introduced in §7.2, the starting point was the expression:

$$P(-1.96 < Z < 1.96) = 0.95$$

The number 1.96 was chosen from the tables of the normal distribution to fix the probability at 0.95 or 95%. This probability can be altered to any other value by choosing the appropriate number from table A3 to replace 1.96. For example, beginning from:

$$P(-2.5758 \leqslant Z \leqslant 2.5758) = 0.99$$

and carrying out a sequence of calculations similar to those in §7.2, we will then arrive at a 99% confidence interval, $14.88 \pm (2.5758 \times 0.5)$ or $(13.59, 16.17)$ for the true population mean. The length of this interval is 2.58 marks $(16.17 - 13.59)$ longer than the 95% interval. That is to be expected. In order to be more certain of including the true value we must include *more* values, thus lengthening the interval. On the other hand, a 90% confidence interval would be $14.88 \pm (1.6449 \times 0.5)$ or $(14.06, 15.70)$, shorter than the 95% interval. Table 7.3 gives a range of confidence intervals all based on the same data.

Is it better to choose a high or a low confidence level? The lower the confidence level the more chance there is that the stated interval does not include the true value. On the other hand, the higher the confidence level, the wider will be the interval and wide intervals are less informative

Table 7.3. *Confidence intervals with different confidence levels*

Confidence level (%)	C*	Confidence interval	Length of interval
50	0.6745	(14.54, 15.22)	0.67
60	0.8416	(14.46, 15.30)	0.84
70	1.0364	(14.36, 15.40)	1.04
80	1.2816	(14.24, 15.52)	1.28
90	1.6449	(14.06, 15.70)	1.64
95	1.9600	(13.90, 15.86)	1.96
99	2.5758	(13.59, 16.17)	2.58
99.9	3.2905	(13.23, 16.53)	3.29
	$\bar{X} = 14.88$	$\sigma = 5$ $n = 100$	

Note: * The number C is obtained from table A3 to give the required confidence level.

than narrow ones. We can be virtually 100% confident that the true value lies between 1.36 and 28.40, but that is hardly a useful statement. Some compromise must be reached between the level of confidence we might like and the narrow interval we would find useful. If a researcher knows, before carrying out an experiment, what level of confidence he requires, he can estimate the sample size, using the methods of the previous section, to obtain the desired width of interval. It is, again, simply a matter of choosing the appropriate number, C, from table 7.3 or table A3. Thus the general formula for choosing sample size to estimate a population mean is:

$$n = \left(\frac{C\sigma}{d}\right)^2$$

where, as before, d is the required precision. In the examples worked through in §7.2 we have used $C = 1.96$ corresponding to a confidence level of 95%.

SUMMARY

This chapter has addressed the problem of using samples to **estimate** the unknown values of population **parameters** such as a population mean or a population proportion.

(1) **Point estimators** were introduced and it was suggested that the sample mean and the sample variance and the sample proportion would be reasonable point estimators for their population counterparts; all of these estimators are **unbiassed** and **consistent**.

(2) The concept of a **confidence interval** was explained and it was shown how to derive a **95% confidence interval for a population mean**, μ. For a large sample such an interval takes the form:

$$\bar{X} \pm 1.96\left(\frac{s}{\sqrt{n}}\right)$$

where $\bar{X}$ is the sample mean, s is the sample standard deviation and n is the sample size.

(3) A **95% confidence interval for the population proportion**, p, was discussed and an example calculated using the formula:

$$\hat{p} \pm \left\{ 1.96 \sqrt{\frac{\hat{p}(1-\hat{p})}{n}} + \frac{1}{2n} \right\}$$

where $\hat{p}$ is the sample proportion and n the sample size.

(4) The problem of obtaining a **confidence interval for μ from a small sample** was discussed and it was shown how this could be done *provided the sample came from a normal distribution* using the tables of the **t-distribution** and the formula:

$$\bar{X} \pm \frac{ts}{\sqrt{n}}$$

where t is the *5% point* from table A4 corresponding to the appropriate number of **degrees of freedom**.

(5) The issue of **sample size** was discussed with its relation to the **Central Limit Theorem** and the **required precision** of a confidence interval.

(6) It was shown how to calculate confidence intervals with different **confidence levels**.

EXERCISES

(1) (a) Using the data of table 3.1, calculate a 95% confidence interval for the mean length of utterance of the observed adult speaking to her child.

(b) Calculate a 99% confidence interval.

(c) Explain carefully what is the meaning of these intervals.

(2) Repeat exercise 7.1 using the data of table 3.3.

(3) In table 3.4 are given the numbers of tokens of words ending *-ing* and the number pronounced [n] by each of ten subjects.

    (a) Calculate 95% confidence intervals for subject 6 for the proportion of [n] endings in all such words the subject might utter (a) spontaneously, (b) when reading from a wordlist.

    (b) Repeat for subject 1.

    (c) Suggest reasons for the differences in the widths of the four confidence intervals.

(4) Ten undergraduate students are chosen at random in a large university and are given a language aptitude test. Their marks are:

$$62, 39, 48, 72, 81, 51, 54, 59, 67, 44$$

Calculate a 95% confidence interval for the mean mark that would have been obtained if *all* the undergraduate students of the university had taken the test.

8

Testing hypotheses about population values

8.1 Using the confidence interval to test a hypothesis

In the previous chapter the confidence interval was introduced as a device for estimating a population parameter. The interval can also be used to assess the plausibility of a hypothesised value for the parameter. Miller (1951) cites a study of the vocabulary of children in which the average number of words recognised by children aged 6–7 years in the USA was 24,000.[1] Suppose that the same test had been carried out in the same year on 140 British children of the same age and that the mean size of vocabulary recognised by that sample was 24,800 with a sample standard deviation of 4,200 words. How plausible is the hypothesis that the population from which the sample of British children was chosen had the same mean vocabulary as the American children of the same age? Admittedly the *sample* of British children had a higher mean vocabulary size, but many samples of American children would also have had a mean score of more than 24,000. We need to rephrase the question. The mean of a sample of British children is 24,800, not 24,000. Is it nevertheless plausible that the mean vocabulary of the British population of children in this age range could be 24,000 words and that the apparent discrepancy is simply due to sampling variation, so that a new sample will have a mean vocabulary size closer to, perhaps less than, 24,000?

Let us begin by using the data obtained on the sample to calculate a 95% confidence interval for the mean vocabulary size of the whole population from which the sample was selected. Let us denote that mean vocabulary size by μ_v. Following the procedure of §7.2 we obtain the interval:

$$\bar{X} \pm 1.96 \frac{s}{\sqrt{n}}$$

$$\text{i.e. } 24\,800 \pm \frac{1.96 \times 4200}{\sqrt{140}} = (24\,104,\ 25\,496)$$

[1] This value was itself based on a sample. However, for the moment we will treat it as though it were the population value, a reasonable enough procedure if the American figure was based on a much bigger sample than the British mean. It is explained in chapter 11 how to compare two *sample* means directly.

At this point we might remind ourselves of the meaning of a 95% confidence interval. If it has been calculated properly, there is only a 5% chance that it will *not* contain the value of the mean of the whole population from which the sample was chosen. So, if the mean vocabulary size for British children aged 6–7 years were in fact 24,000 words, then for 95% of randomly chosen samples, that is for 19 samples out of 20, the 95% confidence interval would be expected to include the value 24,000, while one time in 20 it would not. For the particular sample tested, it turns out that the interval does not include the value 24,000, so *either* the true mean is some value other than 24,000 *or* it really is 24,000 and the sample we have chosen happens to be one of the 5% of samples which result in a 95% confidence interval failing to include the population mean. There is no way of knowing which of these two cases has occurred. There will never be any way of knowing for certain what is the truth in such situations. However, it is intuitively reasonable to suggest that when a confidence interval (based on a sample) fails to include a certain value, then we should begin to doubt that the sample has been drawn from a population having a mean with that value. In the present case, we should begin to doubt that the sample was drawn from a population having a mean of 24,000.

On the basis of what we have said to far, it is possible to develop a formal procedure for the use of observed data in assessing the plausibility of a hypothesis. In particular, let us suppose that the hypothesis we wished to test was that the average size of vocabulary of British children of 6–7 years old was the same as that of their American counterparts. We could decide to make use of a 95% confidence interval based on a sample of British children.

For the moment let us imagine that we do not yet know what that confidence interval is. There are two possible conclusions we could reach on the basis of the confidence interval, depending on whether or not it included 24,000, the mean vocabulary of the American children. If the interval does include 24,000 we could conclude that the data were consistent

Table 8.1. *Possible outcomes from a test of hypothesis*

	True state	
Result of sample	Population mean is 24 000	Population mean is not 24 000
Interval includes the value 24 000	Correct	Error 2
Interval does not include 24 000	Error 1	Correct

with the hypothesis; if the interval does not include 24,000 we would doubt the plausibility of the hypothesis. A convention has been established by which, in the latter case, we would say that we reject the hypothesis as false, while if the interval contains the hypothesised value we simply say that we have no grounds for rejecting it. (This convention and its dangers are discussed further in §8.4, but let us adopt it uncritically for the time being.) Since the hypothesis must be either true or false, there are four possible outcomes, which are displayed in table 8.1. As can be seen, two of these outcomes will lead to correct assessment of the situation, while the other two cause a mistaken conclusion.

The first type of error, referred to as a **type 1 error**, is due to rejecting the value 24,000 when it is the correct value for the population mean. The probability of this type of error is exactly the 5% chance that the true population mean (24,000) accidentally falls outside the interval defined by the particular sample we have chosen.

The second type of error, known as a **type 2 error**, occurs when, although the population mean is no longer 24,000, that value is still included in the confidence interval. In general, the probability of making this type of error will not be known. It will depend on the true value, μ, of the population mean, the sample size, n, and the population variance, σ^2. Sometimes it is possible to calculate it, at least approximately, for different possible values of the population mean. That is true here and some values are given in table 8.2. These values have been calculated assuming that the standard deviations of the sample of vocabulary sizes

Table 8.2. *Probabilities of type 2 error using a 95% confidence interval to test whether* $\mu = 24\,000$

	Sample size		
True mean	n = 140	n = 500	n = 1 000
23 000	0.19	very small	very small
23 500	0.71	0.24	0.04
23 600	0.80	0.39	0.15
23 700	0.87	0.64	0.38
23 800	0.92	0.82	0.67
23 900	0.95	0.92	0.89
24 100	0.95	0.92	0.89
24 200	0.92	0.82	0.67
24 300	0.87	0.64	0.38
24 400	0.80	0.39	0.15
24 500	0.71	0.24	0.04
25 000	0.19	very small	very small
	(In all cases s = 4 200)		

is the correct standard deviation for the population of all British children in the relevant age group. To that extent they are approximate. When the sample size is 140 it can be seen, for example, that if the true population mean is 23,000 there is a probability of about 19% that the hypothesis that $\mu = 24,000$ would still be found acceptable, while if the mean really is 24,500 the probability of making this error is more than 70%. Table 8.2 also demonstrates that the probability of making the second kind of error depends greatly on the size of sample used to test the hypothesis.

Of course, we could decide to use a confidence interval with a different confidence level to assess the plausibility of the hypothesis that the British population mean score was $\mu = 24,000$. In particular, we might decide to reject that hypothesis only if the value $\mu = 24,000$ was not included inside the 99% confidence interval. In that case, the probability of making a type 1 error would reduce to 1% since there is now a 99% probability that the true value will be included by the confidence interval, so that if the true population mean is 24,000 there is only a 1% chance that it will be excluded from the interval. On the other hand, the probability of making a type 2 error will now be increased. A 99% confidence interval will always be wider than a 95% confidence interval based on the same sample of data and therefore it will have more chance of including the value 24,000 even when the population mean has some other value. Table 8.3 gives the probability of making this second kind of error for different true values of the population mean, μ, and for three sample sizes. When n = 140 and the true population mean is 23,000, the probability of the second kind of error is now about 31%; when a 95% confidence interval is used this error would occur with a probability of only 19%. We seem to have reached an impasse. Any attempt to protect ourselves against one type of error will increase the chance of making the other. The conventional way to solve the dilemma is to give more importance to the type 1 error. The argument goes something like this.

The onus is on the investigator to show that some expected or natural hypothesis is untrue. Evidence for this should be accepted only if it is reasonably strong. Let us consider our vocabulary size example in this light. The population mean score over a large number of American children tested is 24,000. If this vocabulary test had never been carried out on British children before we could start out from the point that, in the absence of special circumstances, the mean vocabulary size of the latter population ought to be about the same as that of the former. If we decide to use the 95% confidence interval obtained from the sample of 140 test scores to test this hypothesis, we would conclude that it was false. *The probability*

Table 8.3. *Probabilities of type 2 error using a 99% confidence interval to test whether* $\mu = 24\,000$

	Sample size		
True mean	$n = 140$	$n = 500$	$n = 1\,000$
23 000	0.31	0.001	very small
23 500	0.82	0.37	0.08
23 600	0.88	0.56	0.25
23 700	0.93	0.77	0.53
23 800	0.96	0.90	0.79
23 900	0.98	0.96	0.94
24 100	0.98	0.96	0.94
24 200	0.96	0.90	0.79
24 300	0.93	0.77	0.53
24 400	0.88	0.56	0.25
24 500	0.82	0.37	0.08
25 000	0.31	0.001	very small

(In all cases s = 4 200)

that the conclusion is in error (a type 1 error) *would be only 5%*, or 1 in 20. It would seem that, on balance, the evidence suggests there is something about the education or linguistic environment of the British children which promotes earlier assimilation of vocabulary.

In some cases, the rejection of a hypothesis might lead to some costly action being taken, a change in educational procedures or extra help to some apparently disadvantaged section of the community. In such cases we might feel that a 1 in 20 chance of needlessly spending resources as the result of an incorrect conclusion is too high a probability of error. We could base our decision on a 99% confidence interval since then a conclusion, based on a sample, that a particular subpopulation had a different or unusual mean value, would have a probability of only 1 in 100 of being incorrect. If the hypothesis testing procedure is to be used in this fashion (but see §8.4) we will wish to fix our attention on the probability of wrongly rejecting a hypothesis, and it would be useful to formulate the procedure in such a way that the answer to the following question can be obtained easily: 'If I reject a certain hypothesis on the basis of data obtained from observing a random sample, what is the probability that my rejection of the hypothesis is in error?'

8.2 The concept of a test statistic

Let us recap briefly the procedure presented in §7.2 for calculating the confidence intervals we have been discussing above. We obtain a random sample of 140 vocabulary scores and calculate $\bar{X}$, the sample mean, and s, the sample standard deviation. Provided the sample size is large enough – as it is here – the confidence interval then takes the form:

$$\bar{X} \pm Z\frac{s}{\sqrt{n}}$$

where the value Z is chosen from tables of the standard normal distribution to give the required level of confidence. By an algebraic manipulation of this expression it can be shown that it is not strictly necessary to calculate the confidence interval in order to test a hypothesis. The algebraic argument follows below, in italics, for interested readers.

Suppose we wish to test the hypothesis that the population mean has the value μ. We will reject this if μ is not contained by the confidence interval. *Now, μ **will** be contained inside the interval provided:*

$$\bar{X} - Z\frac{s}{\sqrt{n}} < \mu < \bar{X} + Z\frac{s}{\sqrt{n}}$$

The inequality 'A':

$$\bar{X} - Z\frac{s}{\sqrt{n}} < \mu$$

is the same as:

$$\bar{X} < \mu + Z\frac{s}{\sqrt{n}}$$

is the same as:

$$\bar{X} - \mu < Z\frac{s}{\sqrt{n}}$$

is the same as:

$$\frac{\bar{X} - \mu}{s/\sqrt{n}} < Z$$

Similarly, the inequality 'B':

$$\mu < \bar{X} + Z\frac{s}{\sqrt{n}}$$

is the same as:

$$\frac{\mu - \bar{X}}{s/\sqrt{n}} < Z$$

Thus μ, the postulated value of the population mean, will be included by the confidence interval only if both the inequalities A and B are true.

Taken together, these inequalities can be put into words, as follows. Find the absolute difference between $\bar{X}$ and μ. (That is, take $\bar{X} - \mu$ if $\bar{X}$ is greater, $\mu - \bar{X}$ if μ is greater.) Divide that difference by $s/\sqrt{n}$, the standard error of $\bar{X}$. If the answer is less than the value of Z needed to calculate the confidence interval then the interval will include μ, otherwise it will not.

For our example, $\bar{X}$ is larger than μ, and s = 4,200:

$$\frac{\bar{X} - \mu}{s/\sqrt{n}} = \frac{24\,800 - 24\,000}{4200/\sqrt{140}} = \frac{800}{355} = 2.25$$

Now, to construct a 95% confidence interval, we see from table A3 that we would need to use Z = 1.96; for 99%, Z = 2.58. This tells us that 24,000 will be included in the 99% but *not* the 95% interval, since the Z-value corresponding to the sample is less than 2.58 but greater than 1.96. If we reject the value 24,000 as incorrect, the probability that the rejection is an error (type 1) is less than 5% (since the value falls outside the 95% confidence interval) but greater than 1% (since it does *not* fall outside the value of the 99% confidence interval). Conventionally, we say that the postulated value, μ = 24,000, may be rejected at the 5% significance level but not at the 1% significance level. A common notation used to express this is $0.01 < P < 0.05$, where 'P' is understood to be the probability of making a type 1 error, i.e. P is the significance level.

'At the 5% significance level' is just another way of saying that the postulated mean is not contained by the 95% confidence interval based on the sample. The 'significance level' is then just the probability that this exclusion is due to a sampling accident and not to the failure of the hypothesis. The value:

$$Z = \frac{\bar{X} - \mu}{s/\sqrt{n}}$$

is used as the criterion to assess the degree to which the sample supports, or fails to support, the hypothesis that μ is the mean of the population from which the sample has been selected. Such a value used in such a way is known as a **test statistic**. Every testable statistical hypothesis is judged on the basis of some test statistic derived from a sample.

Every test statistic will be a random variable because its value depends on the results of a random sampling procedure. If we were to repeat our test procedure a number of times, drawing a different sample each time, we would obtain a random sample of values of the test statistic and we could plot its histogram as we did for other variables in chapter 2. A test statistic is always chosen in such a way that a mathematical model for its histogram is known *so long as the hypothesis being tested is true*. In this case the distribution of our test statistic, Z, whenever μ is, in fact, the mean of the population from which the sample is taken, would be the standard normal distribution. It follows that the value $Z = 1.96$ would be exceeded in only 2.5% of samples when we have postulated the correct value of μ. Similarly, only 2.5% of random samples would give a value less than -1.96 when our hypothesis is true. Clearly we are again using the 95% central confidence interval and claiming that values outside this interval are in some sense unusual or interesting since they should result only from 1 random sample in 20.

You should now be ready to understand a complete and formal definition of the classical procedure for a statistical test of hypothesis.

8.3 The classical hypothesis test and an example

A hypothesis is stated about some random variable, for example, that British children of a certain age have a mean vocabulary of 24,000 words. The hypothesis which is taken as a starting point and which often it is hoped will be refuted, is commonly called the **null hypothesis** and designated H_0. We might write: let the variable X with mean μ be the vocabulary size of British children aged 6–7 years. Then we wish to test $H_0 : \mu = 24,000$. The most important requirement to enable the test to take place is the existence of a suitable test statistic whose distribution is known when H_0 is true. In this case there is one, provided we take a large sample of children:

$$Z = \frac{\bar{X} - \mu}{s/\sqrt{n}}$$

where μ is the hypothesised mean and s is the *sample* standard deviation.

For the example we are discussing here:

$$Z = \frac{\bar{X} - 24\,000}{s/\sqrt{n}}$$

Next, we must be able to say what the value of our test statistic would have to be in order for us to reject the null hypothesis. This depends firstly on what **alternative hypothesis** we have in mind, i.e. what we suspect may in fact be the case if the null hypothesis is untrue. There are three obvious possibilities: (i) We believe that British children will have a lower mean vocabulary size as measured by the test used (possibly because the test, devised in the USA, has a cultural bias); (ii) We believe that British children will have a higher mean vocabulary size than American children of the same age (possibly because they start school at an earlier age); (iii) We are simply checking whether there is *any* difference in the mean vocabulary size and have no prior hypothesis about the direction of any difference which might exist.

A full statement of the problem will include a definition of the null hypothesis (H_0) *and* the alternative hypothesis (H_1). In the present case the null hypothesis is $H_0 : \mu = 24,000$ and we have to choose an alternative from:

   (i) $H_1 : \mu < 24\,000$
   (ii) $H_1 : \mu > 24\,000$
  (iii) $H_1 : \mu \neq 24\,000$

Despite its vagueness, the form of H_1 will have a definite bearing on the outcome of a statistical hypothesis test. Consider again the test statistic:

$$Z = \frac{\bar{X} - 24\,000}{s/\sqrt{n}}$$

If (i) is true, the population mean is less than 24,000, so that samples from the population will generally have a sample mean less than 24,000. In that case Z will have a negative value since $\bar{X} - 24,000$ will be less than zero. So large, *negative* values of Z will tend to support H_1 rather than H_0, and positive values, *however large*, cannot be cited as support for the hypothesised alternative. If (ii) is true the argument will be completely reversed so that large, *positive* values of Z should lead to the rejection of H_0 in favour of H_1. If (iii) is true the value of Z will tend to be either negative or positive depending on the actual value of μ. All we can say in this case is that any value of Z which is sufficiently different from zero, *irrespective of sign*, will be support for H_1. Up to this point in our discussion we have tacitly been considering possibility (iii) and have been prepared to reject H_0 if the value of Z is extreme in either direction.

Next, we require tables which will indicate those values of the test statistic which seem to give support to H_1 over H_0. These values are usually referred to as the **critical values of the test statistic**. The tables ought to be in a form which enables us to state the **significance level of the test**. This is simply another name for the probability that we will make a mistake if we decide to reject H_0 in favour of H_1 on the evidence of our random sample of values of the variable we have observed, i.e. the probability of making a type 1 error.

Care is required at this point. The correct way to calculate the significance level of a test depends on the particular form of H_1 which is considered relevant for the test and on the way in which the tables are presented. Some tables are presented in a form suitable for what is often called a **two-tailed test**: our tables A3 and A4 are of that kind. This type of test is so called because values sufficiently far out in either tail of the histogram of the test statistic will be taken as support for H_1. A two-tailed test is the appropriate one to use when the alternative hypothesis does not predict the direction of the difference. In the present case, therefore, a two-tailed test will be called for if our alternative hypothesis is $\mu \neq 24,000$.

A **one-tailed test**, by contrast, is so called because values sufficiently far out in only one tail of the histogram of the test statistic will be taken as support for H_1. A one-tailed test is appropriate when the direction of the difference is specified in the alternative hypothesis. Thus both the following:

$$H_1 : \mu < 24\,000$$
$$H_1 : \mu > 24\,000$$

require a one-tailed test.

As noted above, our treatment of the vocabulary size problem has assumed the alternative hypothesis to be $\mu \neq 24,000$. It follows from this that a two-tailed test has been appropriate. What we have done informally is indeed to carry out a two-tailed test, making use of the significance levels provided in table A3. We will now use another example to demonstrate the procedure formally, step by step, this time with an alternative hypothesis that specifies the direction of the difference.

Let us suppose that there is a proficiency test for students of French as a second language in which students educated to British A level standard are expected to score a mean of 80 marks. In a certain year teaching activities at some schools are disrupted by selective strikes. Ten students are chosen at random from those schools and are administered the test just before the time when they are due to sit the A level examination. (In practice, a much bigger sample would normally be chosen if there were real grounds for believing that the students' performance had been affected by the strikes, but we wish to demonstrate here how a small sample could be analysed.) The scores of the ten students were:

$$62 \quad 71 \quad 75 \quad 56 \quad 80 \quad 87 \quad 62 \quad 96 \quad 57 \quad 69$$

The mean of this sample is 71.5, with a standard deviation of 13.18. Do you think their performance has been affected by the interruption of their studies? One way to answer this question is to test whether the students seem to have achieved results as good as, or worse than, those achieved by the body of students who have taken the same proficiency test in previous years at the same point in their French language education.[2]

The null hypothesis for this test will be that the students tested come from a population whose mean score is 80, the historical mean for students who have had the usual preparation for the A level examination. We would not expect the disruption of teaching to improve students' performance on the whole, so that a one-sided alternative will be appropriate.

We will therefore test the hypothesis that the mean test score of the population from which these mean scores are drawn is 80, against the alternative that the population mean score is less than 80. In other words, we wish to test:

$$H_o : \mu \Sigma 80 \quad versus \quad H_1 : \mu < 80$$

How are we to carry out this test? It looks similar to the test of hypothesis on mean vocabulary size that we carried out in §8.2 – apart from the change in the alternative hypothesis – but there is one very important difference. Here the sample size is too small for the Central Limit Theorem to be invoked safely. In the vocabulary example we did have a large sample and this is what enabled us to be sure that the test statistic, Z, had a standard normal distribution. In small samples that will not be true.

In the last chapter we have already addressed the problem of small sample size in the context of the determination of a confidence interval. The solution which was suggested there carries over to the current problem. First, for small samples, we have to be willing to make an assumption about the distribution of the variable being sampled, namely that it has a normal distribution. Here, for example, in order to make any further progress we must assume that the proficiency test scores would be more or less normally distributed over the whole population of students with disrupted schooling. *Provided that assumption is true*, then the quantity:

$$\frac{\bar{X} - \mu}{s/\sqrt{n}}$$

will still make a suitable test statistic, since its distribution is known and

[2] A better way would be to compare them directly with students who will take the A level in the same year and whose studies were not disrupted. How to do that is explained in chapter 11.

can be tabulated. It is no longer standard normal; rather it has the t-distribution introduced in the previous chapter. For the present example the statistic:

$$\frac{\bar{X} - \mu}{s/\sqrt{n}}$$

will have a t-distribution with 9 (= 10 − 1) degrees of freedom (df). Hypothesis tests are often referred to by the name of the test statistic they use. In this case we might say that we are 'carrying out a t-test' (cf. F-test and chi-squared test in later chapters).

Hence, if the population mean score really is 80 then for *any* sample of ten scores:

$$t = \frac{\bar{X} - 80}{s/\sqrt{10}}$$

will be a random value from the t-distribution with 9 df. If $\mu < 80$, we would expect the test statistic to have a negative value (since then $\bar{X}$ will usually be less than 80), and it will no longer have a t-distribution (since the incorrect value of μ will have been used in its calculation). In other words, if the alternative hypothesis $H_1 : \mu < 80$ is true, then we would expect a value of t which is negative and far out in the tail of the histogram of the t-distribution.

In the test score example we have:

$$n = 10, \quad \bar{X} = 71.5, \quad s = 13.18$$

so that the value of the test statistic is:

$$t = \frac{71.5 - 80}{13.18/\sqrt{10}} = -2.04$$

The value of t is negative. If it had not been so, there could be no question of the data supporting the alternative hypothesis against the null, since a sample mean greater than 80 cannot be claimed as evidence in favour of a population mean less than 80! The question is whether it is a value extreme enough to indicate that the hypothesis $\mu = 80$ is implausible. Figure 8.1 shows the histogram of the t-distribution with 9 df, with the histogram of the standard normal superimposed. They are very similar. Both are symmetric about the value zero but the t-distribution is flatter and spreads more into the tails, reflecting the extra uncertainty caused by the small sample size. If the null hypothesis is true, then $\mu = 80$ and most samples will have a mean of around 80 so that $t = (\bar{X} - \mu)/(s/\sqrt{n})$

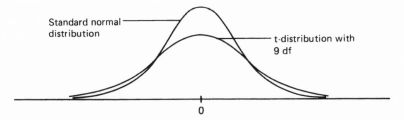

Figure 8.1. Comparison of the histogram of the t-distribution with that of the standard normal distribution.

will have a value around zero. However, even if H_0 is true some samples will correspond to a value of t in the left-hand tail (and so look as if they supported the alternative $H_1 : \mu < 80$). A table of t-distributions, such as table A4, gives values of t which are somewhat unlikely if H_0 is true. These values are often called **percentage points of the t-distribution** since they are the values which will be exceeded in only such and such a per cent of samples *if H_0 is true*. However, the tables are set up to give the percentage points appropriate for a test which involves a two-tailed alternative hypothesis when an extreme value of t, whether positive or negative, could be evidence in favour of the alternative rather than the null hypothesis. For example, for the t-distribution with 9 df the value given as the 10% point is 1.83 and figure 8.2 demonstrates the meaning of the tabulated value. When the null hypothesis is true the value of t will lie in one of the tails – shaded in the figure (i.e. $t > 1.83$ or $t < -1.83$) – for a total of 10% of samples. For half of those samples (5%) the value of t will lie in the left-hand tail, for the other half in the right. Only values in the left-hand tail can support the alternative hypothesis that $\mu < 80$. If we decide to reject the null hypothesis in favour of the alternative whenever the t-value falls in the left-hand tail in figure 8.2, i.e. whenever $t < -1.83$, we would reach this conclusion mistakenly in only 5% of samples when the null hypothesis is actually true. In the present example, $t = -2.04 \, (< -1.83)$. Conventionally, we could say that 'at the 5%

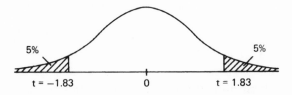

Figure 8.2. The *two-tailed* 10% point of the t-distribution with 9 df.

significance level we can reject $H_0 : \mu = 80$ in favour of the alternative $H_1 : \mu < 80$'. This statement is frequently shortened to 'the value of t is significant at 5%'. The shorter version is acceptable provided the null and alternative hypothesis are stated elsewhere.

It is worth repeating again that the percentage points in the table are relevant for a two-tailed test. The tables say that 1.83 is the 10% value. Since the alternative used in the present example is one-sided only, one of the tails is eliminated from consideration and the use of the 'cut-off' or **critical value** $t = -1.83$ will lead to only a 5% probability of a type 1 error. Notice that if the two-sided alternative $H_1 : \mu \neq 80$ had been relevant here, then, at the 5% significance level, only values of t greater than 2.26 or less than -2.26 would have been significant so that the value obtained here, $t = -2.04$, would no longer be significant at the 5% level! You should find this entirely logical, perhaps after some thought. The significance level is just the probability that the null hypothesis will be (mistakenly) rejected when it is correct. The value that will cut off the 95% of 'acceptable' t-values will be different depending on whether those values are distributed between both tails or are confined to just one. Similar arguments apply to the percentage points corresponding to any other significance level. The 2% point of t with 9 df is given as 2.76 in the tables. But this is, as always, for a two-sided alternative. For a one-sided alternative 2.76 (for $H_1 : \mu > 80$) or -2.76 (for $H_1 : \mu < 80$) is the 1% point.

Note in passing that table A4 does not give all possible degrees of freedom. For example, after 15 df the next tabulated value is 20 df. What happens if you need 18 df, i.e. the sample size is $n = 19$? You will notice that the critical value of t at any significance level decreases as the df increase. In other words, the bigger the sample the smaller are the t-values which are found to be significant. (This reflects the extra confidence we have in s^2 as a measure of *population* variance in bigger samples.) Notice further that the critical values for 20 df are very similar to those for 15 df. For any number of degrees of freedom between 15 and 20 either of those two rows give very close approximations to the correct answer. It is conventional (and conservative) to use the row corresponding to the nearest number of degrees of freedom smaller than those which are required when the latter are not tabulated.

A final point to notice about the t-tables is that as the degrees of freedom increase the values become more and more similar to those of the standard normal distribution. The values in the last row of table A4 are exactly those of the standard normal, i.e. the values in the last row of table A4 correspond to the second column of table A3.

8.4 How to use statistical tests of hypotheses: is significance significant?

Every statistical test of hypothesis has a similar logic whatever are the hypotheses being tested. There will be two hypotheses, one of which, the null, must be precise (e.g. $\mu = 80$) while the other may be more or less vague (e.g. $\mu < 80$). There must be a test statistic *whose distribution is known when the null is true*. Percentage points of that distribution can then be calculated and tabulated. Sometimes the tables will be appropriate to two-sided and sometimes to one-sided alternatives – the rubric will make it clear which is the case. The major constraint on the use of significance tests is that it is generally difficult to discover test statistics with known properties. Such statistics are available for only a few, standard null hypotheses. It frequently happens that a researcher wishes to address a question which is not easily formulated in terms of one of those hypotheses and it would be mistaken to try to force all investigations into this framework. The value of statistical hypothesis testing as a scientific tool has been greatly exaggerated.

In chapter 7 it was argued that a confidence interval gives a useful summary of a data set. We hope it is clear from the development of the hypothesis test from a confidence interval in §8.2 that a test statistic and the result of a test of hypothesis is simply another way of summarising a set of data. It can give a useful and succinct summary, but it is no more than that. Important decisions should not be taken simply on the basis of a statistical hypothesis test. It is a misguided strategy to abandon an otherwise attractive line of research because a statistically significant result is not obtained as the result of a single experiment, or to believe that an unexpected rejection of a null hypothesis means, by itself, that an important scientific discovery has been made. A hypothesis test simply gives an indication of the strength of evidence (in a single experiment) for or against a working hypothesis. The emphasis is always on the type 1 error, error which arises when we incorrectly reject a true null hypothesis on the basis of this one statistical experiment. The possibility of type 2 error tends to be forgotten. If we do not find a highly significant result, this does not mean that the null is correct. Sampling error, small sample size or the natural variability of the population under study may prevent us from *detecting* a substantial failure in the null hypothesis. Furthermore, although we control the probability of type 1 error by demanding that it be small, say 5% or 1% or less, we will not usually know how large is the probability of making a type 2 error. Except when the sample size is very large, the probability of a type 2 error is often rather higher than the probability of a type 1. Hence, there is often a high chance of missing important scientific effects if we rely solely on statistical tests made on small samples to detect them for us.

Hypothesis testing is set up as a conservative procedure, asking for a fairly small probability of a type 1 error before we make a serious claim that the null hypothesis has been refuted. The procedure is designed to operate from the point of view of a single researcher or research team assessing the result of a single experiment. If the experiment is repeated several times, whether by the same or by different investigators, the results need to be considered in a different light. For example, suppose the editors of a scientific journal decide, misguidedly, to publish those papers which contain a statistically significant result and reject all others. They might decide that a significance level of 5% would be required. Now let us suppose that 25 researchers have independently carried out experiments to test a null hypothesis which is, in fact, true. For any one of these individuals it is correct that there is only a 5% chance he will erroneously reject the null hypothesis. However, there is a chance of *greater than 72%* that at least one of the 25 researchers will find an incorrect, but statistically significant, result. If there were 100 researchers, this chance rises to more than 99%! The chance of a research report appearing in the journal would then depend largely on the popularity of the research topic, but there would be no way of assessing how likely to be true are the results in the published articles.

Another point to remember is that no null hypothesis will be exactly true. We tested the hypothesis (in §8.3) that $\mu = 80$; we would probably not wish it to be rejected even if the true value were not 80 but 79.999 since this would not indicate any *interesting* difference in mean scores between the subpopulation and the wider population. On the other hand, if a large enough sample is used such small discrepancies will cause rejection of the null hypothesis. Look back to the example in §8.3. The test statistic was:

$$t = \frac{\bar{X} - \mu}{s/\sqrt{n}}$$

This can be seen to be a quotient of two numbers. The numerator is $\bar{X} - \mu$; the divisor or denominator is $s/\sqrt{n}$. The test statistic will have a large value if *either* the numerator is large *or* the denominator is small. We can make the denominator as small as we please by increasing the value of n. For *very* large values of n, the test statistic can be significant even if the difference between $\bar{X}$ and μ is trivially small. The explicit calculation of a suitable confidence interval would show immediately whether any differences from the hypothesised value were negligible, although the test had rejected the null hypothesis. If a statistical test indicates that some null hypothesis is to be rejected we should always attempt to estimate more likely parameter values to replace those in the rejected null hypothesis. We must keep in mind always the difference between statistical and scientific significance, and we should remember that the latter will frequently have to be assessed further in the light of economic considerations.

Let us consider an example. Suppose that a new method of treatment has been suggested to alleviate a dysphasia. An investigation is carried out whereby an experimental group of n patients is treated for some months by the new method while a matched control group of the same size is treated over the same period by a standard method. We could then test, using one of the tests to be introduced in chapter 11, the null hypothesis that the degree of improvement was the same under both treatment methods against the alternative that the new method caused more improvement. Let us consider the possible outcomes of such a test.

8.4.1   *The value of the test statistic is significant at the 1% level*

What does this tell us? In itself, very little. We have just pointed out that we never expect any null hypothesis to be exactly true. The significant value of the test statistic means that our experiment has been able to discover that. The question is, has the significant value come about because, on average, there is a large benefit from the new method or because, perhaps, a very large sample of subjects was used? If it is the former then it is still possible that this is a sampling phenomenon, that the accidental allocation of patients to the two groups has placed in the experimental group a majority of patients who would have made most improvement under the old method. However, we know, from the significance level, that there is only a one in a hundred chance that the new treatment is in *no* way better than the standard.

Does this then mean that the new treatment should be introduced? Not at all. We must now ask about the relative costs of the two methods. If the new method costs much more than the standard method to administer then it can only be introduced if it causes improvement so much more rapidly that at least the same number of patients annually can be helped to the same level of improvement as under the standard method. It will be necessary to test the new method with a large number and variety of patients before sufficient information can be obtained to assess this properly. Although a small sample might show that there is a statistically significant difference of an apparently interesting magnitude, more information will always be necessary to assess the economic implications of changes of this type.

8.4.2 *The value of the test statistic is not significant*

In itself an 'uninteresting' value of the test statistic should not be the end of the story. Never forget the possibility of type 2 errors, especially if the sample size is very small. At least you should always look at the difference in performance of the two samples and ask 'Would a difference of this magnitude be important if it were genuine?' If the answer is affirmative, then it is worth considering a repetition of the experiment with a larger sample size. You should also take a careful look at some of the details of the data. For example, it could happen that many patients do not improve much under either method but, of those who do, the improvement might be more marked under the new treatment. The average gain of the new method would then be quite small because of the inertia of the 'non-improvers' and the variability in both samples would be increased because they are really mixtures of two types of patient. Both of those conditions would increase the probability of a type 2 error.

In the light of the above comments it should be clear that to report the results of a study by saying that something was significant at the 1% level or was not significant at the 5% level is unsatisfactory. It makes much more sense to discuss the details of the data in a manner which throws as much light as possible on the problem which you intended to tackle. A formal test of hypothesis then indicates the extent to which your conclusions may have been distorted by sampling variability. The occurrence of a significant value of a test statistic should be considered as neither necessary nor sufficient as a 'seal of approval' for the statistical validity of the conclusion. The general rule introduced in chapter 3 still holds good. Any summary of a set of experimental data may be revealing and helpful. This is equally true whether the summary takes the form of a table of means and variances, a graph or the result of a hypothesis test. In all cases, as much as possible of the original data should always be given to enable readers of an article to assess how adequate the summary is and to enable them to carry out a new analysis if they wish.

SUMMARY

This chapter introduces the concepts and philosophy of statistical hypothesis testing.

(1) A **confidence interval** can be used to test the hypothesis that a sample mean takes a particular value; **type 1 errors** and **type 2 errors** were defined.

(2) The concept of a **test statistic** was used to link confidence intervals with hypothesis tests.

(3) The classical hypothesis test was introduced as the test of a **null hypothesis (H_0)** against a specific **alternative hypothesis (H_1)** using as a criterion the value of a **test statistic** whose distribution is known *provided H_0 is true*. The sample value of the test statistic is compared to a table of **critical values** to obtain the **significance level** (probability of a type 1 error) of the test. The meaning of, and need for, **one-tailed** and **two-tailed** tests was explained. To carry out a test of the null hypothesis, $H_0 : \mu = $ specified value, against any of the three common alternatives the relevant statistic is $(\bar{X} - \mu)/(s/\sqrt{n})$. For small samples its value is compared with those of the **t-distribution with ($n - 1$) degrees of freedom**; for large samples it is compared with the critical values of the **standard normal distribution**.

EXERCISES

(1) A sample of 184 children take an articulation test. Their mean score is 48.8 with standard deviation 12.4. Show that these results are consistent with the null hypothesis that the population mean is $\mu = 50$ against the alternative that $\mu \neq 50$.

(2) All the exercises at the end of chapter 7 require the calculation of confidence intervals. Take just one of those confidence intervals and reconsider its meaning in the light of the present chapter. In particular, formulate two different null hypotheses, one of which would be found plausible and the other of which would be rejected as a result of the interval. In both cases state, very precisely, the alternative hypothesis.

(3) An experimenter wants to test whether the mean test score, μ, of a population of subjects has a certain value. In particular he decides to test $H_0 : \mu = 80$ *versus* $H_1 : \mu > 80$. He obtains scores on a random sample of subjects and calculates the sample mean and variance as $\bar{X} = 84.2$ and $s = 14.6$. He omits to report the sample size, n. Show that if $n = 16$, H_0 would *not* be rejected at the 5% level, but that H_0 *would* be rejected if $n = 250$.

(4) In the last example, find the smallest sample size, n, which would lead to the rejection of H_0:

   (i) at the 5% significance level
   (ii) at the 1% level

(5) If $\bar{X} = 80.1$ and $s = 14.6$, show that $H_0 : \mu = 80$ could still be rejected in favour of $H_1 : \mu > 80$ at *any* level of significance.

(6) Discuss the implications of exercises 2, 3 and 4, above.

9
Testing the fit of models to data

9.1 Testing how well a complete model fits the data

In the previous chapter we learned how to test hypotheses concerning the value of important quantities associated with a population. What we tested was whether a *particular* model of the chosen type could be supported or should be rejected on the basis of data observed in a random sample. There are times, however, when we might have doubts about the very form of the model, when, for instance, we are uncertain whether it is appropriate for the population in which we are interested to be modelled as a normally distributed population.

Imagine the case where a School District in the USA wishes to identify those children beginning school who should be provided with speech therapy. Rather than involve themselves in the lengthy and expensive business of constructing a new articulation test, they plan to use a test which is already available. One test which seems on the surface to be suitable for this purpose is British. It has been validated and standardised in Glasgow in such a way that for the whole population of 5-year-old children in Glasgow the scores on the test are normally distributed, with a mean score of 50 and standard deviation of 10. In order to discover whether scores on the test will have similar properties when used with 5-year-old children in its own area, the US School District administers it to a random sample of 184 of these children. The results of this are presented as a frequency table in the first two columns of table 9.1. The mean score of the US children is 48.8 and the standard deviation is 12.4. Using the methods of the previous chapter, it can readily be shown (see exercise 8.1) that the mean of this sample is indeed consistent with a population mean of 50. But this does not tell us whether the complete population of test scores (i.e. those which would be made by all 5-year-old children in the area) could be modelled adequately as a normally distributed population. This question is important to the School District. As we saw in chapter 6, if a population is normally distributed, the proportion of the population

Table 9.1. *Frequency table of scores of 184 children's test scores*

1 Class intervals of scores From → less than		2 Observed number of scores in each class	3 Standardised class intervals $z = \dfrac{X - 50}{10}$ From → less than		4 Expected proportion in each class	5 Expected number of scores in each class
0	30	2	—	−2.0	0.023	4.2
30	35	11	−2.0	−1.5	0.044	8.1
35	40	17	−1.5	−1.0	0.092	16.9
40	45	31	−1.0	−0.5	0.150	27.6
45	50	32	−0.5	0.0	0.191	35.1
50	55	39	0.0	0.5	0.191	35.1
55	60	22	0.5	1.0	0.150	27.6
60	65	19	1.0	1.5	0.092	16.9
65	70	6	1.5	2.0	0.044	8.1
70	75	4	2.0	2.5	0.017	3.1
75 or greater		1	2.5	—	0.006	1.1

lying between any two points is known. If, therefore, the population of scores of the US children on the test *is* normally distributed, it will be possible to calculate what proportion of the population of children will obtain scores within a certain range. More particularly, it will be possible to calculate the proportion of children who will be given speech therapy if a certain (low) score is used as a cut-off point; i.e. only children obtaining a score lower than this will receive therapy. It is in fact quite common practice in the USA in identifying children in need of treatment, to set that cut-off point at two standard deviations below the mean. If the test scores are normally distributed, this means that approximately 2.5% of children will be selected for treatment. But unless we know that the distribution of the US population scores can be modelled on a normal distribution, we cannot ascertain the proportion in this way.

How then do we determine whether or not the sample data obtained are consistent with a normally distributed population of test scores? If the frequency data are represented as a histogram (figure 9.1), it can be seen that they do in fact show some resemblance to a normal curve. But we must go further than this. The question that we have to answer is whether the number of scores in each class is sufficiently similar to that which would result typically when a random sample of 184 observations is taken from a normally distributed population with a mean of 50 and standard deviation of 10. The first step is to calculate the proportion of the model population which would lie in each class interval. To do this, the endpoints of the intervals are standardised to Z-values, as in the third column of table 9.1 (Z-values calculated using the formula $Z = (X - \mu)/\sigma$ presented in chapter 6). In the fourth column are the expected proportions of the model population to be found in each class interval, these proportions being taken from a normal table (table A2) in the way described in chapter 6. In order to calculate the number of scores we would expect in each

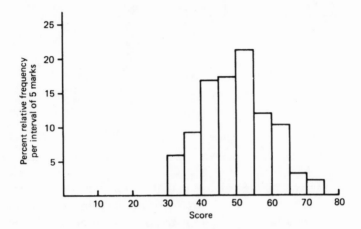

Figure 9.1. Histogram of the data of table 9.1. (Note that the first and last classes are not represented in the diagram.)

class if the sample of 184 scores had been taken from a population with the stated properties, we have only to multiply each expected proportion by 184, the results being given in column 5 (for example, $184 \times 0.023 = 4.2$).

Comparing columns 2 and 5 of the table, we can see that the actually observed number of scores in each class is not very different from what we would expect of a sample of 184 taken from a normal population with a mean of 50 and standard deviation of 10. So far this merely confirms the impression given by the histogram (figure 9.1). But we will now use these observed and expected frequencies to develop a formal test of the fit of the proposed model to the observed data.

Let the null hypothesis (chapter 8), H_0, be that the data represents a random sample drawn from a normally distributed population with $\mu = 50$ and $\sigma = 10$. The alternative, H_1, is that the parent population (the one from which the sample has been drawn) has a distribution different from the one proposed. We must first obtain a measure of the discrepancy between the observed scores and those which would be expected if H_0

Table 9.2. *Calculations for testing the hypothesis that the data of table 9.1 come from a normal distribution with mean 50 and standard deviation 10*

1 Observed frequency, o_i	2 Expected frequency, e_i	3 Discrepancy $(o_i - e_i)$	4 $(o_i - e_i)^2$	5 Relative discrepancy $\dfrac{(o_i - e_i)^2}{e_i}$
$\left.\begin{array}{c}2\\11\end{array}\right\}13$	$\left.\begin{array}{c}4.2\\8.1\end{array}\right\}12.3$	0.7	0.49	0.04
17	16.9	0.1	0.01	0.0006
31	27.6	3.4	11.56	0.42
32	35.1	−3.1	9.61	0.27
39	35.1	3.9	15.21	0.43
22	27.6	−5.6	31.36	1.14
19	16.9	2.1	4.41	0.26
$\left.\begin{array}{c}6\\4\\1\end{array}\right\}11$	$\left.\begin{array}{c}8.1\\3.1\\1.1\end{array}\right\}12.3$	−1.3	1.69	0.14
			Total deviance =	2.70

were true. The most obvious thing to do is calculate for each class the difference between the observed number of scores and the expected number of scores. The expected number can simply be subtracted from the observed number. The result of doing this can be seen in column 3 of table 9.2. (The reason for combining a number of the original classes will be given below.) Some of the discrepancies are positive, the remainder negative. But it is the magnitude of the discrepancy rather than its direction which is of interest to us; the sign (plus or minus) has no importance. What is more, just as with deviations around the mean (chapter 3) the sum of these discrepancies is zero. It will be helpful to square the discrepancies here, just as we did in chapter 3 with deviations around the mean.

It should be clear that it is not the absolute discrepancy between observed and expected frequencies which is important. If, for example, we expected 10 scores to fall in a given class and observed 20 (twice as many), we would regard this as a more important aberration than if we observed 110 where 100 were expected, even though the absolute difference was 10 in both cases. For this reason we calculate the **relative discrepancy** by dividing the square of each absolute discrepancy by the expected frequency. Thus, in the first row: 0.49 (square of discrepancy) ÷ 12.3 (expected frequency) gives a relative discrepancy of 0.04. The results of this and calculations for the remaining rows are found in column 5.

The procedure that we have followed so far has given us a measure of **deviance** from the model for each class which will be zero when the observed frequency of scores in the class is exactly what would be predicted by H_0, and which will be large and positive when the discrepancy is large compared to the expected value. By summing the deviances in column 5 we arrive at the **total deviance**, which is 2.70. Using the total deviance as a test statistic, we are now in a position to decide whether or not the sample scores are consistent with their being drawn from a population of normally distributed scores with $\mu = 50$ and $\sigma = 10$. This is because, provided that all the *expected* frequencies within classes are large enough (in that they are all greater than 5), the distribution of the total deviance is known *when H_0 is true*. It is called a chi-squared distribution (sometimes written χ^2), though, as with the t-distribution, it is really a family of distributions, each member of the family being identified by a number of degrees of freedom. The degrees of freedom depend on the number of classes which have contributed to the total deviance. For the present case there are eight classes, some of the original classes having been grouped together. This was done in order to meet the requirement that the expected frequency in each class should be more than 5 (for example the original classes '70–less than 75' and '75 or greater' did not have sufficiently large values). There are eight classes but the expected frequencies are not all independent. Since their total has to be 184, as soon as seven expected frequencies have been calculated, then the last one is known automatically. There are therefore just 7 df. If H_0 is true, the total deviance will have approximately a chi-squared distribution with 7 df. Critical values of chi-squared are to be found in table A5. We can see there that the 10% critical value for 7 df is 12.0. Since the value we have actually obtained, 2.70, is much smaller than this, there is no real case to be made against the null hypothesis. The scores made by the US children are consistent with those expected from a random sample drawn from a population of scores having a normal distribution with a mean of 50 and a standard deviation of 10. With this knowledge the School District should be able to predict with reasonable accuracy the number of 5-year-old children in their area for whom speech therapy will be indicated by the British articulation test, whatever cut-off point they might wish to select. (Of course, we must not forget the possibility of a type 2 error which would occur when the data really did come from a quite different distribution but the particular sample *happened* to look as though it came from the distribution specified by the null hypothesis. Given the largish sample size and the fact that the value of the test statistic is well below the critical value, it is highly unlikely that any serious error will be committed by accepting that H_0 is true.)

9.2 Testing how well a type of model fits the data

In the previous section we saw how to test the fit of a model with a normal distribution and a given mean and standard deviation. It was because the mean and standard deviation were given that the model was described in the section heading as 'complete', since it was fully specified. But this information is not always available. If the US School District had decided not to use an existing test but to develop one of its own, then there would be no population mean and standard deviation which could be incorporated into the model. Nevertheless, for the reasons given in the previous section, the School District would still be concerned to know whether the population of 5-year-old children on the new test would have a normal distribution, regardless of the mean and standard deviation. How would it find out?

Let us imagine that such a test is produced and administered to a random sample of 341 5-year-old children in the area. The null hypothesis is that the data obtained in this way represent a random sample drawn from a normally distributed population. The alternative hypothesis is that the parent population is not normally distributed. The procedure followed to test the fit of a *type* of model (here one with a normal distribution) is very similar to the one elaborated in the previous section for a complete model. We begin with the sample scores summarised in the first two columns of table 9.3. Since we have not hypothesised a population mean (μ) nor a standard deviation (σ), we will take as our estimate of these

Table 9.3. *Calculations for testing the hypothesis that the scores of 341 children come from a normal distribution*

1 Class interval of scores		2	3 Standardised interval		4	5	6
From→	Less than	Observed frequency	From→	Less than	Proportion expected in each interval	Expected frequency	Deviance
	45	9		−1.83	0.0334	11.4	0.51
45	50	28	−1.83	−1.36	0.0536	18.3	5.14
50	55	28	−1.36	−0.89	0.0992	33.8	1.00
55	60	46	−0.89	−0.41	0.1548	52.8	0.88
60	65	70	−0.41	0.06	0.1829	62.4	0.93
65	70	53	0.06	0.53	0.1780	60.7	0.98
70	75	41	0.53	1.00	0.1394	47.5	0.89
75	80	38	1.00	1.47	0.0879	30.0	2.13
80 and over		28	1.47 and over		0.0708	24.1	0.63

$\bar{X} = 64.36$
$s = 10.6$

Total deviance = 13.09

the sample mean ($\bar{X}$) and standard deviation (s). In the present case $\bar{X} = 64.36$ and s = 10.6. Using these figures, the endpoints of the intervals are standardised (column 3) and the expected proportion of the model population to be found in each class interval is again calculated with the help of a normal table (table A2). Each proportion is then multiplied by 341 to give the number of scores we would expect in each class if the sample were taken from a normally distributed population (column 5). For each class, the deviance is computed by means of the formula:

$$\frac{(o_i - e_i)^2}{e_i}$$

and the deviances are summed to give a total deviance of 13.09 (column 6).

The only difference from what was done in the last section is that this time the sample mean and standard deviation have been used to estimate their population equivalents. This affects the degrees of freedom. As we have said before, the degrees of freedom can be considered in a sense as the number of independent pieces of information we have on which to base the test of a hypothesis. We began here with nine separate classes whose frequencies we wished to compare with expected frequencies. However, we really have only eight separate expected values since the ninth value will be the total frequency less the sum of the first eight expected frequencies. But the degrees of freedom have to be further reduced. In estimating the population mean and standard deviation for the sample, we have, if you like, extracted two pieces of information from the data (one to estimate the mean and another to estimate the standard deviation), reducing by two the number of pieces of information available for checking the fit of the model to the data. The degrees of freedom in this case are therefore 6.

You should not worry if you do not follow the argument in the previous paragraph. The concept of degrees of freedom is difficult to convey in ordinary language and in a book such as this we cannot hope to make it fully understood. So far we have appealed to intuition, using the notion of 'pieces of information'. From now on, however, as the reasoning in particular cases becomes more complex, we shall not always attempt to provide the rationale for the degrees of freedom in a particular example. We shall continue, of course, to make clear exactly how they should be calculated.

As we saw above, the degrees of freedom in this instance are 6 ($9 - 1 - 2$). If H_0 is correct, the total deviance (13.09) will have approximately a chi-squared distribution with 6 df. We see in table A5 that the corresponding 5% critical value is 12.6. Since the total deviance obtained is greater than this, we reject the null hypothesis. From the evidence of the sample scores, it would seem rather unlikely that the population of scores on the test of the 5-year-old children will have a normal distribution. This means that if the School District were to use the test in its present form, it might not be possible to benefit from the known properties of the normal distribution when making decisions about the provision of speech therapy to children in the area. However, we must not forget that there is a probability of 5% that the result of the test is misleading and that the test scores really *are* normally distributed, or at least have a distribution sufficiently close to normal to meet the requirements of the School District authorities. On the other hand, inspection of table 9.3 suggests that the distribution of test scores is rather more spread out then the normal distribution, with higher frequencies than expected in the tails. If a cut-off point of two standard deviations below the mean is used the remedial education services may be overwhelmed by having referred to them many more children than expected.

You will realise that the application of the statistical tests elaborated in this and the previous section are not limited to articulation tests and School Boards in the USA. It should not be difficult to think of comparable examples. What you might not realise is that this idea of testing the fit of models to observed data is not limited to test scores, but can be extended to different kinds of linguistic data. For instance, an assumption underlying factor analysis and regression (chapters 15 and 13) is that the population scores on each variable are normally distributed, and this can be checked in particular cases, when the sample size is large enough, by the method described in this section. If the data do not meet the assumption of normality, the results of factor analysis or regression analysis (if carried out) should be treated with extra caution.

9.3 Testing the model of independence

In this section we will present two examples of a rather different application of the chi-squared distribution. The first example is taken from a study reported by Ferris & Politzer (1981). They wanted to compare the English composition skills of two groups of students with bilingual backgrounds. The children in group A had been born in the USA and educated in English. Those in Group B had been born in Mexico, where they had received their early schooling in Spanish, and had later moved to the USA, where their schooling had been entirely in English. There

Table 9.4. *Contingency table of number of verb tense errors in children's essays*

(a) Observed frequencies*

| | Number of errors in verb tense | | | |
	o	1 error	2–6 errors	Row total
Group A	7	7	16	30
Group B	13	11	6	30
Column total	20	18	22	60

(b) Expected frequencies: (row total) × (column total) ÷ (grand total)

| | Number of errors | | | |
	o	1 error	2–6 errors	Row total
Group A	10	9	11	30
Group B	10	9	11	30
Column total	20	18	22	60

(c) Deviances: $(\text{observed} - \text{expected})^2 \div \text{expected}$

| | Number of errors | | |
	o	1 error	2–6 errors
Group A	0.9	0.44	2.27
Group B	0.9	0.44	2.27

Total deviance = 7.22

* Reproduced from Ferris & Politzer (1981)

were 30 children in each group, all about 14 years old. Each of them wrote a composition of at least 100 words in response to a short film, and the first 100 words of each essay were then scored in several different ways. One of the measures used was the number of verb tense errors made by each child in the composition, and the results of this are shown in table 9.4(a) (such a table is referred to as a **contingency table**). We can see there that there are differences between the two groups in the number of tense errors that they have made. What we must ask ourselves now is whether the differences observed could be due simply to sampling variation, that is, we have two samples drawn from the same population; or whether they indicate a real difference, that is, the two samples are actually from different populations.

To answer this question, we must refer back to chapter 5 and the discussion there about the meaning of statistical independence. If the number of errors scored by an individual is independent of his early experience, then, if the experiment were to be carried out over the entire population, the proportions of individuals scoring no errors, one error, or more than one error would be the same for both subpopulations. Suppose then we set up the null hypothesis, H_0, that the number of errors is independent of the early school experience. If H_0 were true, we could consider that, as regards propensity to make errors in verb tense, the two groups are really a single sample from a single population. The proportion of this single sample making no errors is 20/60 (i.e. 20 of the 60 children make no errors). We consider this as an estimate of the proportion in the complete population who would make no errors of tense under the same conditions. If Group A were chosen from such a population, about how many could be expected to make no errors? Let us assume that the same *proportion*, 20/60, would fall into that category. Since Group A consists of 30 subjects, we would expect about $(20/60) \times 30 = 10$ subjects of Group A to make no errors of tense. This figure is entered as an expected frequency in table 9.4(b). Proceeding in the same way, we obtain the number of subjects in Group A expected to make one verb error (9) and from two to six errors (11). When this process is repeated for Group B, the same expected frequencies (10, 9, 11) are obtained. This is because the two groups contain the same number of subjects, which will not always, or even usually, be the case. It is not necessary that the groups should be of the same size; the test of independence which is developing here works perfectly well on groups of unequal size.

Generalising the above procedure, the expected frequencies of different numbers of errors in each group can be obtained by multiplying the total frequency of a given number of errors over the two groups (the column total) by the number of subjects in each group (the row total) and dividing the result by the grand total of subjects in the experiment. The formula:

$$\frac{\text{column total} \times \text{row total}}{\text{grand total}}$$

will give you the expected frequencies, however many rows and columns you have. You should check that by using it you can obtain all the expected frequencies in table 9.4(b).

Now that we have a table of observed frequencies and another of the corresponding expected frequencies, the latter being calculated by assuming the model of independence, we can test that model in the same way that we have tested models in the previous two sections. The total deviance is computed in 9.4(c), and it then only remains to check whether this value, 7.22, can be considered large enough to call for the rejection of the null hypothesis. As previously, the total deviance will have a chi-squared distribution if the model is correct. The degrees of freedom are easily calculated using the formula:

$$(\text{number of columns} - 1) \times (\text{number of rows} - 1).$$

Table 9.5. *Some typical treatments of English loans in Rennellese*

blade	buleli	half	hapu
cartridge	katalini	matches	masese
crab	kalapu	milk	meleki
cricket	kilikiti	plumber	palama
cross	kolosi	pump	pamu
engine	ininsini	rifle	laepolo
fight	paiti	rugby	laghabi
fishing	pisingi	ship	sipi
fork	poka	story	sitoli

Data from Brasington (1978)

In the present case this means $(3 - 1) \times (2 - 1) = 2$. If we consult the chi-squared tables, we find that, with 2 df, the value 7.22 is significant at the 5% level. This suggests that the null hypothesis may be untenable and that the distribution of errors is different for the two populations. The data point to the population of 14-year-old bilingual children who had early schooling in Spanish in Mexico making more verb errors in compositions than those who were born in the USA and were educated there entirely in English.

The second example concerns the way in which English words borrowed into a Polynesian language have been modified to fit the phonological structure of the language. Brasington (1978) examined the characteristics of vowel epenthesis in loan words from English into Rennellese. This is a language spoken on the island of Rennell, at the eastern edge of the Solomon group. Table 9.5 gives some examples of typical treatments of English loans in this language. It is apparent from the examples that (a) English consonant clusters tend in the Rennellese forms to have a vowel introduced between the two elements of the cluster: the initial /kr/ of *crab* becomes /kal-/, the initial /bl-/ of *blade* becomes /bul-/, the medial -gb-/ of *rugby* becomes /-ghab-/; (b) English final consonants tend to appear in Rennellese supported by a vowel: *ship* becomes /sipi/, *half* becomes /hapu/. These modifications (all referred to by Brasington as 'vowel epenthesis') can plausibly be attributed in general to the phonotactic structure of Rennellese, which exhibits a 'typically Polynesian . . . simple sequential alternation of consonants and vowels' (Brasington 1978:27). The CV syllable structure of the borrowing language modifies the CCV- or -VC or -VCCV- structures of the loaning language in obvious and predictable ways. While this may explain the fact of epenthesis, the selection of particular epenthetic vowels in specific cases remains to be accounted for. The Rennellese vowel system (transcribed as i, e, a, o, u) has three heights and (except for the low vowel) a front/back distinction. Why does the Rennellese version

Table 9.6. *Contingency table of type of epenthesis by position of vowel in English loan words in Rennellese*

(a) Observed frequencies

Position of Epenthetic Vowel	Type of epenthesis	
	Reduplicating	Non-reduplicating
Initial	20	14
Medial	13	6
Final	61	112
	94	132

(b) Expected frequencies and deviances

	Reduplicating		Non-reduplicating	
Initial	14.1	(2.5)	19.9	(1.7)
Medial	7.9	(3.3)	11.1	(2.3)
Final	72.0	(1.7)	101.1	(1.2)

Total deviance = 12.7 on 2 df

of English *plumber*, /palama/, select /a/ as the epenthetic vowel to break up the /pl/ cluster? The most straightforward explanation would be one of reduplication of the non-epenthetic vowel. Rennellese represents the /u/ vowel in English *plumber* as /a/; the same vowel is used as the epenthesised one. The same strategy seems to be followed in the Rennellese word for *crab*: English /æ/ is represented as /a/, and the same vowel epenthesised. We can see similar examples for medial position: *rugby* /laghabi/; and for final position: *ship*/sipi/. There are however counterexamples. In initial position, English *blade* /bleid/ is realised in Rennellese as /buledi/; in final position, *half*/haːf/ appears as /hapu/.

We might ask at this point whether there is any association between the position at which epenthesis occurs and whether or not reduplication is the strategy adopted for selection of the epenthetic vowel. Our null hypothesis would be that reduplication and position are independent. To test this hypothesis of independence we tabulate the observed frequencies of each type of epenthesis, reduplicating and non-reduplicating, in each position, initial, medial and final, as in table 9.6(a). The data for this table were obtained by Brasington from Elbert (1975), a dictionary of Rennell-Bellona, and includes all English loan words entered there – a total of 226. The expected frequencies are calculated in the same way as in the previous example, by multiplying column totals by row totals and dividing by the grand total. Table 9.6(b) shows expected frequencies and deviances. The total deviance of 12.7, with 2 df, exceeds the 1% critical value, 9.21. On this basis we are likely to reject our null hypothesis, and assume that the use of the reduplicating strategy for epenthetic vowel selection is not independent of position. Inspection of the differences between observed and expected frequencies leads us to believe that reduplication is more likely in initial and medial position, and less likely in final position. This does not, of course, exhaust the search for factors relevant to the selection of specific epenthetic vowels, and for full details the reader is urged to consult Brasington (1978). We will, however, leave the example at this point.

9.4 Problems and pitfalls of the chi-squared test

9.4.1 *Small expected frequencies*

We have already noted that, in order for the χ^2 test to have satisfactory properties, all expected frequencies have to be sufficiently large (generally 5 or greater). As we saw with the frequencies in table 9.2, it is sometimes necessary to group categories together to meet this condition. A similar problem may occur with a contingency table, with one or more of the expected frequencies falling below 5. There are two possible ways of dealing with this problem when it arises. The first is to consider whether a variable has been too finely subdivided: if so, then categories can be collapsed so that all the cells of the table do have a sufficiently large expected frequency. Suppose, for example, that in table 9.4(b) we had found that we expected very few people in one of the groups to make exactly one error. Then we could combine the second and third columns and classify degree of error into 'all correct' and 'some errors', and still test whether the two groups were similar with respect to the frequency of their errors. If, on the other hand, a similar problem had arisen in table 9.6(b) – let us say that the expected frequency for reduplicating epenthetic vowels in medial position was too low – it would have been more difficult to decide how to regroup the data. Should the medial position vowels be considered alongside those occurring in initial position, or with those epenthesised finally? Because of the nature of the data, there is no obvious solution to this particular problem.

It may also happen that, in a large table, any problem cells are distributed in a rather haphazard way. In such cases, the collapsing of cells necessary to eliminate all those with small expected frequencies will remove interesting detail. The only really satisfactory approach is to collect more data. It is in fact easy to estimate roughly how much more data we may need to collect. Consider the case where one of the variables classified in the table is controlled experimentally, as in the study of the bilingual schoolchildren where the sizes of the groups were chosen by the experimenter. Suppose that, for one of the groups, some cells have too small an expected value. Let us say that the smallest such value (for a cell we clearly wish to retain in the table) is about 1.25, i.e. a quarter of the required minimum. Then increasing the size of that group to four times its original value will cause all the expected values in that row to be increased by about the same factor provided that the proportions of the new data falling in the different columns are roughly the same as in the original. However, to do this could be extremely expensive in terms of experimental effort, even supposing that the variables are under the experimenter's control. In the Rennellese loans, for example, both the type of epenthesis and its place in the word are language-contact phenomena which are not under the control of the researcher. In such circumstances it would be necessary to increase the *total* number of observations fourfold. Even then success, though likely, is not guaranteed, since we cannot be sure that the new observations will increase the row and column totals relevant to the cell in question as much as we had hoped. When we consider, in addition, that it is impossible in this particular case to find any further loan words from the sources used (since Brasington's data comprise *all* the loan words from English in Elbert 1975), and that further data will require expensive fieldwork, we are likely to conclude that there is little value in trying to augment the observations.

There is, however, a third option. We can go ahead and carry out the chi-squared test *even if some expected frequencies are rather too small*. It can be shown that the likely effect of this is to produce a value of the test statistic which is rather larger than it ought to be when the null hypothesis is true; that is, there is more likelihood of a type 1 error (chapter 8). On the other hand, if *all* the cells with small expected values have an observed frequency *very* similar to the expected and thus contribute relatively little to the value of the total deviance, it is unlikely that the value of the deviance has been seriously distorted, and the result of the test can be accepted, especially if we adopt the attitude to hypothesis testing suggested in §8.5.

Whenever χ^2 values based on expected frequencies of less than 5 are reported, the reader's attention should be drawn to this fact and any conclusions arrived at on the basis of a statistically significant outcome should be expressed in suitably tentative terms. An examination of the use of χ^2 in the applied linguistics literature reveals that this is not always done. Indeed, there is cause to wonder whether the authors are always aware of the failure of the data to meet the requirements of the test.

Table 9.7. *Errors in pronoun agreement for two groups of bilingual schoolchildren*

	Number of errors		
	0	1–3	Row total
Group A	15	15	30
Group B	23	7	30
Column total	38	22	60
	chi-squared = 3.516		

Data from Ferris & Politzer (1981)

9.4.2 *The 2 × 2 contingency table*

Table 9.7 reproduces another section of the results from the paper of Ferris & Politzer (1981), this time comparing the essays of two groups of bilingual children for the number of errors made in pronoun agreement. The authors quite correctly report a chi-squared value, i.e. the value of the total deviance, of 3.516 with 1 df, and this fails to reach the tabulated 5% value, 3.84. If you calculate the total deviance using the method explained above, you will arrive at a value of 4.6, which would apparently lead to the rejection of the null hypothesis at the 5% significance level, the null hypothesis stating that the type of early education does not affect the number of errors in pronoun agreement. Why is there this discrepancy between the statistic derived via the analysis explained earlier, and the value quoted in Ferris & Politzer (1981)? It can be shown mathematically that if the model of independence is correct then the total deviance will have *approximately* a chi-squared distribution with the relevant degrees of freedom. The approximation is very close when the expected frequencies are large enough and *the table is larger than 2 × 2*. When the table has only two rows and two columns the total deviance tends to be rather larger than it ought to be for its distribution to be modelled well as a chi-squared variable with 1 df. Thus a correction (referred to as 'Yate's correction') is needed, and takes the following form.

As always, for each of the four cells, you must find the difference between expected and observed frequency. Then, ignoring the sign of that difference, reduce its magnitude by 0.5, square the result and divide by the expected value as before. For example, for the cell giving the number of subjects in Group A who make no errors with agreement of pronouns (table 9.7) the expected frequency is 19 while 15 instances were actually observed. The **magnitude** of the difference (15 − 19) is 4. We reduce

Table 9.8. *Corrected deviances for table 9.7, using the formula:* ({*observed frequency* − *expected frequency*} − 0.5)² ÷ *expected frequency*

	Number of errors	
	o	1–3
Group A	0.645	1.113
Group B	0.645	1.113
	Total = 3.516	

this to 3.5 and calculate the deviance $(3.5)^2 \div 19 = 0.645$. The remainder of the individual deviances are given in table 9.8 and we see that the chi-squared value of 3.516 is correct. Note that, in this example, the un-modified value of the total deviance would have led us to conclude, incorrectly, that the result was significant at the 5% level.

9.4.3 *Independence of the observations*

It is quite common in the study of first or second language learning to analyse a series of utterances from the speech of an individual in order to ascertain the incidence of various grammatical elements and/or errors of a particular kind. Hughes (1979) provides a simple example of this. In his study of the learning of English through conversation by a Spanish speaker (referred to in chapter 3) one of the features that he investigated was noun phrases of the type possessor–possessed, e.g. *Marta('s) bedroom*. Over one period covered in the study the learner used a total of 81 constructions of this type. Of these, 55 showed correct English ordering (e.g. *Marta('s) bedroom*), while the remainder (26) reflected Spanish constituent order (e.g. *bedroom Marta*). On the lexical dimension, 23 of the 81 collocations involved pairings of words that were referred to as 'novel', since these particular pairings had not been used previously by the learner. The remaining 58 pairs were non-novel. An interesting question, relating to productivity in the learner's languge, is whether the novel and non-novel instances manifest different error rates. The data are entered in table 9.9, which looks similar in structure to the 2 × 2 contingency table (table 9.7). However, it would be mistaken to use the chi-squared test on this data, because the separate utterances which were analysed to obtain the data for the table **were not independent of each other**. We have already stressed in earlier chapters that the data we use to estimate a parameter of a population, or to test a statistical hypothesis, must come from a random sample of the population. This is no less true

Table 9.9. *The relation between the novelty of word pairings and ordering errors in the English of a native Spanish speaker*

	Novel pairings	Non-novel pairings	Row total
Correct order	8	47	55
Incorrect order	15	11	26
Column total	23	58	81

of the chi-squared test for association between the rows and columns of a contingency table. In particular, all the instances which have been recorded must be separate and not linked in any way. For example, in spontaneous data from language learners it is not uncommon for instances of the same structure to occur at points close in time, though not as part of the same utterance. It would be naive to suppose that the form which the structure takes on a second occasion is quite independent of the form it took in an utterance occurring a few seconds earlier (see also §7.5.2). This is particularly important in situations like the one under discussion where some cell frequencies are likely to be more affected than others by the lack of independence. Instances of novel pairings of nouns cannot, by definition, be affected by repetition since when a word pair is repeated it is no longer novel. However, instances of non-novel noun pairings could occur in successive utterances. Whenever it is not clear that the observations are completely independent, if a chi-squared value is calculated it should be treated very sceptically and attention drawn to possible defects in the sampling method.

Consider the following example. A researcher is interested in the frequency with which two groups of learners of English supply the regular plural morpheme (realised as /s/, /z/, /ɪz/) in obligatory contexts. One group of learners has had formal lessons in English, the other group has not. Each learner is interviewed for one hour and the number of times he supplies and does not supply the morpheme is noted. The results are reported in table 9.10.

The researcher would be completely mistaken to use the group total in order to carry out a χ^2 test. For one thing, two members of the group that had received instruction contributed many more tokens than anyone else in the study. Their performance had undue influence on the total for their group. But even if all learners had provided an equal number of tokens, it would still not be correct to make use of the group totals in calculating χ^2. This is because an individual's performance with respect

Table 9.10. *Frequency with which two groups of learners of English supply and fail to supply regular plural morphemes in obligatory contexts during interview*

	Group with instruction		Group without instruction	
	Morpheme supplied	Morpheme not supplied	Morpheme supplied	Morpheme not supplied
	32	28	42	36
	112	24	39	28
	106	39	31	29
	42	40	55	37
	26	24	62	55
Group totals	318	155	229	185

to the plural morpheme on one occasion cannot be seen as independent of his performance on all the other occasions within a single hour.

If we seem to have laboured the point about independence in relation to χ^2, there is a reason. There is evidence in applied linguistics publications that the requirement of independence is not generally recognised. The reader is therefore urged to exercise care in the use of χ^2 and also to be on the alert when encountering it in the literature. Whenever an individual's contribution to a contingency table is more than 'one', then there must be suspicion that the assumption of independence has not been met.

9.4.4 *Testing several tables from the same study*

In the Ferris & Politzer study, the essays of the 60 students were marked for six types of error in all, and for each type of error a contingency table was presented in the original paper. Each table was analysed to look for differences between groups at the 5% significance level. There are two points to watch when several tests are carried out based on data from the same subjects.

First, the risk of spurious 'significant' results (i.e. type 1 errors) increases with the number of tests. If we carry out six independent chi-squared tests at the 5% significance level then, for *each* test it is true that the probability of wrongly concluding that the groups are different is only 0.05. However, the probability that *at least one* test will lead to this wrong conclusion is $1 - (0.95)^6 = 0.26$. In fact the errors in verb tense which we analysed in table 9.4 were the only set of errors which gave a significant difference at the 5% level. From the above argument the true significance (taken in conjunction with all the other tests) could be 0.26, or 26%, and we might conclude that there is no strong evidence that the groups are more different than might have occurred by random sampling from the same population. (We cannot be sure of the exact value since the contingency tables, being used all on the same subjects, will not be independent. The true significance level will be somewhere between 5% and 26%.)

A second problem that may occur when one analyses the same scripts or the same set of utterances for a number of different linguistic variables is that these variables may not be independent. Even though we may have, say, yes/no questions and auxiliaries as separate categories in our analysis it is unlikely that these variables are entirely unconnected. Analysing sets of dependent tables can cause the groups to appear either more or less alike than they really are, depending on the relationship between the different variables. Again, in practice one may very well carry out many tests based on a single data set, but it is important to realise that the results cannot be given as much weight as if each table were based on an independent data source.

9.4.5 *The use of percentages*

We have already seen that the data in table 9.7, when tested for independence, produced a non-significant value of chi-squared, suggesting no evidence of any association between rows and columns. Consider now table 9.11(a), which provides a chi-squared value of 6.18, significant at the 0.01 level (for 1 df). This table is, however, 'identical' to the first

Table 9.11. *Data of table 9.7 restated as percentages*

(a) Percentage of total number of subjects

	Number of errors		
	0	1–3	Row total
Group A	25	25	50
Group B	38	12	50
Column total	63	37	100

(b) Percentage of number of subjects in each group

	Number of errors		
	0	1–3	Row total
Group A	50	50	100
Group B	76	24	100
Column total	126	74	200

except that the cell frequencies have been converted to percentages of the total frequency. Table 9.11(b), where an alternative method of calculating the frequencies of table 9.7 in terms of percentages is used, gives an even more dramatic result. Here the frequencies are given as percentages of the row totals, and the resulting chi-square of 13.4 appears to be highly significant. Both examples serve to underline how misleading the conversions of **raw observed frequencies** into percentages can be. The effect can operate in the other direction, disguising significant results, if the true total frequency is greater than 100.

SUMMARY

The previous chapter dealt with the situation where the underlying model was taken for granted (e.g. the data came from a normal distribution) or did not matter (because the sample size was so large). This chapter discussed the problem of testing whether the model itself was adequate, at least for a few special cases.

(1) It was shown how to test H_0: a sample is from a normal distribution with a specific mean and standard deviation *versus* H_1: the sample is not from that distribution, by constructing a frequency table and comparing the **observed class frequencies**, o_i, with the **expected class frequencies**, e_i, if H_0 were true. The test statistic was the **total deviance**, $\chi^2 = \Sigma\{(o_i - e_i^2/e_i\}$, which would have a **chi-squared distribution** with $k - 1$ degrees of freedom where k is the number of classes in the frequency table.

(2) A test was presented of H_0: the sample comes from a normal distribution with no specified mean and standard deviation *versus* H_1: it comes from some other distribution. The procedure and test statistic were the same except that the degrees of freedom were now $(k - 3)$.

(3) The **contingency table** was introduced together with the **chi-squared test**, to test the null hypothesis H_0: the conditions specified by the rows of the table are independent of those specified by the columns or H_0: there is no association between rows and columns *versus* the alternative, which is the simple negation of H_0. The expected and observed frequencies are again compared using the total deviance which has a chi-squared distribution when H_0 is true. The number of degrees of freedom is obtained from the rule:

$$df = (\text{no. of rows} - 1) \times (\text{no. of columns} - 1)$$

(4) It was pointed out that the chi-squared test of contingency tables is frequently misused: all the **expected frequencies** must be 'reasonably large' (generally 5 or more); the **2 × 2 contingency table** requires special treatment; the **observations must be independent** of one another – the only completely safe rule is that each subject supplies just a single token; the **raw observed frequencies** should be used, *not* the relative frequencies or percentages.

EXERCISES

(1) Lascaratou (1984) studied the incidence of the passive in Greek texts of various kinds. Two types of text that she looked at were scientific writing and statutes. Out of a sample of 1,000 clauses from statutes, 698 were passive (incidentally, she included only those clauses where a choice was possible, eliminating active clauses which could not be passivised); out of a sample of 999 clauses of scientific writing, 642 were passive. Knowing that sampling has been very careful, what conclusions would you come to regarding the relative frequency of the passive in texts of the two types?

(2) A group of monolingual native English speakers and a group of native speakers, bilingual in Welsh and English, were shown a card of an indeterminate colour and asked to name the colour, in English, choosing between the names blue, green or grey. The responses are given below. Does it appear that a subject's choice of colour name is affected by whether or not he speaks Welsh?

	Blue	Green	Grey
Monolingual:	28	41	16
Welsh:	40	38	29

(3) An investigator examined the relationship between oral ability in English and extroversion in Chinese students. Oral ability was measured by means of an interview. Extroversion was measured by means of a well-known personality test. On both measures, students were designated as 'high', 'middle' or 'low' scorers. The results obtained are shown separately for males and females in table 9.12. Calculate the two χ^2 values, state the degrees of freedom, and say whether the results are statistically significant. What conclusion would you come to on the basis of this data?

Table 9.12. *Data on relationship of oral ability in English and extroversion (Chinese students)*

Female subjects		Oral proficiency scores		
		High	Middle	Low
Extroversion	High	2	6	4
	Middle	1	3	3
	Low	2	1	2
Male subjects		Oral proficiency scores		
		High	Middle	Low
Extroversion	High	2	0	0
	Middle	2	7	0
	Low	3	1	2

(4) An investigator asked English-speaking learners of an exotic language whether sentences he presented to them in that language were grammatical or not.

Amongst his results he reports the following: for sentences containing one kind of error, there was a 33% rejection rate; for sentences containing a related error, the rejection rate was only 13%. In both cases N is said to be 60. Is the rejection rate for one kind of error significantly different from that for the other kind?

10

Measuring the degree of interdependence between two variables

In chapters 5 and 6 we introduced a model for the description of the random variation in a single variable. In chapter 13 we will discuss the use of a linear model to describe the relationship between two random variables defined on the same underlying population elements. In the present chapter we introduce a measure of the degree of interdependence between two such variables.

10.1 The concept of covariance

A study by Hughes & Lascaratou (1981) was concerned with the evaluation of errors made by Greek learners of English at secondary school. Three groups of judges were presented with 32 sentences from essays written by such students. Each sentence contained a single error. The groups of judges were (1) ten teachers of English who were native speakers of the language, (2) ten Greek teachers of English, and (3) ten native speakers of English who had no teaching experience. Each judge was asked to rate each sentence on a 0–5 scale for the seriousness of the error it contained. A score of 0 was to indicate that the judge could find no error, while a score of 5 would indicate that in the judge's view it contained a very serious error. Total scores assigned for each sentence by the two native English-speaking groups are displayed in table 10.1. One question that can be asked of this data is the extent to which the groups agree on the relative seriousness of the errors in the sentences overall. In this case we wish to examine the degree of association between the total error scores assigned to sentences by the two native-speaker groups.

As a first step in addressing this question, we construct the kind of diagram to be seen in figure 10.1, which is based on the data in table 10.1, and is referred to as a scatter diagram, or **scattergram**. Each point has been placed at the intersection on the graph of the total error score for a sentence by the English teachers (the X axis) and the English non-

Table 10.1. *Total error scores assigned by ten native English teachers (X) and ten native English non-teachers (Y) for each of 32 sentences*

Sentence	English teachers (X)	English non-teachers (Y)
1	22	22
2	16	18
3	42	42
4	25	21
5	31	26
6	36	41
7	29	26
8	24	20
9	29	18
10	18	15
11	23	21
12	22	19
13	31	39
14	21	23
15	27	24
16	32	29
17	23	18
18	18	16
19	30	29
20	31	22
21	20	12
22	21	26
23	29	43
24	22	26
25	26	22
26	20	19
27	29	30
28	18	17
29	23	15
30	25	15
31	27	28
32	11	14

$\bar{X} = 25.03$ $\quad$ $s_X = 6.25$
$\bar{Y} = 23.63$ $\quad$ $s_Y = 8.26$

teachers (the Y axis). So, for example, the point for sentence 12 is placed at the intersection of $X = 22$ and $Y = 19$. The pattern of points on the scattergram does not appear to be haphazard. They appear to cluster roughly along a line running from the origin to the top right-hand corner of the scattergram. There are three possible ways, illustrated in figure 10.2, in which a scattergram with this feature could arise:

(a)   There is an exact linear (i.e. 'straight line') relationship between X and Y, distorted only by measurement error or some other kind of random variation in the two variables.

155

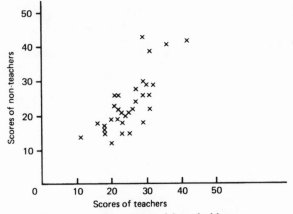

Figure 10.1. Scattergram of data of table 10.1.

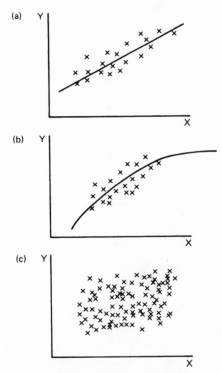

Figure 10.2. Three hypothetical relationships which might give rise to the data of table 10.1 and figure 10.1.

(b)   There is a non-linear relationship between X and Y which, especially in the presence of random error, can be represented quite well by a linear model.

(c) There is no degree of linear relation between X and Y and any apparent linearity in the way the points cluster in figure 10.1 is due entirely to random error.

As usual there will be no way to decide *with certainty* between these different hypotheses. We must find some way of assessing the degree to which each of them is supported by the observed evidence. To do this we first of all require some measure of the extent to which a linear relationship between two variables is implied by observed data. We have already developed measures of 'average' (the mean and the median), measures of dispersion (variance and standard deviation), and now we will introduce a measure of **linear correlation**.

This will be done in two stages, the first of which is to define a rather general measure of the way and the extent to which two variables, X and Y, vary together. This is known as the **covariance**, which we will designate COV(X,Y), and is defined by:[1]

$$COV(X,Y) = \frac{1}{n-1}\Sigma(X_i - \bar{X})(Y_i - \bar{Y})$$

In table 10.2 we have shown what this formula would mean for the data of table 10.1. For both of the variables X, the total error score for each sentence given by the English teachers, and Y, the total error score for the same sentence given by the English non-teachers, we start as though we were about to calculate the variance (cf. §3.7). For example, we find $\bar{X}$, the mean of the 32 X observations, and calculate the difference $d_i(X)$ between each observed value, X_i, and the mean. We then carry out a similar operation on the 32 Y values to obtain the $d_i(Y)$. We then multiply $d_1(X)$ by $d_1(Y)$, $d_2(X)$ by $d_2(Y)$ and so on. We finish by adding the 32 products together and then divide by 31 to find the 'average product of deviations from the mean'. The results of these calculations can be found in table 10.2. (Note that the column of this table giving the cross-products of X and Y, is not used here, but is made use of in table 10.3 to calculate the covariance by an alternative method.)

The reason for doing all this may not immediately seem obvious. It may become clearer, however, when it is recognised that three distinct patterns in the data are translated by this process into three rather different outcomes:

Pattern 1

X and Y tend to increase together. In this case, when X is bigger

---

[1] There is a degree of arbitrariness about the choice of the divisor; some authors may use n, others n − 2. The choice we have made simplifies later formulae. Of course, for largish samples the results will be effectively the same.

Table 10.2. *Covariance between the error scores assigned by ten native English teachers and ten native English non-teachers on 32 sentences*

	1	2	3	4	5	6
Sentence	X	Y	XY	d(X) X − X̄	d(Y) Y − Ȳ	d(X)d(Y)
1	22	22	484	−3.03	−1.63	4.94
2	16	18	288	−9.03	−5.63	50.84
3	42	42	1764	16.97	18.37	311.74
4	25	21	525	−0.03	−2.63	0.08
5	31	26	806	5.97	2.37	14.15
6	36	41	1476	10.97	17.37	190.55
7	29	26	754	3.97	2.37	9.41
8	24	20	480	−1.03	−3.63	3.74
9	29	18	522	3.97	−5.63	−22.35
10	18	15	270	−7.03	−8.63	60.67
11	23	21	483	−2.03	−2.63	5.34
12	22	19	418	−3.03	−4.63	14.03
13	31	39	1209	5.97	15.37	91.76
14	21	23	483	−4.03	−0.63	2.54
15	27	24	648	1.97	0.37	0.73
16	32	29	928	6.97	5.37	37.43
17	23	18	414	−2.03	−5.63	11.43
18	18	16	288	−7.03	−7.63	53.64
19	30	29	870	4.97	5.37	26.69
20	31	22	682	5.97	−1.63	−9.73
21	20	12	240	−5.03	−11.63	58.50
22	21	26	546	−4.03	2.37	−9.55
23	29	43	1247	3.97	19.37	76.90
24	22	26	572	−3.03	2.37	−7.18
25	26	22	572	0.97	−1.63	−1.58
26	20	19	380	−5.03	−4.63	23.29
27	29	30	870	3.97	6.37	25.29
28	18	17	306	−7.03	−6.63	46.61
29	23	15	345	−2.03	−8.63	17.52
30	25	15	375	−0.03	−8.63	0.26
31	27	28	756	1.97	4.37	8.61
32	11	14	154	−14.03	−9.63	135.11

$$\text{COV}(X,Y) = 1231.49 \div 31 = 39.73$$

$$r = \frac{\text{COV}(X,Y)}{s_X s_Y} = \frac{39.73}{6.25 \times 8.26} = 0.772$$

than the X average, Y will usually be bigger than the Y average, so that the product $d_i(X)d_i(Y)$ will tend to be positive. Whenever X is less than the X average, Y will usually be smaller than the Y average. *Both* deviations $d_i(X)$ and $d_i(Y)$ will then be negative so that their product will again be positive. Since most of the products will be positive, their sum (and mean) will be positive and (possibly) quite large.

Pattern 2

There is a tendency for Y to decrease as X increases and vice versa. Now we will find that when X is below average, Y will usually be above average and vice versa. The two deviations $d_i(X)$ and $d_i(Y)$ will usually have opposite signs so that their product will be negative. The sum of the products will then be large and negative.

Pattern 3

There is no particular relation between X and Y. This implies that the sign of $d_i(X)$ will have no influence on the sign of $d_i(Y)$ so that for about half the subjects they will have the same sign and for the remainder one will be negative and the other positive. As a result, about half the products $d_i(X)d_i(Y)$ will be positive and the rest negative so that the sum of products will tend to give a value close to zero.

The covariance between two random variables is a useful and important quantity and we will make use of it directly in this and later chapters. However, its use as a descriptive variable indicating the degree of linearity in a scatter diagram is made difficult by two awkward properties it possesses.

The first we have met before when the variance was introduced (see § 3.7). The units in which covariance is measured will normally be difficult to interpret. In the example of table 10.1 both $d_i(X)$ and $d_i(Y)$ will be a number designating assigned error score so that the product will have units of 'error score × error score' or 'error score squared'. The second is more fundamental. Look at figure 10.3 which shows the scatter diagram of height against weight of 25 male postgraduate students of a British university. As we would expect and can see from the data, taller students *tend* to be heavier, but it is not invariably true that the taller of two students is the heavier. In figure 10.3(a) heights are measured in metres and weight in kilos. In figure 10.3(b) the units used are, respectively, centimetres and grams. (If you think the two diagrams are identical look carefully at the scales marked on the axes.) Clearly the *relationship* between the two variables has not changed in the sample, but the covariances corresponding to the two diagrams are 0.275 metre-kilos and 27,500 centimetre-grams, respectively. Changing the units from metres to centimetres and kilos to grams causes the covariance to be increased by a factor of 100,000. (We would say that covariance is a **scale-dependent** measure.) Surely if we can plot graphs of identical shape for two sets of data, we would want any measure of that shape to give the same value both times? Fortunately, both these defects in the covariance statistic are removed by making a single alteration, which we will present in the next section.

(a)

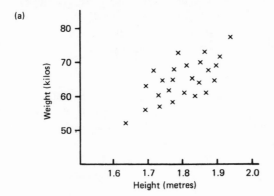

(b)

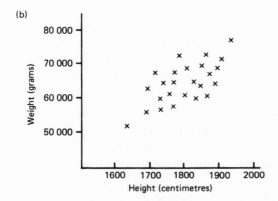

Figure 10.3. Scattergram of height and weight of 25 students.

10.2 **The correlation coefficient**

The standard deviation was calculated of both the heights and the weights from the data on which the scatter diagrams of figure 10.3 were based. They are (s_X and s^*_X are actually the same length – the star simply indicates a change in units):

Set a: fig. 10.3(a)	$s_X = 0.051$ metres	$s_Y = 6.2$ kilos	
Set b: fig. 10.3(b)	$s^*_X = 5.1$ centimetres	$s^*_Y = 6200$ grams	

As we would expect from our knowledge of the properties of the sample standard deviation, $s^*_X = 100s_X$ and $s^*_Y = 1,000s_Y$.

Now consider the product $s_X s_Y$. Its value for Set b is exactly 100,000 times its value for Set a (cf. the covariance) and the units of this product are exactly the same as the units of the covariance in both cases: metre-kilos and centimetre-grams respectively. This suggests that to describe, in some sense, the 'shape' of the two scatter diagrams of figure 10.3, we might try the quantity r, known as the **correlation coefficient**, in which we use the product $s_X s_Y$ as a denominator:

For Set a:

$$r(X,Y) = \frac{COV(X,Y)}{s_X s_Y} = \frac{0.275 \text{ metre-kilos}}{0.051 \text{ metres} \times 6.2 \text{ kilos}} = 0.87$$

and for Set b:

$$r(X,Y) = \frac{COV(X,Y)}{s^*_X s^*_Y} = \frac{27\,500 \text{ cm-grams}}{5.1 \text{ cms} \times 6200 \text{ grams}} = 0.87$$

First note that r does not have any units. It is a dimensionless quantity like a proportion or a percentage. (The units in the numerator 'cancel out' with those in the denominator.) Second, it has the same value for both scattergrams of figure 10.3. Changing the scale in which one, or both, variables are measured does not alter the value of r. It can also be shown that the value of the numerator, ignoring the sign, can never be greater than $s_X s_Y$, and hence the value of r can never be greater than 1.

We can then sum up the properties of $r(X,Y)$ as follows:

(1) $\quad r = r(X,Y) = \dfrac{COV(X,Y)}{s_X s_Y}$

(2) The units in which the variables are measured does not affect the value of r (the correlation coefficient is **scale-independent**)

(3) $\quad -1 \leqslant r \leqslant 1$ (i.e. r takes a value between plus and minus one)

The quantity r is sometimes referred to formally as the 'Pearson product–moment coefficient of liner correlation'.[2] There are other ways of measuring the degree to which two variables are correlated (we will meet one shortly), but we will adopt the common practice of referring to r simply

---

[2] The terminology of statistics is often obscure. Many of the terms were chosen from other branches of applied mathematics. Pearson is the name of the statistician credited with the discovery of r and its properties; many simple statistics like the mean, variance and covariance are called 'moments' by analogy with quantities in physics which are calculated in a similar fashion, e.g. moment of inertia, and 'product' refers to the multiplication of the two factors $(X_i - \bar{X})$ and $(Y_i - \bar{Y})$ in the calculation of the covariance.

Table 10.3. *Example of the rapid method to calculate r*

From the data of table 10.2 we can obtain:

$\bar{X} = 25.03$ $\qquad\qquad$ $s_X = 6.25$
$\bar{Y} = 23.63$ $\qquad\qquad$ $s_Y = 8.26$
$\Sigma X^2 = 21\,261$ $\qquad\qquad$ $\Sigma Y^2 = 19\,978$

$$COV(X,Y) = \frac{\Sigma(X_i - \bar{X})\,(Y_i - \bar{Y})}{n-1} \text{ or, for calculation,}$$

$$COV(X,Y) = \frac{\Sigma XY - n\bar{X}\bar{Y}}{n-1}$$

$$= \frac{20\,155 - (32 \times 25.03 \times 23.63)}{31}$$

$$= \frac{1\,228.32}{31}$$

$$= 39.62$$

$$r = \frac{39.62}{6.25 \times 8.26}$$

$$= 0.767$$

as the (linear) correlation coefficient and give a special name to any other statistics measuring correlation.

A more convenient formula for the *calculation* of the numerator in the formula for r is presented and the calculations are demonstrated in table 10.3 for the data of table 10.2. Note that the value of $COV(X,Y)$ obtained in this table is slightly different from that obtained in table 10.2. This is due to rounding errors, especially in the latter table. Differences of this magnitude can be expected whenever two different methods of calculation are used. They are unimportant. The value of ΣXY in these calculations is determined by summing the values of column 3 in table 10.2.

10.3 Testing hypotheses about the correlation coefficient

Simply by looking at the value of r, can we make statements such as 'The two variables are strongly (weakly) correlated' or 'These two variables are unrelated to one another'?

The first point to notice here is that, even if two variables are completely uncorrelated, the value of r calculated from any random sample of pairs of observations on the variables will not be exactly zero. Simply because of the randomness of the sampling process the value of r will be different from one sample to another. Suppose we take a number of random samples and calculate r for each sample. If the two variables being studied are quite independent of one another we will find that the value of r is sometimes positive, sometimes negative. The mean of the different r values should be close to zero, but some of the individual values might be quite large in magnitude. This type of variation should not surprise us by now; it occurs every time we attempt to estimate any parameter of a statistical population by looking at samples. As usual, the problem lies partly in the fact that we will often try to assess the situation on the basis of a single sample. If we could obtain the *complete* population of all the possible pairs (X,Y) which could ever occur together, we could calculate the exact *population* value of the correlation coefficient. We will denote this value by ρ. The value of r obtained by calculating from a sample of pairs (X,Y) is then an estimate of ρ (cf. the relationship between $\bar{X}$ and μ).

A population in which X and Y are mutually independent would have $\rho = 0$ and this hypothesis is frequently tested. But probably *no* single sample of pairs (X,Y) will give a value of r which is exactly zero. We are back in the situation of chapter 8 where, using a random sample of observations, we considered how to test hypotheses about the values of population parameters. To follow the general procedure for testing a statistical hypothesis which was introduced in chapter 8, we need a null hypothesis, H_0, an alternative hypothesis, H_1, a test statistic and tables which give critical values of the test statistic for different levels of significance. Here we have:

$$H_0: \rho = 0 \qquad H_1: \rho \neq 0$$

Provided that both the variables involved have a normal distribution, r can itself be used as the test statistic, though critical values will depend on the sample size. Table A6 gives critical values of r for different significance levels and sample sizes. In §10.6 we will suggest a different test which can be applied even when the variables have a decidedly non-normal distribution.

For the error gravity example of table 10.3 we discovered that the correlation between the error scores of the English teachers and non-teachers was 0.77. Looking at table A6 we see that, for a sample size of 32, this result is significant beyond the 1% level. In other words, we can quite confidently reject the hypothesis that $\rho = 0$. We could interpret this to mean that there is some agreement between the two groups on the relative seriousness of the errors.

10.4 A confidence interval for a correlation coefficient

When hypothesis tests were introduced in chapter 8 we emphasised that the statement that a result was significant at the such and such level is not normally a sufficiently informative summary of a data set.

The same applies here. It is one thing to show that the hypothesis that two variables have *no* correlation can be rejected; it is quite another to argue that either variable contains an important amount of information about the other. In other words, it is not so much the existence of correlation between two variables that is important but rather the magnitude of that correlation. A sample correlation coefficient is a point estimator (chapter 7) of the population value, ρ, and may vary considerably from one sample to another. A confidence interval would give much more information about the possible value of ρ.

Unfortunately, there is no simple way to obtain a **confidence interval for the true correlation** ρ, in samples of less than 50 or so, even if both variables have a normal distribution. For larger samples and normally distributed variables a 95% confidence interval can be calculated as follows:[3]

$$\frac{e^X - 1}{e^X + 1} < \rho < \frac{e^Y - 1}{e^Y + 1}$$

$$\text{where } X = 2\left(Z - \frac{1.96}{\sqrt{n - 3}}\right)$$

$$Y = 2\left(Z + \frac{1.96}{\sqrt{n - 3}}\right)$$

$$\text{and } \quad Z = \frac{1}{2}\log_e\left(\frac{1 + r}{1 - r}\right)$$

The sample size is n and r is the sample correlation coefficient. The quantity e has the value 2.71828 .... and logarithms to the base e are known as natural logarithms; sometimes $\log_e$ is written 'ln'. It is possible that some of the symbols used here are unfamiliar to you, so we will work through an example, step by step, which you should be able to follow on a suitable calculator.

Suppose, in a sample of 60 subjects, a correlation of r = 0.32 has been observed between two variables. Let us calculate the corresponding 95% confidence interval for the true correlation, ρ. First calculate:

$$Z = \frac{1}{2}\log_e\left(\frac{1 + r}{1 - r}\right)$$

[3] This interval is obtained by relying on a device known as **Fisher's Z-transformation** – see, for example, Downie & Heath (1965: 156).

$$= \frac{1}{2} \log_e \left(\frac{1.32}{0.68} \right)$$

$$= 0.5 \log_e (1.9412)$$

$$= 0.5 \times 0.6633 = 0.3316$$

Now,

$$X = 2 \left(Z - \frac{1.96}{\sqrt{n-3}} \right)$$

$$= 2 \left(0.3316 - \frac{1.96}{\sqrt{57}} \right)$$

$$= 0.1440$$

and

$$Y = 2 \left(Z + \frac{1.96}{\sqrt{n-3}} \right) = 1.1824$$

Next we have $e^X = e^{0.1440} = 1.155$ (the relevant calculator key may be marked e^X or perhaps exp) and $e^Y = e^{1.1824} = 3.2622$.

$$\frac{e^X - 1}{e^X + 1} = \frac{0.155}{2.155} = 0.072$$

$$\frac{e^Y - 1}{e^Y + 1} = \frac{2.2622}{4.2622} = 0.531$$

The value of the 95% confidence interval is then:

$$0.072 < \rho < 0.531.$$

10.5 Comparing correlations

Using Fisher's Z-transformation it is also possible to test whether two correlation coefficients, *estimated from independent samples*, have come from populations with equal population correlations. Suppose the correlations r_1 and r_2 have been calculated from samples of size n_1 and n_2 respectively. For both correlations, calculate the value:

$$Z = \frac{1}{2} \log_e \left(\frac{1+r}{1-r} \right)$$

The statistic:

$$(Z_1 - Z_2) \sqrt{\frac{(n_1 - 3)(n_2 - 3)}{n_1 + n_2 - 6}}$$

is approximately standard normal provided the null hypothesis: $\rho_1 = \rho_2$ is true. For sample sizes greater than 50 the statistic has a distribution very close to that of the standard normal and the hypothesis H_0: $\rho_1 = \rho_2$ *versus* H_1: $\rho_1 \neq \rho_2$ can be tested by comparing the value of the statistic to percentage points of the normal distribution. A simple example will show how the arithmetic is done.

A sample of $n_1 = 62$ subjects is used to estimate the correlation between two variables X and Y. In a sample of $n_2 = 69$ different subjects the variables X and W are measured. The first sample has a correlation $r_1 = 0.83$ between X and Y, the second has a correlation of $r_2 = 0.74$ between X and W. Test the hypothesis that the population correlations are equal (i.e. the correlation between X and Y is equal to the correlation between X and W).

$$Z_1 = \frac{1}{2}\log_e \left(\frac{1.83}{0.17}\right) = 1.1881$$

$$Z_2 = \frac{1}{2}\log_e \left(\frac{1.74}{0.26}\right) = 0.9505$$

$$(Z_1 - Z_2) \sqrt{\frac{59 \times 66}{125}} = 1.326$$

The 10% point of the standard normal distribution for a two-tailed test is 1.645 so that the value 1.326 is not significant. It is perfectly possible that the correlation between X and Y is the same as the correlation between X and W.

The test we have just described is relevant only if the correlations r_1 and r_2 are based on independent samples. If X, Y and W were all measured on the same n subjects the test would not be valid. Downie & Heath (1955) give a test statistic for comparing two correlations obtained on the same sample. Their test is relevant when exactly three variables are involved, X, Y and W say, and it is required to compare the correlations of two of the variables with the third. To test whether r_{XW} and r_{YW} are significantly different they suggest the statistic:

$$t = \frac{(r_{XW} - r_{YW})\sqrt{(n-3)(1 + r_{XY})}}{\sqrt{2(1 - r_{XW}^2 - r_{YW}^2 - r_{XY}^2 + 2r_{XW}r_{YW}r_{XY})}}$$

This test should not be used for small samples. For samples with $n > 100$ the value of t should be compared with percentage points of the standard normal distribution.

10.6 **Interpreting the sample correlation coefficient**

It is rather difficult at this stage to explain precisely how to interpret a statement such as 'the correlation coefficient, r, between X and Y was calculated from a sample of 32 pairs of error scores and $r = 0.722$'. We will be able to reveal its meaning more clearly after we have discussed the concept of linear regression in chapter 13. However, for the moment we will attempt to explain the essential idea in a somewhat simplistic way, at least for the case where both variables are normally distributed.

We show three different sample scattergrams in figure 10.4. Now, let us suppose for the moment that the three samples which gave rise to

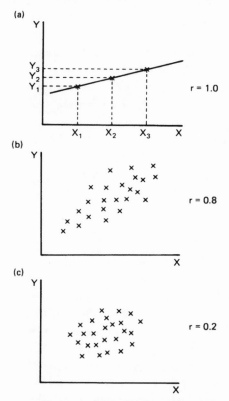

Figure 10.4. Three hypothetical scattergrams with associated value of the correlation coefficient.

the graphs produce values of r close to the true value ρ for their respective populations. In the first diagram, figure 10.4(a), the plotted points lie exactly on a straight line so that $r = 1.0$, i.e. the sample points are perfectly correlated. Now, if this is true of the population from which the sample was drawn then there is a sense in which either of the variables X or Y is redundant once we know the value of the other. Suppose that we have three observations (X_1, Y_1), (X_2, Y_2), (X_3, Y_3), with the property, for example, that the difference $X_3 - X_1$ is exactly twice as large as the difference $X_2 - X_1$. Then it will follow that the difference $Y_3 - Y_1$ is also exactly twice as large as the difference $Y_2 - Y_1$. We could say that variations in Y (or X) are accounted for 100% by variations in X (or Y).

Now consider figure 10.4(b). Because the points do not lie exactly on a straight line, it will not be true that variations in X will be associated with exactly predictable variation in Y. However, it is clear from the scattergram that if we know how the X values vary in a sample we ought to be able to guess quite well how the corresponding Y values will vary in relation to them. With the case shown in figure 10.4(c) we will not be able to do that nearly so well.

The correlation coefficient is often used to describe the extent to which knowledge of the way in which the values of one variable vary over observed units can be used to assess how the values of the other will vary over the same units. This is frequently expressed by a phrase such as 'the observed variation in X (or Y) accounts for P% of the observed variation in Y (or X)'. The value of P is obtained by squaring the value of r. The reason for this is explained in chapter 13.

For the three examples pictured in figure 10.4 we have:

$$
\begin{array}{lll}
\text{(a) } r = 1.0 & r^2 = 1.00 & (= 100\%) \\
\text{(b) } r = 0.8 & r^2 = 0.64 & (= 64\%) \\
\text{(c) } r = 0.2 & r^2 = 0.04 & (= 4\%).
\end{array}
$$

For example, for case (b) we might say that '64% of the variation in Y is accounted for (or 'is due to') the variation in X'.

As always, it is important to keep in mind that another random sample of values (X_i, Y_i) from the same population will lead to a different value of r and r^2, so that the 64% mentioned above is only an estimate. How good that estimate is will, as usual, depend on the sample size. An important point to realise here is that by a 'random sample' we mean a sample chosen randomly with respect to both variables.

It is worth noting that just a few unusual observations can affect greatly the value of r. This is the situation in the scattergram of figure 10.5 where, although most points are distributed in apparently random fashion, there are three obviously extreme points. That these would greatly influence the estimated correlation can be seen from exercise 10.4. This is an additional reason for drawing a graph of the data. We have stressed at various times the value of *looking* closely at the data before carrying out any analysis.

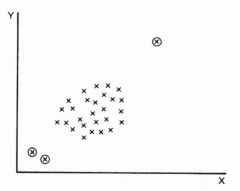

Figure 10.5. A hypothetical scattergram. Most of the points are dotted about as though there were very little correlation – see figure 10.4(c) – but the presence of the circled points will produce a large value of r.

A highish correlation apparently due to only two or three observations ought to be treated with great caution. Apart from any other reason, if both variables come from normally distributed populations it will be extremely rare for a random sample of moderate size to contain two or three unusually extreme data values – often called **outliers**.

10.7 **Rank correlations**

The statements made in the previous two sections about the meaning of r and how to test it all depend on the assumption that both the variables being observed follow a normal distribution. There will be many occasions when this assumption is not tenable. For example, in a study of foreign language learners' performance on a variety of tests, one of the variables might be the score on a multiple choice test with a maximum score of 100 (and perhaps with a distribution, over the whole population, approximately normal), while the other might be an impressionistic score out of 5 given by a native-speaking judge for oral fluency in an interview. The latter, principally because of the small number of possible categories (i.e. 0–5), will be distributed in a way very unlike a normal distribution. There will be times when the data do not consist of scores at all, for example when several judges are asked to rank a set

Table 10.4. *Calculating the rank correlation coefficient*

Sentence	X	Y	R (Rank of X)	S (Rank of Y)	R − S
1	22	22	11.0	17.0	−6.0
2	16	18	2.0	9.0	−7.0
3	42	42	32.0	31.0	1.0
4	25	21	17.5	14.5	3.0
5	31	26	28.0	22.5	5.5
6	36	41	31.0	30.0	1.0
7	29	26	23.5	22.5	1.0
8	24	20	16.0	13.0	3.0
9	29	18	23.5	9.0	14.5
10	18	15	4.0	4.0	0.0
11	23	21	14.0	14.5	−0.5
12	22	19	11.0	11.5	−0.5
13	31	39	28.0	29.0	−1.0
14	21	23	8.5	19.0	−10.5
15	27	24	20.5	20.0	0.5
16	32	29	30.0	26.5	3.5
17	23	18	14.0	9.0	5.0
18	18	16	4.0	6.0	−2.0
19	30	29	26.0	26.5	−0.5
20	31	22	28.0	17.0	11.0
21	20	12	6.5	1.0	5.5
22	21	26	8.5	22.5	−14.0
23	29	43	23.5	32.0	−8.5
24	22	26	11.0	22.5	−11.5
25	26	22	19.0	17.0	2.0
26	20	19	6.5	11.5	−5.0
27	29	30	23.5	28.0	−4.5
28	18	17	4.0	7.0	−3.0
29	23	15	14.0	4.0	10.0
30	25	15	17.5	4.0	13.5
31	27	28	20.5	25.0	−4.5
32	11	14	1.0	2.0	−1.0

$$\Sigma(R_i - S_i)^2 = 1\,413.5$$

$$r_s = 1 - \frac{6 \times 1413.5}{32 \times (32^2 - 1)} = 0.741$$

of texts on perceived degree of difficulty. In such cases there is an alternative method for measuring the relationship between two variables which does not assume that the variables are normally distributed. This method depends on a comparison of the **rank orders** rather than numerical scores.

Let us go back to the example on error gravity and change the pairs of values (X_i, Y_i) into (R_i, S_i) where R_i gives the rank order of X_i in an ordered list of all the X values, S_i is the rank order of Y_i in a list of all the Y values – see table 10.4. It should be clear to you that if X and Y are perfectly positively correlated $(r = 1.0)$ then $S_i = R_i$ always – see figure 10.6(a). For perfect negative correlation ($r = -1.0$), $S_i = n + 1 - R_i$, where n is the sample size – see figure 10.6(b). If X and Y vary independently of one another, there ought to be no relation between the rank of a particular X_i among the Xs and the rank of the associated Y_i among

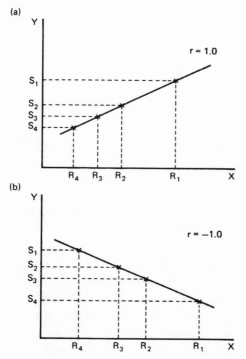

Figure 10.6. The relation between (X_i, Y_i) and (R_i, S_i) for perfectly correlated data.

the Ys. It ought therefore to be possible to derive a measure of the correlation between X and Y by considering the relationship between these rankings. One such measure is r_s, the **Spearman rank correlation coefficient**.

Suppose a random sample of n pairs has been observed and let R_i and S_i be the ranks of the Xs and Ys as we have defined them above. Let $D = \Sigma(R_i - S_i)^2$. Then r_s is calculated by the formula:

$$r_s = 1 - \frac{6D}{n(n^2 - 1)}$$

It may look to you at first sight as though r_s is simpler to calculate than r. This is not usually the case. First, except for very small samples, it is a time-consuming exercise, unless it can be done by computer, to calculate all the ranks. Second, there is the problem of tied ranks. This arises when one of the variables has the same value in two or more of the pairs. Suppose in a sample of five observations we have:

$$X_1 = 6, X_2 = 3, X_3 = 4, X_4 = 3, X_5 = 1$$

How should we calculate the ranks, R_i?

$R_1 = 1$ (X_1 has the largest value)
$R_2 = ?$ (Should X_2 be ranked third or fourth?)
$R_3 = 2$
$R_4 = ?$
$R_5 = 5$

Clearly, R_2 has to have the same value as R_4 since $X_2 = X_4$, and its value must lie between 2 and 5. The way to deal with this is to take the average of the 'missing' ranks, in this case take the average of 3 and 4, which is 3.5. Then $R_2 = R_4 = 3.5$. We can then calculate r_s in the usual way.

Unfortunately, the problem does not end here. Tied ranks cause bias in the value of r_s. If we use mean ranks and calculate r_s by the usual formula we will tend to overestimate the true correlation. A full discussion of this problem can be found in Kendall (1970). However, unless a very high proportion of ranks is tied, the bias is likely to be *very* small. Siegel (1956) gives a formula to adjust the value of r_s for tied ranks. He then gives an example with a number of tied ranks for which $r_s = 0.617$ if the usual formula is used and $r_s = 0.616$ if the exact (and more complex) formula is used. Our advice is to use the formula we have given even in the presence of ties, but to suspect that the apparent correlation may be very slightly exaggerated in the presence of a substantial proportion of tied ranks. The data on sentence error gravity are analysed in this way in table 10.4.

In this case, the Spearman correlation coefficient $r_s = 0.741$, quite close to the value of the Pearson correlation coefficient $r = 0.772$ calculated on the same sample. Does this mean that r_s can be interpreted in much the same way as r? In particular will r_s^2 still indicate the extent to which one variable 'explains' the other? Unfortunately, the answer to this question is an unequivocal 'No'. For moderate-sized samples from a population in which the variables are normally distributed the Spearman coefficient can be interpreted in roughly this way. However, even then r_s will tend to underestimate the true correlation and will be more variable from one sample to another than the Pearson correlation coefficient. Besides, r_s was designed to cope with data sets which are not normally distributed or whose exact values are not known (e.g. when only the ranks are known in the first place) and should not be used on data which have a more or less normal distribution. Furthermore, for certain kinds of data the population value, ρ_s, of the Spearman coefficient is very different from that of ρ, the Pearson correlation coefficient, in the same population. Since r_s is often calculated rather than r precisely in those situations where the underlying distribution of the data is unknown it is never safe to try to interpret r_s as a *measure* of correlation. In fact its only legitimate use is as a test statistic for testing the hypothesis that two variables are independent of one another. Consider the following example. Two different judges are asked to rank ten texts in order of difficulty.

Text:	A	B	C	D	E	F	G	H	J	K
Judge: 1	1	2	3	4	5	6	7	8	9	10
Judge: 2	4	2	7	1	3	10	8	9	6	5

Test the hypothesis that the judges are using entirely unrelated criteria and hence that their rankings are independent.

H_0: There is no interdependence in the sets of judgements
H_1: There is interdependence in the sets of judgements

Here we have:

$$D = 3^2 + 0^2 + 4^2 + 3^2 + \ldots + 5^2 = 90$$

and

$$r_s = 1 - \frac{6 \times 90}{10 \times 99}$$

$$= 0.4545$$

From table A7 we can see that this value of r_s is *just* significant at the 10% level. There is, therefore, somewhat weak evidence of some measure of agreement between the judges. However, nothing else can be said. It is not possible, for example, to calculate a confidence interval for the population value, ρ_s, and there is therefore no way of knowing how precise is the estimate 0.4545. This is a general deficiency of rank correlation methods.

Table A7 gives percentage points of r_s for sample sizes up to n = 30. For sample sizes greater than this it is safe to use table A6 of percentage points of the Pearson correlation coefficient. *In large samples and when the two variables are actually independent* (so that $\rho = \rho_s = 0$) the values of r_s and r will be very similar. In the case of correlated variables our previous statement holds: there is no simple relationship, in general, between r and r_s, nor between the population correlation coefficients ρ and ρ_s. There is no simple way to interpret the 'strength' of correlation implicit in a sample value of r_s.

SUMMARY

(1) The **covariance**, $\mathrm{COV}(X,Y) = \Sigma(X_i - \bar{X})(Y_i - \bar{Y})/(n-1)$, was introduced and exemplified as a measure of the degree to which two quantities vary in step with one another. The covariance was shown to be **scale-dependent**.

(2) The **correlation coefficient** (Pearson's product-moment coefficient of linear correlation) between two variables, X and Y, was defined by $r(X,Y) = \dfrac{\mathrm{COV}(X,Y)}{s_X s_Y}$ and was shown to be independent of the scales in which X and Y were measured. The value of r^2 could be interpreted as the proportion of the variability in either variable which was 'explained' by the other.

(3) The test statistic for the hypothesis H_0: $\rho = 0$ was r itself: the critical values to be found in table A6.

(4) It was shown how to calculate a **confidence interval for the true correlation** from large samples using **Fisher's Z-transformation**.

(5) A test for the hypothesis that two population correlations were equal was presented.

(6) The **Spearman rank correlation coefficient**, r_s, was defined. It was explained that it would usually be difficult to interpret r_s as a measure of 'degree of interdependence' but that a test of the hypothesis H_0: two variables are independent could be based on r_s even when the data are decidedly non-normal.

EXERCISES

(1) Draw a scattergram to examine the relationship between the assigned error scores in the columns headed 'X' and 'Y' of table 11.5 on page 186, that is, between the scores of the Greek teachers and the English teachers. Compare your scattergram with figure 10.1. What do you notice?

(2) (a) Now calculate the covariance of these two sets of scores, using the method of table 10.2, and then determine the correlation coefficient.

(b) Recalculate the correlation coefficient using the rapid method of table 10.3. What does this value tell you about the linear relationship between the scores of the Greek teachers and those of the English teachers?

(3) Is the correlation coefficient obtained in exercise 10.2 significant?

(4) In the original study from which this data were taken, judges were presented with some sentences which were correct. For two of these sentences English and Greek teachers were in complete agreement and assigned the following scores:

Sentence no.	Greek teachers	English teachers
33	3	3
34	0	0

Include this data in the set you used for your calculations in exercise 10.2 and recalculate the correlation coefficient. What difference does the addition of these two data points for each group make?

(5) Calculate the Spearman rank order correlation coefficient for the data you used in exercise 10.2.

(6) Twenty-five non-native speakers of English took a 50-item cloze test. The exact word method of scoring was used. Without warning, a few days later, they were presented with the same cloze passage, but this time for each blank they were given a number of possible options (i.e. multiple choice), these including all the responses they had given on the first version with the addition of the correct answer, if this had not been amongst their responses. The results were:

1st version	Multiple choice version	1st version	Multiple choice version
33	27	25	20
31	31	24	25
32	29	24	24
30	33	23	32
29	31	23	23
29	30	22	24
28	30	21	15
29	23	22	24
27	30	21	23
28	29	17	18
27	26	16	17
26	27	16	24
25	24		

Twenty-five native speakers of English also took the first version of the test. Their scores were:

36 35 33 34 34 33 33 32 32 32 32

31 31 31 31 31 31 30 30 29 28 28

26 25 24

(a) Are the two sets of scores for the non-native speakers related? How do you interpret the correlation coefficient you have calculated?

(b) What is the relationship between non-native-speaker scores, and native-speaker scores, on the first version of the test?

11

Testing for differences between two populations

It is often the case in language and related studies that we want to compare population means on the basis of two samples. In a well-known experiment in foreign language teaching (Scherer & Wertheimer 1964), first-year undergraduates at the University of Colorado were divided into two groups. One group was taught by the audiolingual method, the other by the more traditional grammar–translation method. The intention was to discover which method proved superior in relation to the attainment of a variety of language learning goals. The experiment continued for two years, and many measurements of ability in German were taken at various stages in the study. For our present purpose we will concentrate on just one measurement, that of *speaking ability*, made at the end of the experiment. Out of a possible score on this speaking test of 100, the traditional grammar–translation group obtained a mean score of 77.71 while the audiolingual group's mean score was 82.92. Thus the sample mean of the audiolingual group was higher than that of the grammar–translation group. But what we are interested in is whether this is due to an accidental assignment of the more able students to the audiolingual group or whether the higher mean is evidence that the audiolingual method is more efficient. We will address this question by way of a formal hypothesis test.

11.1 Independent samples: testing for differences between means

The notation we will use is displayed in table 11.1. We wish to test the null hypothesis:

$$H_0 : \mu_1 = \mu_2$$

Our alternative hypothesis is:

$$H_1 : \mu_1 \neq \mu_2$$

176

Table 11.1. *Notation used in the formulation of a test of the hypothesis that two population means are equal*

	First population	Second population
Population mean	μ_1	μ_2
Population standard deviation	σ_1	σ_2
Sample size	n_1	n_2
Sample mean	$\bar{X}_1$	$\bar{X}_2$
Sample standard deviation	s_1	s_2

(At the outset of the experiment there was no compelling reason to believe that the audiolingual group would do better on this test after two years; it was not inconceivable that the grammar–translation group would do better. For this reason a non-directional alternative hypothesis is chosen.) A test statistic can be obtained to carry out the hypothesis test provided two assumptions are made about this data:

1. The populations are both normally distributed. (As before, this will not be necessary if the sample size is large since then the Central Limit Theorem assures the validity of the test.)
2. $\sigma_1 = \sigma_2$; that is, the population standard deviations are equal. This point is discussed further below. The value of the common standard deviations is estimated by:

$$s = \sqrt{\frac{(n_1 - 1)s_1^2 + (n_2 - 1)s_2^2}{n_1 + n_2 - 2}}$$

This estimate is used in the calculation of the test statistic, t, as follows:

$$t = \frac{\bar{X}_1 - \bar{X}_2}{\sqrt{\dfrac{s^2}{n_1} + \dfrac{s^2}{n_2}}}$$

This statistic has a t-distribution (the same as that met in chapter 7) with $n_1 + n_2 - 2$ df *whenever the null hypothesis is true*. The value of t can be compared with the critical values in table A4 to determine whether the difference between the sample means is significantly large.

The data in table 11.2 are taken from table 6-5 of Scherer & Wertheimer (1964).

We first estimate the population standard deviation using the formula presented above:

Table 11.2. *Group differences in speaking ability at the end of two years*

Audiolingual		Grammar–translation	
$\bar{X}_1$	82.92	$\bar{X}_2$	77.71
s_1	6.78	s_2	7.37
n_1	24.00	n_2	24.00

Data from Scherer & Wertheimer (1964: table 6–5)

$$s = \sqrt{\frac{(23 \times 6.78^2) + (23 \times 7.37^2)}{46}}$$

$$= \sqrt{\frac{1057.27 + 1249.29}{46}}$$

$$= 7.08$$

This estimate of the population standard deviation is then used to calculate t:

$$t = \frac{82.92 - 77.71}{\sqrt{\frac{7.08^2}{24} + \frac{7.08^2}{24}}}$$

$$= \frac{5.21}{\sqrt{2.09 + 2.09}}$$

$$= \frac{5.21}{2.04}$$

$$= 2.55$$

If we enter table A4 with 46 df ($n_1 + n_2 - 2$), we discover that the t-value of 2.55 is significant at the 2% level (which is what was reported by Scherer & Wertheimer). The probability of the two sample means coming from populations with the same mean is less than 2 in 100 (which is the same as 1 in 50). There then appears to be support for the belief that the audio-lingual method is superior to the grammar–translation method in developing speaking ability in German. However, various difficulties encountered by Scherer and Wertheimer in conducting the experiment mean that this result should be treated with caution.

Let us look now at another piece of research where it is appropriate to test for differences between means on the basis of two samples. Macken & Barton (1980a) investigated the acquisition of voicing contrasts in four English-speaking children whose ages at the beginning of the study ranged from 1;4.28 to 1;7.9. Each child was then seen every two weeks over an eight-month period, and recordings made of conversations between

Table 11.3. *Mean VOT values (in milliseconds), standard deviations and number of tokens for a single child at different ages*

	Age 1;8.20		Age 1;11.0	
	Consonant		Consonant	
	/d/	/t/	/d/	/t/
Mean VOT (ms)	14.25	22.30	7.67	122.13
Standard deviation	15.44	13.50	19.17	54.19
Number of tokens	8	10	15	15

Data from Macken & Barton (1980a: table 5).

the child and its mother. The focus of the instrumental analysis of this data was the measurement of voice onset time (VOT) in initial stops in tokens produced by the children. On the assumption that VOT is the major determinant of a voiced/voiceless contrast in initial stops, its values were examined, separately for each child, to identify the point at which the child became capable of making a voicing contrast. The data in table 11.3 were extracted from Macken & Barton's table 5, which presents a summary of measurements on their subject, Jane.

In normal, adult spoken English, the mean VOT for /t/ is higher than for /d/. Children have to learn to make the distinction. For the data in table 11.3 we can test the null hypothesis that there is no detectable difference in the mean VOT against the natural alternative that the mean VOT is higher for /t/. Using the formulae given above, we find the standard deviation estimate:

$$s = \sqrt{\frac{(7 \times 15.44^2) + (9 \times 13.50^2)}{16}} = 14.38 \text{ milliseconds}$$

and evaluate the test statistic as:

$$t = \frac{14.25 - 22.30}{\sqrt{\frac{s^2}{8} + \frac{s^2}{10}}} = -1.18 \text{ with } 16 \text{ df}$$

On this occasion it can be argued that the natural alternative hypothesis is directional: we may discount the possibility that the VOT for /d/ could be greater than the VOT for /t/. The 5% critical value for t with 16 df would be 1.75 (= for 15 df). The t-value we have calculated is less than this; indeed it is less than the 10% critical value (1.34). We will therefore be unwilling to claim that the population mean VOT for /t/ is greater than that for /d/. We will not wish to claim that the child has learned to distinguish the two sounds successfully in terms of VOT, despite the difference of more than 8 ms in the sample means. This is due partly to the large standard deviations and partly to the small number of tokens observed. If we carry out a similar analysis on the VOTs observed on the same child at age 1;11.0 we find $t = -7.71$, which is highly significant and indicates that the child is now making a distinction between the two consonants.

Having discovered that it seems likely that a difference may exist between two means, it will usually make good sense to estimate how *large* that difference seems to be. A 95% confidence interval for the *difference* $\mu_1 - \mu_2$ is given by:

$$\bar{X}_1 - \bar{X}_2 \pm \left(\text{constant} \times \sqrt{\frac{s^2}{n_1} + \frac{s^2}{n_2}} \right)$$

where the constant is the 95% critical value of the t-distribution with $(n_1 + n_2 - 2)$ df. The data imply that there is a difference between Jane's two mean VOTs at age 1;11.0. To estimate the size of this difference we first calculate:

$$s = \sqrt{\frac{(14 \times 19.17^2) + (14 \times 54.19^2)}{28}}$$

$$= 40.65$$

A 95% confidence interval for the difference in the mean VOTs would then be:

$$X_1 - X_2 \pm \left(2.04 \times \sqrt{\frac{s^2}{14} + \frac{s^2}{14}} \right)$$

or 114.46 ± 31.34

i.e. 83.12 to 145.80 milliseconds

We calculate therefore that we can be 95% certain that the difference between the population mean VOT for /d/ and that for /t/, for this child at this age, is somewhere between 83.12 and 145.80 ms. In view of the comment in the next paragraph concerning the variances of the VOTs of the two consonants, this interval is probably not quite correct, but it is unlikely to be far wrong and certainly gives a good idea of the order of difference between the mean VOTs.

The correctness of the above analysis depends on the two assumptions we have made: that the variable, VOT, is normally distributed for this subject at the two ages when the observations were taken and that, at both ages, the VOT was equally variable for either sound.[1] Since the full data set is not published in the source paper we cannot judge whether the VOTs seemed to be normally distributed. With the small number of tokens observed it would be rather difficult to judge anyway and the investigators would have had to rely on their experience of such data as a guide to the validity of the assumption. If we had, say, 30 tokens at each age instead of 15, modest deviations from normality would be unimportant. On the other hand, turning to the second assumption, there is always information contained in the values of the two sample standard deviations about the variability of the populations. In the test related to the VOTs at age 1;11.0, the sample standard deviations of the VOTs for /d/ and /t/ were 19.17 and 54.19, the larger being almost three times the value of the former. In the light of this, were we justified in carrying out the test? In the following section we give a test for comparing two variances and it will be seen that we will reject decisively the assumption that VOT for /t/ has the same variance as VOT for /d/. This is serious and would remain so even if the sample sizes were much larger.[2]

There is a further problem which may arise with this kind of data where several tokens are elicited from a single subject in a short time period. Every method of statistical analysis presented in this book presupposes that the data consist of a set of observations on one (or several) simple random samples with the value of each observation quite independent of the values of others. If a linguistic experiment is carried out in such a way that several tokens of a particular linguistic item occur close together the subject may, consciously or not, cause them to be more similar than they would normally be. Such a lack of independence in the data will distort the results of any analysis, including the tests discussed in this chapter. This point has already been discussed in chapter 7.

[1] We did not question these assumptions in the case of the language teaching example above. First, though we do not have access to the complete data set, it is not unreasonable to expect the distribution of scores on a language test with many items to approximate normality. Secondly, the F-test (see below) did not indicate a significant difference in variances.

[2] However, *provided the sample sizes are equal*, as they are here, it can be shown mathematically that the test statistic will still have a t-distribution when H_0 is true but with fewer degrees of freedom – though never less than the number of tokens in just one of the samples, i.e. 15. The value of −7.71 is still highly significant even with only 15 df, so that the initial conclusion stands, that the population mean VOT for /t/ is larger at age 1;11.0 than the population mean VOT for /d/. If the sample variances are such that we have to reject the hypothesis of equal population variances *and* the sample sizes are unequal then a different test statistic with different properties has to be used. The relevant formulae, with a discussion, can be found in Wetherill (1972: §6.6).

11.2 Independent samples: comparing two variances

We have seen that it is necessary to assume that two populations have the same standard deviation or, equivalently, the same variance before a t-test for comparing their means will be appropriate. It is possible to check the validity of this assumption by testing $H_0 : \sigma_1^2 = \sigma_2^2$ (see table 11.1) against $H_1 : \sigma_1^2 \neq \sigma_2^2$ using the test statistic:

$$F = \frac{\text{larger sample variance}}{\text{smaller sample variance}}$$

In the example of the previous section, two samples of 15 tokens of /t/ and /d/ from a child aged 1;11.0 gave standard deviations of 19.17 and 54.19 ms respectively. The larger sample variance is therefore $54.19^2 = 2936.56$ and the smaller is $19.17^2 = 367.49$, so that:

$$F = 2936.56 \div 367.49 = 7.99$$

If the null hypothesis is true and the population variances are equal the distribution of this test statistic is known. It is called the **F-distribution** and it depends on the degrees of freedom of both the numerator and the denominator. In every case the relevant degrees of freedom will be those used in the divisors of the sample standard deviations. Since both samples contained 15 tokens, the numerator and denominator of the F statistic, or **variance ratio statistic** as it is often called, will both have 14 df, and the statistic is denoted $F_{14,14}$. In general we write F_{m_1,m_2} where m_1 and m_2 are the degrees of freedom of numerator and denominator respectively. In the tables of the F-distribution (table A8) we find that no value is given for 14 df in the numerator or in the denominator. To give all possible combinations would result in an enormous table. However, the 1% significance value for $F_{12,15}$ is 3.67 and that for $F_{24,15}$ is 3.29 so the value for $F_{14,14}$ must be close to 3.6. The value obtained in the test is much larger than this so that the value is significant at the 1% level and it seems highly probable that the VOT for /t/ has a much higher variance than that for /d/. Note, however, that this test (frequently referred to as the **F-test**) also requires that the samples be from normally distributed populations and it is rather sensitive to failures in that assumption.

11.3 Independent samples: comparing two proportions

We have already established a test for comparing two proportions. In table 9.7 we presented, as a contingency table, data from a study by Ferris & Politzer (1981) of pronoun agreement in two groups of bilingual children. The data in that table can be presented in a different form as

Proportion of error free cases

Group A $15/30 = 0.5$ $(\hat{p}_1)$
Group B $23/30 = 0.7667$ $(\hat{p}_2)$
Overall $38/60 = 0.6333$ $(\bar{p})$

Now $\hat{p}_1$ and $\hat{p}_2$ are estimates of the true population proportions p_1 and p_2. We can test the hypothesis that $H_0 : p_1 = p_2$ using the test statistic.

$$Z = \frac{|\hat{p}_1 - \hat{p}_2| - \frac{1}{2}\left(\frac{1}{n_1} + \frac{1}{n_2}\right)}{\sqrt{\bar{p}(1 - \bar{p})\left(\frac{1}{n_1} + \frac{1}{n_2}\right)}}$$

where n_1 and n_2 are the sample sizes. (Remember that $|\hat{p}_1 - \hat{p}_2|$ means the absolute magnitude of the difference between $\hat{p}_1$ and $\hat{p}_2$ and is always a positive quantity.) When the null hypothesis is true Z will have a standard normal distribution.[3] Here we have:

$$Z = \frac{|0.5 - 0.7667| - \frac{1}{2}\left(\frac{1}{30} + \frac{1}{30}\right)}{\sqrt{(0.6333 \times 0.3667)\left(\frac{1}{30} + \frac{1}{30}\right)}}$$

$$= \frac{0.2667 - 0.0333}{0.1244} = 1.876$$

The 5% significance value of the normal distribution for a two-sided test is 1.96 so that this result just fails to be significant at that level, exactly the conclusion reached by the chi-squared test of section 9.4.2. Furthermore, $1.876^2 = 3.519$, almost exactly the value of the chi-squared statistic in that analysis and the relevant 5% significance value of chi-squared was 3.84, which is 1.96^2. Because of this correspondence, the two methods will always give identical results. The only real difference is that with the test we have presented in this section it is possible to consider a one-sided alternative such as $H_1 : p_1 < p_2$ while the chi-squared test will always require a two-sided alternative.

It will usually be helpful to estimate *how* unlike two proportions may

[3] Note that it is always the normal distribution that is referred to when testing for differences between two simple proportions – never the t-distribution. However, as when using the chi-squared test, care must be taken if there are fewer than five tokens in any of the four possible categories.

be whenever a test has found them to be significantly different. An approximate 95% confidence interval for the difference in two proportions is calculated by the formula:

$$|\hat{p}_1 - \hat{p}_2| \pm \left\{ 1.96 \times \sqrt{\frac{\hat{p}_1(1 - \hat{p}_1)}{n_1} + \frac{\hat{p}_2(1 - \hat{p}_2)}{n_2}} \right\}$$

i.e. $0.2667 \pm \left(1.96 \times \sqrt{\frac{0.5 \times 0.5}{30} + \frac{0.7667 \times 0.2333}{30}} \right)$

i.e. 0.032 to 0.501

Note that this interval does not include the value zero, which we would expect since the hypothesis that $p_1 = p_2$, or $p_1 - p_2 = 0$, was not rejected at the 5% level (see chapter 7). This occurs because the confidence interval is not exact. It will not be sufficiently incorrect to mislead seriously, especially if the exact test of hypothesis is always carried out first.

11.4 Paired samples: comparing two means

Table 11.5 presents data on the error gravity scores of ten native English-speaking teachers and ten Greek teachers of English for 32 sentences which appeared in the compositions of Greek-Cypriot learners of English. (Note that the data for Greek teachers is adapted from that presented in Hughes & Lascaratou 1981, for purposes of exposition.) A summary of the data in the notation of the present chapter appears in table 11.4.

First let us test the assumption that the variances in the two populations are equal, $H_0 : \sigma_1 = \sigma_2$, against the hypothesis $H_1 : \sigma_1 \neq \sigma_2$. The test statistic is:

$$F = \frac{\text{larger } s^2}{\text{smaller } s^2} = \frac{7.85^2}{6.25^2} = \frac{61.62}{39.06} = 1.58$$

with 31 df in both numerator and denominator. From tables of the F-distribution we can see that this is not significant and we will assume that the population variances are equal.

Let us now test the hypothesis that the two groups of teachers give the same error gravity scores on average, i.e. $H_0 : \mu_1 = \mu_2$ against $H_1 : \mu_1 \neq \mu_2$. The situation is different from the previous examples in this chapter inasmuch as it is possible to compare the scoring of Greek teachers and the English teachers in respect of each of the 32 sentences, not only in terms of their overall scoring. There is likely, on average, to be some correlation between scores awarded by different groups of judges on the

Table 11.4. *Summary of data from table 10.1*

	Group 1 (English)	Group 2 (Greek)
Sample mean	$\bar{X}_1 = 25.03$	$\bar{X}_2 = 28.28$
Sample standard deviation	$s_1 = 6.25$	$s_2 = 7.85$
Sample size	32	32

same error. It is in this sense that we refer to the samples as 'correlated'. When we have correlated samples we follow a rather different procedure in tests for a difference between population means. This will be detailed below, but first of all let us see what results we would obtain if (mistakenly!) we proceeded as if, as in the above examples, the samples were independent (i.e. uncorrelated). The test statistic would be:

$$t = \frac{\bar{X}_1 - \bar{X}_2}{\sqrt{\dfrac{s^2}{32} + \dfrac{s^2}{32}}}$$

where:

$$s^2 = \frac{31s_1^2 + 31s_2^2}{62}$$

i.e.

$$t = -1.83 \text{ with 62 df.}$$

This is not significant at the 5% level. Apparently there is little evidence that errors are judged more severely by the Greek teachers. However, we have not used all the information in the experiment. The test we have carried out would be the only one possible if we had only the summary values of table 11.4. It ignores the fact that since each group of teachers assessed the *same* 32 sentences, and we know their scores on each sentence, we can compare their severity scores for the individual errors. In table 11.5 we present the total data set. In the last column of the table we have given the value obtained by subtracting the total score of the Greek teachers from the total score of the English teachers for each sentence individually. Some of these differences will be positive and others negative – it is important to be consistent in the order of subtraction and evaluate the sign properly. Now, the null hypothesis we wanted to test was that, on average, the English and the Greek teachers give equal scores for the same errors, $H_o : \mu_1 = \mu_2$. This is logically equivalent to testing the hypothesis that, on average, the differences in item scores is zero. Since $d_i = X_i - Y_i$, the population mean difference, μ_d, will have the value $\mu_d = \mu_1 - \mu_2$.

185

Table 11.5. *Total error gravity scores of ten native English teachers (X) and ten Greek teachers of English (Y) on 32 English sentences*

Sentence	X	Y	d = X − Y
1	22	36	−14
2	16	9	7
3	42	29	13
4	25	35	−10
5	31	34	−3
6	36	23	13
7	29	25	4
8	24	31	−7
9	29	35	−6
10	18	21	−3
11	23	33	−10
12	22	13	9
13	31	22	9
14	21	29	−8
15	27	25	2
16	32	25	7
17	23	39	−16
18	18	19	−1
19	30	28	2
20	31	41	−10
21	20	25	−5
22	21	17	4
23	29	26	3
24	22	37	−15
25	26	34	−8
26	20	28	−8
27	29	33	−4
28	18	24	−6
29	23	37	−14
30	25	33	−8
31	27	39	−12
32	11	20	−9

$H_0 : \mu_1 = \mu_2$ is the same hypothesis as $H_0 : \mu_1 - \mu_2 = 0$ which in turn can be written as $H_0 : \mu_d = 0$.

We already know how to test the last hypothesis. In chapter 8 we introduced a test of the null hypothesis that a sample was drawn from a population with a given population mean. The 32 differences in the last column of table 11.5 can be considered as a sample of the differences that would arise from two randomly chosen groups of these types assessing these errors. Following the procedure of §8.3, a suitable statistic to test the null hypothesis $H_0 : \mu_d = 0$ is:

$$t = \frac{\bar{d} - 0}{\dfrac{s}{\sqrt{n}}} = \bar{d} \div (s/\sqrt{n}), \text{ with 31 df}$$

where $\bar{d}$ is the mean of the observed differences, s is the standard deviation of the sample of 32 differences and n is the sample size, 32.

We find:

$$\bar{d} = -3.25 \qquad s = 8.32$$

and therefore that $t = -2.21$ with 31 df. From tables of the t-distribution we find that this value is significant at the 5% level, giving some reason to believe that there is a real difference between the scores of the teachers of the different nationalities.

Let us summarise what has occurred here. In the opening section of the chapter we presented a procedure for testing the null hypothesis that two population means are equal. We began the present section by carrying out that test on the error gravity score data of table 11.5. The conclusion we reached was that the null hypothesis of equal scores for the two groups could not be rejected even at the 10% level. We then carried out another test of the same hypothesis using the same data and found we could reject it at the 5% significance level. Is there a contradiction here?

There is none. It is important to realise that the second test made use of information about the differences between individual items which was ignored by the first. Indeed the first test could have been carried out in exactly the same way even if the two groups had scored *different* sets of randomly chosen student errors. By matching the items for the groups we have eliminated one source of variability in the experiment and increased the sensitivity of the hypothesis test.

This **paired comparison** or **correlated samples t-test** will frequently be relevant and it is usually good experimental practice to design studies to exploit its extra sensitivity. However, it requires exactly the same assumptions as the test which uses independent samples; the two populations being compared should be approximately normally distributed and have equal variances.

A 95% confidence interval for the difference between the two population means can be calculated as:

$$|\bar{d}| \pm (\text{constant} \times s/\sqrt{n})$$

where the constant is the 5% significance value of the t-distribution with $(n - 1)$ df. For this example we have:

$$|-3.25| \pm (2.04 \times 8.32 \div \sqrt{31})$$

or $\qquad 3.25 \pm 3.05$

i.e. $\qquad 0.2$ to 6.3

11.5 Relaxing the assumptions of normality and equal variance: nonparametric tests

We have seen that experimental situations do arise (§11.2) where the assumption that two populations have equal variances may be untenable, and that this will affect the validity of some of the tests introduced above. We may also have doubts about the other assumption, necessary except for large samples, that both samples are drawn from normally distributed populations. Occasions will arise when we have samples which are so small that there is a need to worry about this assumption as well. It is possible to carry out a test of the hypothesis that the samples come from two populations with similar characteristics without making any assumptions about their distribution. It will, of course, still be necessary that our data consist of proper random samples in which the values are independent observations. There is a great number of such tests, collected under the general heading of **nonparametric tests** – tests which require no special distributional assumptions – and we will present just two examples here. The χ^2 test for association in contingency tables in chapter 9 and the test for significant rank correlation in chapter 10 are two nonparametric tests we have already presented. A larger selection can be found in Siegel (1956).

Suppose that, as part of a study like that of Macken & Barton (1980a) (see §11.1), a child aged 2;0 is observed for tokens of /g/ and /k/ in the same phonological environment, and that the VOTs in milliseconds for the observed tokens were:

for /g/: 38, 195, 56, 3, 51, 89   (six tokens)
for /k/: 125, 73, 138, 35, 51, 190, 169   (seven tokens)

Despite the small number of tokens, we can test the null hypothesis that the VOTs for the two consonants are centred on the same value by means of a **two-sample Mann-Whitney rank test**. We begin by putting all 13 observations into a single, ranked list, keeping note of the sample in which each observation arose, as in table 11.6. It will not matter whether the ranking is carried out in ascending or descending order. Note how we have dealt with the tied value of 51 ms (see §10.6).

Now, sum the ranks for the smaller of the two samples. If both samples are the same size then sum the ranks of just one of them. In this case the smaller sample consists of the VOTs for the child's six tokens of /g/; T, the sum of the relevant ranks, is given by:

$$T = 1 + 3 + 4.5 + 6 + 8 + 13 = 35.5$$

Table 11.6. *Ranking of VOTs for /g/ and /k/ from a single child*

Value	3	35	38	51	51	56	73	89	125	138	169	190	195
Source	/g/	/k/	/g/	/k/	/g/	/g/	/k/	/g/	/k/	/k/	/k/	/k/	/g/
Rank	1	2	3	4.5	4.5	6	7	8	9	10	11	12	13

If m is the size of the sample whose ranks have been summed (m = 6 in this example) and n is the size of the other sample (n = 7) we calculate *two* statistics, U_1 and U_2, as follows:

$$U_1 = mn + \frac{m(m+1)}{2} - T$$

$$U_2 = mn - U_1$$

Here we have:

$$U_1 = 6 \times 7 + \frac{6 \times 7}{2} - 35.5 = 27.5$$

$$U_2 = 6 \times 7 - 27.5 = 14.5$$

We then refer the *smaller* of these values to the corresponding value of table A9. (We have given the 5% significance values in this table; see Siegel if other critical values are required.) Since 14.5 is greater than the tabulated value of 6 we do not reject the equality of mean VOTs at the 5% significance level. The table of critical values we have supplied allows only for the situation where the larger of the two samples contains a maximum of 20 observations. For larger samples the sum of the ranks, T, can be used to create a different test statistic:

$$Z = \frac{T - \frac{m}{2}(m + n + 1)}{\sqrt{\frac{mn}{12}(m + n + 1)}}$$

which can then be compared with critical values of the standard normal distribution (table A3) to see whether the null hypothesis of equal population means can be rejected.

There are likewise various nonparametric tests which can be used to test hypotheses in paired samples. Suppose that 22 dysphasic patients have the extent of their disability assessed on a ten-point scale by two different judges. Suppose that for 13 patients judge A assessed their condition to be much more serious (i.e. have a higher score) than judge B, for five patients the reverse is true and for the remaining four patients the judges agree. We can test the null hypothesis H_0: the judges are giving the same assessment scores, on average, *versus* the two-sided alternative H_1: on average the assessment scores of the judges are different, although it is unlikely that the assessment scores are normally distributed and the size of the sample is not large enough for us to rely on the Central Limit Theorem.

The procedure is to mark a subject with a plus sign if the first judge gives a higher score, or with a minus sign if the first judge gives a lower score. Subjects who receive the same score from both judges are left out of the analysis. Note the number of times, S, that the less frequent sign appears and the total number, T, of cases which are marked with one or other sign. Here $S = 5$ and $T = 18$.

Now enter table A10 using the values of S and T. Corresponding to $S = 5$ and $T = 18$ we find the value 0.096. These tabulated values are the significance levels corresponding to the two-tailed test. Hence we could say here that H_0 could be rejected at the 10% significance level but not at the 5% level ($P = 0.096 = 9.6\%$). For the one-sided alternative we first of all have to ask whether there are *any* indications that the alternative is true. For example, if we had used in the above example the one-sided alternative H_1: judge B scores more highly, on average, there would be no point in a formal hypothesis test since judge B has actually scored *fewer* patients more highly than judge A. If the *direction* of the evidence gives some support for a one-sided alternative, then table A10 should be entered as before using the values of S and T *but the significance level should be halved*. We have seen this before with table A3 and table A4.

Only values of T up to $T = 25$ are catered for by table A10. If T is greater than 25, the test can still be carried out by calculating S and T in the same way and then using the test statistic:

$$Z = \frac{T - 2S - 1}{\sqrt{T}}$$

which should be referred to table A3, critical values of the standard normal distribution. For example, if we carry out a sign test on the error gravity scores of table 11.5 we have $T = 32$, $S = 11$ (there are 11 positive and 21 negative differences) so that $Z = (32 - 22 - 1)/\sqrt{32}$, i.e. $Z = 1.59$, which is not a significantly large value of the standard normal distribution (table A3).

11.6 **The power of different tests**

In chapter 8, where the basic concepts of statistical hypothesis testing were introduced, we discussed the notion of the two types of error which were possible as a result of a test of hypothesis: type 1 error, the incorrect rejection of a valid null hypothesis, and type 2, the failure to reject the null when it is mistaken. Let us recapitulate the results of the tests we have carried out in the current chapter on the error gravity scores of the two groups of judges (table 11.5). The **paired sample t-test** which we carried out in §11.4 resulted in the conclusion that there was a difference, significant at the 5% level, between the mean scores of the two groups. The **sign test** carried out on the *same* data in §11.5 could not detect a difference, not even at the 5% significance level, which is the weakest level of evidence which, by general convention, most experimenters would require in order to claim that 'the null hypothesis can be rejected'. It is important to understand why this has come about. Assessing a statistical hypothesis is similar to many other kinds of judgement. The correctness of the conclusion will depend on two things: the quantity of the information available *and* its quality. The two tests in question use different information.

It is an assumption of both tests that the observations were collected as an independent random sample. The fact that the observations were collected in this way can therefore be seen as a piece of information that both tests use. A second piece of information that both tests use is the direction of the difference in each pair (represented simply by plus or minus in the case of the sign test). But the paired sample t-test makes use of additional, different, information. First, it makes use of the fact that the populations of scores are normally distributed (one of its necessary assumptions). Secondly, it uses not only the direction but also the *size* of the difference in pairs (the information contained in the last column of table 11.5). Since the t-test is based on richer information, it is more sensitive to differences in the population means and will more readily give a significant value when such differences exist (and for this reason may be referred to as a more **powerful** test). In other words, for any set of data the sign test will be more likely than the t-test to cause a type 2 error. However, if the assumption about the parent population which underlies the t-test, i.e. that they are normally distributed, is not justified, the likelihood of a type 1 error will be higher than the probability indicated by the t-value. The *apparent* significance of the test result can be exaggerated.

Which test then is it more appropriate to use? There is no simple answer.

Testing for differences between two populations

A sensible procedure might be first to use the sign test. If a significant result is thereby obtained there is really no need to go on to carry out a t-test. However, there is no way to calculate a confidence interval for the *size* of the difference without assuming normality anyway. If a t-test *is* carried out, the researcher should be aware of the consequences of the possible failure to meet the assumptions of the test.

SUMMARY

This chapter has looked at various procedures for testing for differences between two groups.

(1) The **t-test for independent samples** to test $H_0 : \mu_1 = \mu_2$ uses the test statistic:

$$t = \frac{(\bar{X}_1 - \bar{X}_2)}{\sqrt{\dfrac{s^2}{n_1} + \dfrac{s^2}{n_2}}}$$

where:

$$s^2 = \frac{(n_1 - 1)s_1^2 + (n_2 - 1)s_2^2}{n_1 + n_2 - 2}$$

which has a t-distribution with $(n_1 + n_2 - 2)$ df when H_0 is true.

(2) To compare **two proportions estimated from independent samples** the statistic:

$$Z = \frac{|\hat{p}_1 - \hat{p}_2| - \dfrac{1}{2}\left(\dfrac{1}{n_1} + \dfrac{1}{n_2}\right)}{\sqrt{\bar{p}(1 - \bar{p})\left(\dfrac{1}{n_1} + \dfrac{1}{n_2}\right)}}$$

should be referred to tables of the standard normal distribution.

(3) The **F-test for comparison of two variances** was explained. The test statistic was $F = (\text{larger } s^2)/(\text{smaller } s^2)$ to be compared with critical values of the F-distribution with (n_2, n_2) df.

(4) The **paired samples t-test** for testing for differences between two means was presented. The test is carried out by calculating $\bar{d}$ and s from the differences and then comparing $t = \bar{d}/(s/\sqrt{n})$ with tables of the t-distribution with $(n - 1)$ df.

(5) Two **nonparametric tests** were explained. The **Mann-Whitney test** for independent samples and the **sign test** for paired samples.

EXERCISES

(1) In chapter 8 we discussed a sample of British children whose comprehension vocabularies were measured. The mean vocabulary for a sample of 140 children was 24,800 words with a standard deviation of 4,200. If a random sample of 108 American children has a mean vocabulary of 24,000 words with a standard deviation of 5,931, test the hypothesis that the two samples come from populations with the same mean vocabulary.

(2) Table 10.1 gives the total error gravity scores for ten native English speakers who are not teachers. In table 11.5 can be found the scores of ten Greek teachers of English on the same errors. Test the hypothesis that the two groups give the same error gravity scores, on average.

(3) Calculate a 95% confidence interval for the difference between the mean error gravity scores of the two groups in exercise 11.2.

(4) For the data of table 9.6 on vowel epenthesis in Rennellese, use the procedure of §11.3 to test whether reduplication is equally likely in initial and medial position.

(5) Using the same data as in exercise 11.2, test whether the two sets of error scores come from populations with equal variance.

(6) A sample of 14 subjects is divided randomly into two groups who are asked to learn a set of 20 vocabulary items in an unfamiliar language, the items being presented in a different format to the two groups but all subjects being allowed the same time to study the items before being tested. The numbers of errors recorded for each of the subjects are:

$$
\begin{array}{llllllll}
\text{Format A:} & 3 & 4 & 11 & 6 & 8 & 2 & \\
\text{Format B:} & 1 & 5 & 8 & 7 & 9 & 14 & 6 & 8
\end{array}
$$

(Two of the students in the first group dropped out without taking the test.) Test whether the average number of errors is the same under both formats.

12

Analysis of variance – ANOVA

In the last chapter we explained how it was possible to test whether two sample means were sufficiently different to allow us to conclude that the samples were probably drawn from populations with different population means. When more than two different groups or experimental conditions are involved we have to be careful how we test whether there might be differences in the corresponding population means. If all possible pairs of samples are tested using the techniques suggested in the previous chapter, the probability of type 1 errors will be greater than we expect, i.e. the 'significance' of any differences will be exaggerated. In the present chapter we intend to develop techniques which will allow us to investigate possible differences between the mean results obtained from several (i.e. more than two) samples, each referring to a different population or collected under different circumstances.

12.1 Comparing several means simultaneously: one-way ANOVA

Imagine that an investigator is interested in the standard of English of students coming to Britain for graduate training. In particular he wishes to discover whether there is a difference in the level of English proficiency between groups of distinct geographical origins – Europe, South America, North Africa and the Far East. As part of a pilot study he administers a multiple choice test to 40 graduate students (10 from each area) drawn at random from the complete set of such students listed on a central file. The scores obtained by these students on the test are shown in table 12.1. The means for the four samples do not have exactly the same value – we would not expect that. However, we might ask if the observed variation in the means is of the order that we could expect from four different random samples, each drawn from the same population of test scores, or are the differences sufficiently large to indicate that students from certain areas are more proficient in English, on average,

Table 12.1. *Marks in a multiple choice vocabulary test of candidates for the Cambridge Proficiency of English examination from four different regions*

	Groups			
	1 Europe	2 South America	3 North Africa	4 Far East
	10	33	26	26
	19	21	25	21
	24	25	19	25
	17	32	31	22
	29	16	15	11
	37	16	25	35
	32	20	23	18
	29	13	32	12
	22	23	20	22
	31	20	15	21
Total	250	219	231	213
Mean	25.0	21.9	23.1	21.3
Sample standard deviation	8.138	6.607	5.915	6.897
Sample variance	66.222	43.655	34.988	47.567

than students from other areas? This is a generalisation of the problem discussed in §11.1 for the comparison of two samples to test whether they were drawn from populations with different mean values. It might seem that the solution presented there could be applied here, by comparing these groups of candidates in pairs: the Europeans with the North Africans, the South Americans with the Europeans, and so on. Unfortunately, it can be demonstrated theoretically that doing this leads to an unacceptable increase in the probability of type 1 errors. If all six different pairs are tested at the 5% significance level there will be a much bigger than 5% chance that *at least one* of the tests will be found to be significant even when no population differences exist. The greater the number of samples observed, the more likely it will be that the difference between the largest sample mean and the smallest sample mean will be sufficiently great – even when all the samples are chosen from the same population – to give a significant value when a test designed for just two samples is used. We need a test which will take into account the total number of comparisons we are making. Such a test can be constructed by means of an **analysis of variance**, usually contracted to **ANOVA** or **ANOVAR**.

As usual, there will be some assumptions that must be met in order for the test to be applied, i.e. that each sample comes from a normally distributed population and that the four populations of candidates' scores all have the same variance, σ^2. The data in table 12.1 consist of four groups of scores from four populations. Suppose that the i-th population has mean μ_i, so that Group 1 is a sample of scores from a population of scores, normally distributed with mean μ_1 and variance σ^2, and so on. The null hypothesis we will test shortly is H_0: $\mu_1 = \mu_2 = \mu_3 = \mu_4$ against the alternative that not all the μ_i have the same value.

Assuming that each sample comes from a population with variance σ^2, the four different sample variances are four independent estimates of the common population variance. These can be combined, or **pooled**, into a single estimate by multiplying each estimate by its degrees of freedom (the sample size minus one) summing the four products and dividing the total by the sum of the degrees of freedom of the four sample variances, thus:

$$\text{pooled variance estimate} = \frac{(n_1 - 1)s_1^2 + (n_2 - 1)s_2^2 + (n_3 - 1)s_3^2 + (n_4 - 1)s_4^2}{n_1 + n_2 + n_3 + n_4 - 4}$$

(If you glance back to §11.1 you will recognise this as a direct generalisation of the method we used to estimate the common variance when we wished to compare only two samples.)

This estimate of the population variance is often called the **within-samples estimate of variance** since it is obtained by first calculating the variances within each sample and then combining them. We will refer to this as s_w^2. In the example of table 12.1, all the samples are the same size, $n_1 = n_2 = n_3 = n_4 = 10$, so that:

$$s_w^2 = \frac{(9 \times 66.222) + (9 \times 43.655) + (9 \times 34.988) + (9 \times 47.567)}{36} = 48.11$$

Now, let us suppose for the moment that the null hypothesis is true, and that the common population mean value is μ. In that case (chapter 5), each of the four sample means is an observation from a normal distribution with mean μ and variance $\sigma^2/10$. (Since we know that in general the standard deviation of a mean has the value $\sigma/\sqrt{n}$ its variance will be σ^2/n). In other words, the four sample means constitute a random sample from that distribution and the variance of this random sample of four means is an estimate of the population variance, $\sigma^2/10$. The sample means are 25.0, 21.9, 23.1, 21.3. Treating these four values as a random sample of four observations, we can calculate the sample standard deviation in the normal way. We find that it is 1.632, and hence the sample variance,

s^2, is $1.632^2 = 2.662$. Since this is an estimate of $\sigma^2/10$, multiplying it by 10 gives a new estimate of σ^2 called the **between-groups estimate of variance**, s_b^2, since it measures the variation across the four sample means. We now have calculated $s_w^2 = 48.11$ and $s_b^2 = 10 \times 2.662 = 26.62$. If the null hypothesis is true, both of these are estimates of the same quantity, σ^2, and it can be shown that the ratio of the estimates:

$$F = s_b^2 \div s_w^2$$

has an F-distribution with 3 and 36 df. There are 3 df in the numerator since it is the sample variance of four observations, and 36 in the denominator since it is a pooled estimate from four samples each of which had 10 observations and each of which hence contributed 9 df to calculate the sample variance. The F-distribution has appeared already in §11.2 as the test statistic for comparing two variances.

If the null hypothesis is not true, s_b^2 will tend to be larger than s_w^2 because the variability in the four sample means will be inflated by the differences between the population means. Large values of the F statistic therefore throw doubt on the validity of the null hypothesis. In the case of the multiple choice test scores, we have $s_b^2 \div s_w^2 = 26.62 \div 48.11 = 0.55$. The 5% critical value of $F_{3,36}$ is just bigger than $F_{3,40}$, which is 2.84, so that the value obtained from the data is not significant and there are no grounds for claiming differences between the groups. In other words, these data do not support the view that graduate students coming to Britain differ in their command of English according to their geographical origin.

The description just given of the analysis of variance procedure is not the most usual way in which the technique is presented. ANOVA, as we will see, is a rather general technique which can be applied to the comparison of means in data with quite complex structure. It is convenient, therefore, to have a method of calculating all the required quantities which will generalise easily. For this reason we will now repeat the analysis of the multiple choice test scores using the more common and general method. The analysis is a particular example of a **one-way analysis of variance** – the comparison of the means of groups which are classified according to a single (hence 'one-way') criterion variable, linguistic/geographical origin in this example. During the presentation of the alternative analysis we will take the opportunity to state the problem in a completely general way.

Suppose that samples of size n have been taken from each of m populations. We will write Y_{ij} for the j-th observation in the i-th group. For example, in table 12.1, $Y_{4,7} = 18$, the score of the seventh Far Eastern (group 4) candidate. As is common when analysis of variance is presented, we write $Y_{i.}$ to mean the *total* of the observations of group i. That is:

$$Y_{i.} = \sum_{j=1}^{n} Y_{ij}$$

For our example:

$$Y_{1.} = \sum_{j=1}^{10} Y_{1j} = 250, \ Y_{2.} = 219, \ Y_{3.} = 231, \ Y_{4.} = 213$$

The grand total of all the observations is designated $Y_{..}$ so that:

$$Y_{..} = 913$$

Since we have m samples (m = 4) each[1] of size n (n = 10) we have mn (4 × 10 = 40) observations in all. A term, usually called the **correction factor** or CF, is now calculated by:

$$CF = \frac{Y_{..}^{2}}{mn} = \frac{913^2}{40} = 20\,839.225$$

(It is often necessary, when calculating for an ANOVA, to keep a large number of figures in the intermediate calculations.)

We now calculate the **total sum of squares**, TSS, which is the sum of the **between-groups sum of squares** and the **within-groups sum of squares**. (The latter is often called the **residual sum of squares** (RSS) for a reason which will become apparent shortly.)

$$\begin{aligned}
\text{TSS (total sum of squares)} &= \Sigma Y_{ij}^{2} - CF \\
&= 10^2 + 19^2 + \ldots + 22^2 + 21^2 - CF \\
&= 22\,651 - 20\,839.225 \\
&= 1811.775
\end{aligned}$$

$$\begin{aligned}
\text{between-groups SS} &= \frac{\Sigma Y_{i.}^{2}}{n} - CF \\
&= (250^2 + 219^2 + 231^2 + 213^2) \div 10 - CF \\
&= 79.875
\end{aligned}$$

$$\begin{aligned}
\text{within-groups SS} &= \text{total SS} - \text{between-groups SS} \\
&= 1811.775 - 79.875 \\
&= 1731.9
\end{aligned}$$

The within-groups sum of squares is the quantity left when the between-groups sum of squares is subtracted from the total sum of squares – hence

---

[1] It is not necessary that the samples be of the same size, though experiments are often designed to make such groups equal. However, the general exposition becomes rather cumbersome if the sample sizes are different.

Table 12.2. *ANOVA table for the data of table 12.1*

Source	df	SS	MSS	F-ratio
Between groups	3	79.875	26.62	$F_{3,36} = 0.55$
Within groups (residual)	36	1731.9	48.11	
Total	39	1811.775		

the term 'residual sum of squares'. An ANOVA table is now constructed
– table 12.2.

The first column in the table gives the source of the sums of squares
– between-groups, residual and total. The second column gives the degrees
of freedom which are used to calculate the different variance estimates
i.e. 3 for between-groups and 36 (4×9) for the within-groups estimates,
as we had in the first analysis above. Generally the between-groups degrees
of freedom will be $m - 1$, one less than the number of groups, the total
available degrees of freedom will be $mn - 1$, one less than the total number
of observations, and the residual degrees of freedom are obtained by subtraction (see table 12.3, which is a general ANOVA table for one-way
ANOVA of m samples each containing n observations). The fourth column
of table 12.2, the **mean sum of squares**, is obtained by dividing each
sum of squares by its degrees of freedom. Note that the values obtained
at this stage are exactly the between-groups variance estimate and within-
groups variance estimate that we calculated previously. The final column
then gives, on the row corresponding to the source which is to be tested
for differences (in this case between-groups) the F-ratio statistic required
for the hypothesis test. It is important that you learn to interpret such
tables, for two reasons. The first is that researchers often present their
results in this way. The second is that, especially for complex data structures, you may perhaps not carry out the calculations by hand, leaving
that to a computer package. The output from the package will usually
contain an ANOVA table of some form.

Table 12.3. *General ANOVA table for one-way ANOVA of m samples each
containing n observations*

Source	df	SS	MSS	F-ratio
Between groups	$m - 1$	BSS	$s_b^2 = \dfrac{BSS}{m-1}$	$\dfrac{s_b^2}{s_r^2}$
Within groups (residual)	$m(n - 1)$	RSS	$s_r^2 = \dfrac{RSS}{m(n-1)}$	
Total	$mn - 1$	TSS		

12.2 Two-way ANOVA: randomised blocks

In chapter 10 we saw that the sensitivity of a comparison between two means could be improved by pairing the observations in the two samples. This idea can be extended to the comparison of several means. Table 12.4 repeats the data on gravity of errors analysed in chapter 11, but now extended to three groups of judges, the third group consisting of the ten English non-teachers. There are now three ways to divide up the variability: variation in scores between m groups of judges, variation in scores between the n different errors and residual, random variation. The necessary calculations and the resulting table are similar to those found in the one-way case, but with an extra item, between-errors sum of squares, added.

We begin by calculating the totals, displayed in table 12.4:

$Y_{i.}$ the total for the i-th error
$Y_{.j}$ the total for the j-th set of judges
$Y_{..}$ the grand total

We calculate, as before, a correction factor by:

$$CF = \frac{Y_{..}^2}{mn} = \frac{2462^2}{3 \times 32} = 63\,140.04$$

Then the total sum of squares:

$$\begin{aligned} TSS &= \Sigma Y_{ij}^2 - CF \\ &= 22^2 + 16^2 + \ldots + 28^2 + 14^2 - CF \\ &= 68\,742 - 63\,140.04 \\ &= 5601.96 \end{aligned}$$

Between-errors sum of squares:

$$\begin{aligned} ESS &= \frac{\Sigma Y_{.j}^2}{m} - CF \\ &= (80^2 + 43^2 + \ldots + 94^2 + 45^2) \div 3 - CF \\ &= 198\,096 \div 3 - CF \\ &= 2891.96 \end{aligned}$$

Between-groups (of judges) sums of squares:

$$\begin{aligned} GSS &= \frac{\Sigma Y_{i.}^2}{n} - CF \\ &= (801^2 + 905^2 + 756^2) \div 32 - CF \\ &= 365.02 \end{aligned}$$

Note that the divisor in each sum of squares calculation is just the number

Table 12.4. *Total error gravity scores of ten native English teachers (1), ten Greek teachers of English (2) and ten native English non-teachers (3) on 32 English sentences*

Sentence	Group			Total ($Y_{i.}$)
	1	2	3	
1	22	36	22	80
2	16	9	18	43
3	42	29	42	113
4	25	35	21	81
5	31	34	26	91
6	36	23	41	100
7	29	25	26	80
8	24	31	20	75
9	29	35	18	82
10	18	21	15	54
11	23	33	21	77
12	22	13	19	54
13	31	22	39	92
14	21	29	23	73
15	27	25	24	76
16	32	25	29	86
17	23	39	18	80
18	18	19	16	53
19	30	28	29	87
20	31	41	22	94
21	20	25	12	57
22	21	17	26	64
23	29	26	43	98
24	22	37	26	85
25	26	34	22	82
26	20	28	19	67
27	29	33	30	92
28	18	24	17	59
29	23	37	15	75
30	25	33	15	73
31	27	39	28	94
32	11	20	14	45
Total ($Y_{.j}$)	801	905	756	2462

of observations which have gone into each of the values being squared. For example, in GSS we have $(801^2 + 905^2 + 756^2) \div 32$ because each of the values 801, 905 and 756 is the sum of 32 data values. The corresponding ANOVA is presented in table 12.5.

As before, the residual sum of squares and the residual degrees of freedom are calculated by subtraction from the total sum of squares and total degrees of freedom respectively. The F-ratio for groups of judges is 4.85 with 2 and 62 df and this is significant beyond the 2.5% level, clearly indicating differences in the scores of the three sets of judges. The question

Table 12.5. *ANOVA for data of table 12.4*

Source	df	SS	MSS	F-ratio
Between errors	31	2891.96	93.29	$F_{31,62} = 2.47$
Between groups of judges	2	365.02	182.51	$F_{2,62} = 4.83$
Residual	62	2344.98	37.82	
Total	95	5601.96		

remains whether this is due to the Greek judges scoring differently from English judges (whether teachers or not), teachers (whether Greek or English) scoring differently from non-teachers, and so on. We will return to this question in §12.5.

Note that the F-ratio for comparing errors is significant beyond the 1% level, but to investigate this was not an important part of this analysis. We have simply taken account of the variability that this causes in the scores so that we can make a more sensitive comparison between groups. This type of experimental design is often called a **randomised block design**.

12.3 Two-way ANOVA: factorial experiments

It is often convenient and efficient to investigate several experimental variables simultaneously. The sociolinguist, for example, may be interested in both the linguistic context and the social context in which a linguistic token is used; a psycholinguist may wish to study how word recognition reaction times vary in different prose types and with subjects in different groups. Indeed it will only be possible to study the interaction between such variables if they are observed simultaneously. We will use again the multiple choice test scores of the four groups of graduate students to introduce the terminology and demonstrate the technique.

In table 12.6 we have given the same data as in table 12.1 but now **cross-classified** by geographical origin *and* sex. The style of presentation of this table is quite a common one for cross-classified data, with various totals given in the margins of the table (they are often referred to as **marginal totals**): total scores by sex, total scores by geographical location and subtotals by the origin by sex cross-classification. To discuss these data and describe any formulae for their analysis it is convenient to refer to them by means of three suffixes; Y_{ijk} will refer to the score of the k-th subject of the j-th sex who belongs to the i-th geographical location. Generalising the use of the **dot notation** introduced in the previous section we write:

Table 12.6. *Marks of 40 subjects in a multiple choice test (the subjects are classified by geographical location and sex)*

| Sex | Geographical location | | | | Total |
	Europe (1)	South America (2)	North Africa (3)	South East Asia (4)	
Male (1)	10	33	26	26	
	19	21	25	21	
	24	25	19	25	
	17	32	31	22	
	29	16	15	11	
Subtotal	99	127	116	105	447
Female (2)	37	16	25	35	
	32	20	23	18	
	29	13	32	12	
	22	23	20	22	
	31	20	15	21	
Subtotal	151	92	115	108	466
Total	250	219	231	213	913

$Y_{ij.}$ = total score of subjects belonging to the i-th location and j-th sex (e.g. $Y_{31.} = 116$)

$Y_{i..}$ = total score of subjects at i-th location ($Y_{2..} = 219$)

$Y_{.j.}$ = total score of subjects of j-th sex ($Y_{.2.} = 466$)

$Y_{...}$ = grand total = 913

An experiment designed to give this kind of data structure is usually called a **factorial experiment**, the different criterion variables being called **factors**. These 'factors' are entirely unrelated to those of **factor analysis**, a technique discussed in chapter 15. Here there are two factors, sex and geographical origin. The different values of each factor are often referred to as the **levels of the factor**. Sex has two levels, male and female, and geographical location has four.

We can use this single set of data to test *independently* two different null hypotheses: whether mean scores are the same between geographical origins and whether mean scores are the same for the two sexes. The calculations required are similar to those of the example in the previous section. We begin by calculating the correction factor, CF:

$$CF = \frac{Y_{...}^2}{40} = \frac{913^2}{40} = 20\,839.225$$

and continue by obtaining the various sums of squares:

$$\text{total SS} = \Sigma Y_{ijk}^2 - CF$$
$$= (10^2 + 19^2 + \ldots + 22^2 + 21^2) - CF$$
$$= 1811.775$$

$$\text{between-locations SS} = \frac{\Sigma Y_{i..}^2}{10} - CF$$
$$= (250^2 + 219^2 + 231^2 + 213^2) \div 10 - CF$$
$$= 79.875$$

$$\text{between-sexes SS} = \frac{\Sigma Y_{.j.}^2}{20} - CF$$
$$= (447^2 + 466^2) \div 20 - CF$$
$$= 9.025$$

and this leads to the ANOVA in table 12.7(a) from which we conclude from the small F-ratios that there is no significant difference between geographical locations (we came to the same conclusion in §12.1), and none between sexes. However, the analysis carried out thus tests the differences between the sample means of the locations calculated over all the observations for an origin irrespective of the sex of the subject. Likewise, the sample means for the sexes are calculated over all 20 observations for each sex ignoring any difference in location. Calculated in that way, the sample mean score for males is $447 \div 20 = 22.35$ and for females it is 23.30, so that they are rather similar. However, suppose we look to see if there are differences between sexes within some of the locations (refer back

Table 12.7.

(a) ANOVA of main effects only from data of table 12.6

Source	df	SS	MS	F-ratio
Between locations	3	79.875	26.62	$F_{3,35} = 0.54$
Between sexes	1	9.025	9.025	$F_{1,35} = 0.18$
Residual	35	1722.875	49.225	
Total	39	1811.775		

(b) ANOVA of main effects and interaction from data of table 12.6

Source	df	SS	MS	F-ratio
Between locations (L)	3	79.875	26.62	$F_{3,32} = 0.68$
Between sexes (S)	1	9.025	9.025	$F_{1,32} = 0.23$
Interaction (L×S)	3	473.775	157.925	$F_{3,32} = 4.05$
Residual	32	1249.100	39.03	
Total	39	1811.775		

to table 12.6). For the North Africa and South East Asia samples the mean scores of the two sexes are still very similar, but among European students the females have apparently done rather better, while for the South Americans the reverse is the case. These differences cancel out when we look at the sex averages over all the locations simultaneously. What we are possibly seeing here is an interaction between the two factors. In other words, it may be that there is a difference between the mean scores of the sexes, but the extent of the difference depends on the geographical location of the subjects. Any difference between the levels of a single factor which is independent of any other factor is referred to as a **main effect**. Differences which appear only when two or more factors are examined together are called **interactions**. As a form of shorthand, main effects are often designated by a single letter, e.g. L for the variation in mean score of students from different locations, and S for the variation between sexes. Interaction effects are designated by the use of the different main effects symbols joined by one (or more) crosses, e.g. L×S for the interaction between location and sex. Provided there is more than one observation for each combination of the levels of the main factors it is possible to test whether significant interaction effects are present. For the multiple choice test scores data of table 12.6 we have observed five scores for each of the eight combinations of the levels of sex and location. (For factorial experiments it is important that each combination has been observed the same number of times. If that has not happened it is still possible to carry out an analysis of variance but the main effects cannot then be tested independently of one another and there may be difficulties of interpretation of the ANOVA. Furthermore, the calculations become much more involved and it is not really feasible to carry them out by hand – see §13.12.) To test for a significant interaction we simply expand the ANOVA to include an interaction sum of squares calculated by:

$$\text{interaction SS} = \frac{\Sigma Y_{ij.}^2}{5} - CF$$
$$= (99^2 + 127^2 + \ldots + 115^2 + 108^2) \div 5 - CF$$
$$= 473.775$$

The relevant ANOVA appears in table 12.7(b). The only extra feature requiring comment is that the degrees of freedom for the interaction term are obtained by multiplying the degrees of freedom of the main effects included in the interaction (here, $3 \times 1 = 3$): the symbol for the interaction effect, L×S, is a useful mnemonic for this. The F-ratio for testing the interaction effect is significant at the 1% level, showing that such effects

205

need to be considered. The practical implication of this would be that when considering possible differences between the scores of subjects of different sex we should not leave out of consideration their geographical origin.[2]

We now go on to consider more generally the interpretation of main effects and interaction in ANOVA.

12.4   ANOVA models: main effects only

Let us reconsider the first problem we discussed in this chapter – the one-way ANOVA of four independent samples of students from four locations. We wished to test the hypothesis that the population mean score of students from all geographical locations was the same, and we assumed that, at all locations, the scores were from a normal distribution with variance σ^2. All this can be summarised neatly in a simple mathematical model:

$$Y_{ij} = \mu_i + e_{ij}$$

where Y_{ij} is the j-th score observed at the i-th location, μ_i is the population mean at the i-th location, and e_{ij} is the random amount by which the j-th score, randomly chosen at the i-th location, deviates from the mean score. Our earlier assumption that the scores of students from the i-th location were normally distributed with mean μ_i and variance σ^2 is equivalent to the assumption that, for each geographical location the 'error' or 'residual', e_{ij}, was normally distributed with mean zero and variance σ^2. We then tested the null hypothesis that $\mu_i = \mu$, the same value, for all locations.

Although this simple model is perfectly adequate for the one-way ANOVA problem, it does not generalise easily to more complex cases such as the factorial experiment. In order to make that possible a slight modification is needed. Suppose we ignore the existence of the four different locations. We could then consider the 40 scores as having come from a single population with mean μ, say. Now write $L_i = \mu_i - \mu$. That is, L_i is the difference between the mean of the overall population (that is, the grand population mean, μ) and the mean score of the population of scores of students from the i-th location, μ_i. Equivalently we can write $\mu_i = \mu + L_i$, and substituting this into the previous model we now have:

$$Y_{ij} = \mu + L_i + e_{ij}$$

---

[2] In this case the division of subjects into 'male' and 'female' was entirely hypothetical, carried out to demonstrate the basic concept of 'interaction'.

Some values in such a model, Y_{ij} and e_{ij}, depend on the specific data values observed in the experiment. Others, μ and L_i, are assumed to be fixed for all the different samples that might be chosen; they are population, as opposed to sample, values and are referred to as the **parameters of the model**. μ is usually called the **grand mean** and L_i the **main effect** of origin i.

The previous null hypothesis that all the μ_i had the same value, μ, can now be restated as H_o: $L_i = o$, for every value of i (that is, the main effect of geographical location is zero). This model can be generalised to cover a huge variety of situations. For example, consider the randomised block experiment of table 12.4. The observations are arranged in 32 'blocks', i.e. the errors. Within every block we have a score from each set of judges. A suitable model would be:

$$Y_{ij} = \mu + b_i + g_j + e_{ij}$$

which says that each score, Y_{ij}, is composed of four components summed together, the grand mean, μ, the **block effect**, b_i, the **group effect**, g_j, and the random variation e_{ij} about the mean score of judges of type j scoring the error i for its gravity.

It may be easier to understand what this means if we fit the model to the observed data and estimate values for the parameters. Each parameter is estimated by the corresponding sample mean: μ is estimated by $Y_{..} \div 96$, since there is a total of 96 observations. We will use a circumflex to designate an estimate and write:

$\hat{\mu} = Y_{..} \div 96 = 2462 \div 96 = 25.65$

$\hat{g}_1 = $ (total for group 1 $\div$ number of scores for group 1) $- \hat{\mu}$

     $= Y_{.1} \div 32 - 25.65 = (801 \div 32) - 25.65 = -0.62$

(suggesting that group 1 scores *may* be smaller than the overall average)

$\hat{b}_1 = Y_{1.} \div 3$ (each 'block' contains three scores – one from each group of judges) $- 26$

     $= (80 \div 3) - 25.65 = 26.66 - 25.65 = 1.01$

(so that the first error *may* be reviewed as more serious than average)

The complete set of parameter estimates is given in the margins of table 12.8. The values of these estimates are useful when discussing the data. For example, we can say that the English teachers' group gives 0.62 ($\hat{g}_1$) marks per error less than the mean ($\hat{\mu}$) while the Greek teachers' group gives 2.63 ($\hat{g}_2$) marks per error more than the average. Error number 2 receives 11.32 ($\hat{b}_2$) marks per group of judges less than the mean gravity

Table 12.8. *Total error gravity scores of ten native English teachers (1),
and ten Greek teachers of English (2), and ten native English non-teachers
(3), on 32 English sentences*

Sentence	Group 1	Group 2	Group 3	Total ($Y_{i.}$)	Mean	$\hat{b}$
1	22	36	22	80	26.67	1.02
2	16	9	18	43	14.33	−11.32
3	42	29	42	113	37.67	12.02
4	25	35	21	81	27.00	1.35
5	31	34	26	91	30.33	4.68
6	36	23	41	100	33.33	7.68
7	29	25	26	80	26.67	1.02
8	24	31	20	75	25.00	−0.65
9	29	35	18	82	27.33	1.68
10	18	21	15	54	18.00	−7.65
11	23	33	21	77	25.67	0.02
12	22	13	19	54	18.00	−7.65
13	31	22	39	92	30.67	5.02
14	21	29	23	73	24.33	−1.32
15	27	25	24	76	25.33	−0.32
16	32	25	29	86	28.67	3.02
17	23	39	18	80	26.67	1.02
18	18	19	16	53	17.67	−7.98
19	30	28	29	87	29.00	3.35
20	31	41	22	94	31.33	5.68
21	20	25	12	57	19.00	−6.65
22	21	17	26	64	21.33	−4.32
23	29	26	43	98	32.67	7.02
24	22	37	26	85	28.33	2.68
25	26	34	22	82	27.33	1.68
26	20	28	19	67	22.33	−3.32
27	29	33	30	92	30.67	5.02
28	18	24	17	59	19.67	−5.98
29	23	37	15	75	25.00	−0.65
30	25	33	15	73	24.33	−1.32
31	27	39	28	94	31.33	5.68
32	11	20	14	45	15.00	−10.65
Total ($Y_{.j}$)	801	905	756	2462		
Mean	25.03	28.28	23.63		25.65	
$\hat{g}$	−0.62	2.63	−2.03			

score ($\hat{\mu}$), but error number 11 is seen to be of about average seriousness
since $\hat{b}_{11}$ is very close to zero, and so on. We can also examine the degree
to which a particular score is well or badly fitted by the model, by calculating the value of the **random** or **residual** component of the score, e_{ij}.
For example, $Y_{20,2}$, the observed score on error number 20 of the Greek
judges is 41, while $\hat{Y}_{20,2}$, the value obtained from the **fitted model** is:

$$\hat{Y}_{20,2} = \hat{\mu} + \hat{b}_{20} + \hat{g}_2 = 25.65 + 5.68 + 2.63 = 33.96$$

so that the so-called **residual error**, the difference:

$$e_{20,2} = Y_{20,2} - \hat{Y}_{20,2} = 41 - 33.96$$

between the observed and fitted values is 7.04, which seems rather large, while:

$$e_{20,1} = Y_{20,1} - \hat{Y}_{20,1} = 31 - (25.65 + 5.68 - 0.62) = 0.29$$

which suggests a good correspondence between the observed and fitted values of the score of the English teachers on the error number 20. This brings us to the last parameter which apparently has not yet been estimated, namely σ^2, the **random error variance** or **residual variance**. A good estimate of its value is given by the residual mean square error in the ANOVA displayed in table 12.5, i.e. $\hat{\sigma}^2 = 37.82$, so that the standard deviation is estimated by $\sqrt{37.82} = 6.15$. This value is important when it comes to deciding which types of judges do seem to be giving different scores, on average, for the errors used in the study. In chapter 11 we gave the formula for a 95% confidence interval for the size of the difference between the two means:

$$\text{(difference between sample means)} \pm \left(\text{constant} \times \sqrt{\frac{s^2}{n_1} + \frac{s^2}{n_2}} \right)$$

where s^2 was an estimate of the common standard deviation and n_1 and n_2 were the sample sizes. Let us use this to estimate how much difference there seems to be between the mean scores of English and Greek teachers. Applying the above formula gives the interval:

$$\bar{Y}_{.2} - \bar{Y}_{.1} \pm \left(\text{constant} \sqrt{\frac{37.82}{32} + \frac{37.82}{32}} \right)$$

Each of the sample sizes is 32, since both means are based on the scores for 32 different errors. The constant used in the formula is the 5% significance value of the t-distribution with the same number of degrees of freedom as there are for the residual in the ANOVA table – 62 in this case (see table 12.5). The interval will then be:

$$(28.28 - 25.03) \pm (2.0 \times \sqrt{2.36})$$

or $\qquad 3.25 \pm 3.07$

i.e. $\qquad 0.18$ to 3.62

Similar confidence intervals for the other possible differences in means are as follows. For English teachers *versus* English non-teachers:

$$25.03 - 23.63 \pm 3.07$$

i.e. $\qquad -1.67$ to 4.47

and for Greek teachers *versus* English non-teachers:

$$28.28 - 23.63 \pm 3.07$$

i.e.   1.58 to 7.72

It might seem safe now, following the procedure of chapter 5 for carrying out tests of hypotheses using confidence intervals, to conclude that, at the 5% significance level, we can reject the two hypotheses that Greek teachers give the same scores as English teachers and non-teachers. On the other hand, there does not seem to be a significant difference between the mean scores of English teachers and English non-teachers. *However, this procedure is equivalent to carrying out three pair-wise tests* and, at the beginning of this chapter, we denied the validity of such an undertaking. There are theoretically correct procedures for making **multiple comparisons** – comparing all the possible pairs of means – but they are not simple to carry out. A frequently adopted rule of thumb is the following. *Provided that the ANOVA has indicated a significant difference between a set of means*, calculate the standard error s* for the comparison of any pair of means by:

$$s^* = \sqrt{\frac{2 \times \text{residual mean square}}{n}}$$

where n is the number of observations which have been averaged when calculating each mean. Then find the difference between each pair of means. If the difference between a pair of means is greater than 2s*, take this as suggesting that the corresponding population means may be different. If the difference in two sample means is greater than 3s*, take this as reasonably convincing evidence of a real difference.

For the three groups of judges, we know (see table 12.5) that the residual mean square is 37.82 and therefore:

$$s^* = \sqrt{2.36} = 1.54, \; 2s^* = 3.07 \text{ and } 3s^* = 4.61$$

mean of Greek teachers − mean of English teachers   = 3.25
mean of English teachers − mean of English non-teachers = 1.40
mean of Greek teachers − mean of English non-teachers   = 4.65

from which we might conclude that Greek and English teachers probably give different scores on average and the Greek teachers and English non-teachers almost certainly do. However, this seems a suitable moment to reiterate our comment about the difference between statistical significance and scientific importance (chapter 7). It is important always to consider the observed magnitude of the differences in the means as estimated from the data and ask whether they seem large enough to be important, *whether or not* they are found to be significant by a statistical hypothesis test.

12.5 ANOVA models: factorial experiments

In §12.4 we introduced the concept of a factorial experiment, using as an example vocabulary test scores classified by two factors, the sex of the subject who supplied the score and his or her geographical location. A model which we might try to fit to these data is:

$$Y_{ijk} = \mu + L_i + S_j + e_{ijk}$$

where Y_{ijk}, as before, is the score of the k-th subject who is of the i-th location and is of the j-th sex, μ is the grand population mean, L_i is the main effect of the i-th location, S_j is the main effect of the j-th sex and e_{ijk} is the random amount by which this subject's score is different from the population mean of all scores of subjects of the j-th sex of the i-th origin. As before, we assume that all the values of e_{ijk} are from a normal distribution with mean zero and variance, σ^2. Use of this model would lead to the analysis of table 12.6. The values of the various parameters can be estimated using exactly the same steps as in the analysis of the error gravity scores above (see exercise 3). The residual variance, σ^2, is estimated by $\hat{\sigma}^2 = 49.225$, the residual mean square of the ANOVA table 12.7(a). We have already seen that neither of the main effects is significant, i.e. there is no obvious difference in mean scores for the two sexes nor in the mean scores at the four different locations.

However, look again at the model:

$$Y_{ijk} = \mu + L_i + S_j + e_{ijk}$$

There is an assumption here that, apart from the random variation, e_{ijk}, each score can be reconstructed by the addition of three parameters, the grand mean plus the effect of having origin i (assumed equal for both sexes) plus the effect of the subject being of sex j (assumed equal for all locations). We have already demonstrated in §12.3 that this model will not give an adequate description of the data. There is an additional effect to consider. There seems to be an interaction between sex and location, males scoring better, on average, in one location and females scoring better in another. The model can be expanded to cope with this as follows:

$$Y_{ijk} = \mu + L_i + S_j + a_{ij} + e_{ijk}$$

where the parameter a_{ij} is the additional correction which should be made for the interaction between the effects of the i-th origin and the j-th sex. We have already seen in table 12.7(b) that this interaction effect is significant. Table 12.9 gives the parameter estimates and the sample means for

211

Table 12.9. *Estimation of the model* $Y_{ijk} = \mu + L_i + S_j + a_{ij} + e_{ijk}$ *to the data of table 12.6*

Sex	Geographical location					
	1	2	3	4		
1	$\bar{Y}_{11.} = 19.80$	$\bar{Y}_{21.} = 25.40$	$\bar{Y}_{31.} = 23.20$	$\bar{Y}_{41.} = 21.00$	$\bar{Y}_{.1.} = 22.35$	
	$\hat{a}_{11} = -4.72$	$\hat{a}_{21} = 3.98$	$\hat{a}_{31} = 0.58$	$\hat{a}_{41} = 0.18$	$\hat{S}_1 = -0.48$	
2	$\bar{Y}_{12.} = 30.20$	$\bar{Y}_{22.} = 18.40$	$\bar{Y}_{32.} = 23.00$	$\bar{Y}_{42.} = 21.60$	$\bar{Y}_{.2.} = 23.30$	
	$\hat{a}_{12} = 4.72$	$\hat{a}_{22} = -3.98$	$\hat{a}_{32} = -0.58$	$\hat{a}_{42} = -0.18$	$\hat{S}_2 = 0.48$	
	$\bar{Y}_{1..} = 25.0$	$\bar{Y}_{2..} = 21.9$	$\bar{Y}_{3..} = 23.1$	$\bar{Y}_{4..} = 21.3$	$\bar{Y}_{...} = 22.83$	
	$\hat{L}_1 = 2.17$	$\hat{L}_2 = -0.93$	$\hat{L}_3 = 0.27$	$\hat{L}_4 = -1.53$	$\hat{\mu} = 22.83$	

$\hat{\sigma}^2$ = residual mean square = 39.03 – see table 12.7(b)

standard error for comparing origin means = $\sqrt{39.03 \times 2 \div 10} = 2.79$

standard error for comparing sex means = $\sqrt{39.03 \times 2 \div 20} = 1.98$

standard error for comparing interaction means = $\sqrt{39.03 \times 2 \div 5} = 3.95$

the different mean effects and interactions. In this table, $\bar{Y}_{ij.}$ represents the sample mean score of subjects from location i and sex j, etc. When the interaction effect is significant there is not a great deal of point in examining the main effects. In this example it is quite unhelpful to say that the mean scores for the different sexes are about equal when that hides the fact that, between some origins, there seems to be an important difference of scores. It makes more sense to compare sexes within origins and origins within sex. In order to make this comparison we have to use the standard error for comparing *interaction* means, which has the value 3.95 (see table 12.9). For example, for origin 1 the difference in the sex means is 30.2 – 19.8 = 10.4, which is 2.6 times the relevant standard error. Using the guidelines proposed in the previous section, this suggests a real difference. In any case, an *observed* average difference of 10 marks in a test which was scored out of 50 is sufficiently large to merit further investigation. On the other hand, in the case of origin 4, the difference is only 0.6 which is certainly not significant compared to the standard error and is in any case hardly large enough to have any practical importance.

12.6 Fixed and random effects

In the example analysed in the previous section, students had been sampled from four different locations. We reached the conclusion that there was no main effect of location. Ignoring for the moment the important interaction effects, we might conclude that the mean mark of students having one of these locations would be very similar to the mean mark of students having another. How wide is the scope of this conclusion? Does it apply only to the four locations actually observed or can we extend it to students from other locations? The analysis we have carried out above is correct only if we do not wish to extend the results, formally, beyond the four locations involved in the experiment. If we intend these locations to serve as representatives of a larger group of locations, the model has to be conceptualised differently and a different analysis will be required.

The model fitted to multiple choice test scores, ignoring interactions for the moment, was:

$$Y_{ijk} = \mu + L_i + S_j + e_{ijk}$$

for which we tested the hypotheses $H_0 : L_i = 0$ for all four locations and $H_0 : S_j = 0$ for both sexes. We reached the conclusion that both these hypotheses seemed reasonable. With this formulation of the model the results will not extend to other origins. This is known as a **fixed effects model**.

If we wish to widen the scope of the experiment we have to construct a mechanism to relate the effect of the locations actually involved to the effects of those not included in the experiment. This is usually done by assuming that there is a very large number of possible locations each with its own location effect, L, on the mean score of students having that location. We then have to assume further that the different values of L can be modelled as a normal distribution with mean zero and some standard deviation, σ_L. The null hypothesis for a location effect will now be formulated somewhat differently, as $H_0 : \sigma_L = 0$ since if there is no variation in the values of L the variance of the distribution of L values would be zero. It will now be assumed that the four locations we have chosen for the experiment have been randomly sampled from all the possible locations we could have chosen. This is an example of a **random effect**, the four levels of the factor 'locations' being chosen randomly from a population of possible levels.

For a one-way ANOVA (see §12.1) the calculations and the F-test are carried out exactly the same whether or not origin is viewed as a fixed or random effect. The difference lies in the conclusion we can reach and the kind of estimation possible in the model. The small F-value (table 12.2) would indicate that location effects were not important and, *provided the four locations in the experiment had been randomly chosen from a large set of possible locations*, this conclusion would apply to the whole population of locations. However, we have frequently indicated that, whatever the results of a hypothesis test, it is always advisable to *estimate*

Table 12.10. *ANOVA of main effects and interaction from data of table 12.6 with location as a random effect*

Source	df	SS	MS	F-ratio
Between locations (L)	3	78.875	26.62	$F_{3,32} = 0.68$
Between sexes (S)	1	9.025	9.025	$F_{1,32} = 0.06$
L×S	3	473.775	157.925	$F_{3,32} = 4.05$
Residual	32	1249.100	39.03	
Total	39	1811.775		

the parameters of any model in case important effects have been missed by the statistical test or unimportant effects exaggerated. In this model an important parameter is σ_L, the standard deviation of the location effects. It is estimated by subtracting the residual mean square from the between-locations mean square and taking the square root of the answer. From table 12.2 we would estimate:

$$\hat{\sigma}_L = \sqrt{26.62 - 48.11}$$

Unfortunately the square root of a negative number does not exist, so that we cannot estimate σ_L, and this is a not infrequent outcome in random effects ANOVAs. The best we can say is that we are fairly certain that the value of $\sigma_L{}^2$ is about zero.

With higher order ANOVA (that is, two-way and more), even the F-tests will differ, depending on which effects we assume to be random or fixed, though the actual calculations of the sums of squares and mean squares will always be the same. In the previous section we carried out an ANOVA of data classified by sex and location. The table for that analysis (table 12.7(b)) is correct assuming that both sex and location are fixed effects. Clearly sex will always be a fixed effect – there are only two possible levels – but we could have chosen location as a random effect. The revised ANOVA table is given in table 12.10. You may have to look very hard before you find the only change that has occurred in the table. It is in the F-ratio column; the F-value for testing the main effect of sex is now obtained by dividing the sex mean square by the mean square for the L×S interaction and *not* by the residual mean square. This has caused the F-value to decrease. In this example that was unimportant but it is in general possible that the apparent significance of the effect of one factor may be removed by assuming that another factor is a random rather than a fixed effect.

Further discussion of this problem in general terms is beyond the scope of this book. Every different mixture of random and fixed effects gives rise to different sets of F-ratios and the greater the number of factors the greater is the number of possible combinations. Many books on experimental design or ANOVA give the details (e.g. Winer 1971). It is sensible to avoid the random effects assumption wherever possible, choosing levels of the different factors for well-considered experimental reasons rather than randomly. The fixed effects model is always easier to interpret because all the parameters can always be estimated. However, there are situations in linguistic studies where it may be difficult to avoid the use of the random effects model. It could be argued, for example, that in the analysis presented in §12.2 the 32 errors whose gravity was assessed by sets of judges are representatives of a population of possible errors and that 'error' should be considered as a random effect. This problem is discussed at length by Clark (1973), who advocates that random effects models should be used much more widely in language research.

Clark's suggestion is one way to cope with a complex and widespread problem, but it does seem a pity to lose the simplicity of the fixed effects model and replace it with a complicated variety of models containing various mixtures of fixed and random effects. There are other possible solutions. One is to claim that any differences found relate only to the particular language examples used. We could conclude that the Greek and English teachers give different scores on this particular set of errors. Though this may seem rather weak it may serve as an initial conclusion, allowing simple estimation of how large the differences seem to be and at least serving as a basis for the decision on whether further investigation is warranted. A second solution would be to identify classes of error into which all errors could be classified. If each of the 32 errors in the study were a representative of one of the, say, 32 possible classes of error, then we would be back to a fixed effects model.

There may still be a problem. Remember that an important assumption of the ANOVA model is that the variability should not depend on the levels of the factors. It may very well be that, say, different sets of judges find it easier to agree about the gravity of one type of error than the gravity of another. The variance of scores on the latter error would then be greater than on the former. If the difference is large this could have serious implications for the validity of the ANOVA (see §12.8). There is one area where random effects models occur naturally – in the assessment of the reliability of language tests.

12.7 Test score reliability and ANOVA

Language testers are quite properly interested in the 'reliability' of any test which they may administer. A completely reliable test would be one in which an individual subject would always obtain exactly the same score if it were possible for him to repeat the test several times. How can reliability be measured? Several indices have been proposed (e.g. Ghiselli, Campbell & Zedeck 1981) but the most common is the following.

Assume that for the i-th subject in a population there is an underlying true score, μ_i, for the trait measured by the test. The 'true' scores (chapter 6) will form a statistical population with mean μ and variance σ_b^2, the b signifying that the variability is measured between subjects. In fact, a subject taking the test will not usually express his true score exactly, due to random influences, such as the way he feels on a particular day and so on. The score actually observed for the i-th subject will be $Y_i = \mu_i + e_i$ where the error, e_i, is usually assumed to be normally distributed with mean zero and some variance, σ^2. If this subject takes the same test several times, his observed score on the j-th occasion will be $Y_{ij} = \mu_i + e_{ij}$, where e_{ij} is the error in measuring the true score of the i-th student on the j-th occasion when he takes the test. This model can be written.

$$Y_{ij} = \mu + a_i + e_{ij}$$

where μ is the mean 'true' score of all the students in the population and a_i is the difference between the 'true' score of the i-th student and the mean for all students. Since we had previously assumed that true scores were normally distributed with mean μ and variance σ_b^2, the values a_i will be from a normal distribution with mean zero and variance σ_b^2. Now, if the measurement error variance is close to zero, all the variability in scores will be due to differences in the true scores of students. A common **reliability coefficient** is:

$$rel = \frac{\sigma_b^2}{\sigma_b^2 + \sigma^2}$$

which is the proportion of the total variability which is due to true differences in the subjects. If $rel = 1$, there is no random error. If rel is close to zero, the measurement error is large enough to hide the true differences between students. How can we estimate rel? It can be shown that $rel = \rho$, the correlation between two repetitions of the *same* test over all the subjects, and rel is frequently estimated by r, the correlation between the scores of a sample of subjects each of whom takes the test twice. However, there is a problem with this. It is simply not possible to administer exactly the same test to a group of subjects on different occasions. It is much more common to administer two *forms* of the same test. The tester hopes

Table 12.11. *Scores of ten subjects on two parallel forms of the same test*

Subject	Form 1	Form 2	Total
1	63	67	130
2	41	39	80
3	78	71	149
4	24	21	45
5	39	48	87
6	53	46	99
7	56	51	107
8	59	54	113
9	46	37	83
10	53	61	114
Total	512	495	1007

that the two different versions of the test will be measuring the same trait in the same way – quite a large assumption. The correlational method of estimating the reliability makes no check on this assumption. If the second version of the test gave each subject exactly 10 marks (or 50 marks) more than the first version, the correlation would be 1, and the reliability would be apparently perfect, though the marks for each subject are quite different on the two applications of the test. The random effects ANOVA model provides a different method for estimating the reliability and also offers the possibility of checking the assumption that the 'parallel forms' of the test do measure the same thing in the same way.

Table 12.11 shows the hypothetical marks of ten subjects on two forms of a standard test. There are two ways to tackle the analysis of this data. One is to *assume* that the parallel forms are equivalent so that the data can be considered as two independent observations of the same trait score on ten students. This is equivalent to assuming that any student has the same *true* score on both forms of the test. The observed scores can then be analysed using the model:

$$Y_{ij} = \mu + a_i + e_{ij}$$

where μ is the common mean of all parallel forms of the test over the whole population of students, a_i is the amount by which the score of the i-th student in the sample differs from this mean, and e_{ij} is the random error in measuring the score of the i-th student at the j-th test. The corresponding ANOVA is given in table 12.12(a).

The random error variance σ^2 is estimated by the residual mean square, $s^2 = 31.95$. It can be shown that the between-students mean square is an estimate of $\sigma^2 + k\sigma_b^2$ where k is the number of parallel forms used,

217

Table 12.12. *ANOVA for data in table 12.11 allowing for differences in supposed parallel forms when assessing test reliability*

(a) One-way ANOVA of data in table 12.11

Source	df	SS	MS
Between students	9	3655.05	406.12
Residual	10	319.50	31.95
Total	19	3974.55	

(b) Two-way ANOVA of data in table 12.11

Source	df	SS	MS	F-ratio
Between students	9	3655.05	406.12	
Between forms	1	186.05	186.05	$F_{1,9} = 12.55$
Residual	9	133.45	14.83	
Total	19	3974.55		

here two. The quantity s_b^2, an estimate of σ_b^2, can be obtained by putting $s^2 + 2s_b^2 = 406.12$ which gives $s_b^2 = 187.085$. An estimate of the reliability is given by:

$$rel = \frac{s_b^2}{s_b^2 + s^2} = 0.854$$

On the other hand, the correlation between the two sets of scores is 0.93 and frequently this would have been used as an estimate of the reliability. Why is there this discrepancy? The ANOVA table 12.12(b) gives a clue. The sample correlation will be a good estimator of the reliability only if it is true that the parallel forms of the test really do measure the same trait on the same scale. To obtain this second ANOVA we have assumed the model:

$$Y_{ij} = \mu + a_i + f_j + e_{ij}$$

where f_j is the difference between the overall mean score μ of all forms of the test over the whole population and the mean of the j-th form used in this study over the whole population, i.e. the main effect of forms (a random effect). The F-ratio corresponding to this effect is highly significant, showing that the mean marks of different forms is *not* the same. In the sample the means for the two forms are 51.2 and 49.5. This suggests that the sample correlation is not appropriate as an estimate of the reliability since its use in that way *assumes* equivalence of parallel forms. In fact the use of the correlation coefficient ignores entirely the variability caused by using different forms. From table 12.12(b) we can re-estimate $s^2 = 14.83$, $s^2 + 2s_b^2 = 406.12$ so that $s_b^2 = 195.64$. This is a new estimate of σ_b^2, which we have already estimated, above, as 187.085. These two estimates for the same quantity, both calculated from the same data, have slightly different values because of the different models assumed for their calculation. The variance in the mean scores of different parallel forms, σ_f^2, can be estimated in a similar way by:

$$s^2 + ks_f^2 = \text{mean square for forms}$$

where k is the number of subjects in the sample. This gives $14.83 + 10s_f^2 = 186.05$, or $s_f^2 = 17.12$. Now, the total variance of any score will be the sum of these three variances:

$$s^2 + s_b^2 + s_f^2 = 14.83 + 195.64 + 17.12 = 227.59$$

Using the definition of reliability that says:

$$rel = \frac{\text{between-subjects variance}}{\text{total variance}} = \frac{195.64}{227.59} = 0.860$$

which is very close to the estimate of 0.854 we obtained previously. However, if the variability due to parallel forms is wrongly assumed to be part of the true scores variance, we would obtain:

$$rel = \frac{195.64 + 17.12}{227.59} = 0.93$$

which is the correlation between the scores on the two forms of the test! Thus the use of the correlation to estimate reliability is likely to cause its overestimation. Furthermore, the ANOVA method extends with no difficulty to the case where several parallel forms have been used. Further discussion of the meaning and dangers of reliability coefficients can be found in Krzanowski & Woods (1984).

12.8 Further comments on ANOVA

In this, already rather long, chapter we have covered only the basic elements of ANOVA models. The possible variety of models is so large, with the details being different for each different data structure or experimental design, that it is neither possible nor appropriate to attempt a complete coverage here. The general principles are always the same and the details for most designs can be found in any of several books. However, there are two special points, of some importance in linguistic research, which need to be mentioned.

12.8.1 Transforming the data

The first point is the possibility of transforming data which do not meet the assumptions required for ANOVA to a different form which do. There are many possibilities, depending on the specific feature of the original data which might cause problems. However, one special case which may arise fairly frequently in applied language studies is data in the form of proportions or percentages, e.g. the proportion of correct insertions in a cloze test with 20 deletions. In this example, a sample of native speakers would be expected to score higher than second language learners. In an 'easy' cloze test native speakers might achieve very high scores, many getting all or almost all items correct, with a few perhaps scoring less well. Such data would lack symmetry and could not be normally distributed. Furthermore, since most of the subjects would then have very similar scores, the sample variance would be small. A sample of second language learners might show much greater spread of ability with a lower mean. In general, with this kind of data, the nearer the mean score is to 50% correct the greater will be the variance, while the symmetry and variance of the sample scores will both decrease as the mean approaches one of the extremes of 0% or 100%. It may not be legitimate in such cases to carry out a t-test or ANOVA to investigate whether there was a significant difference in the average scores of the two groups or to estimate what the difference might be, using the methods of chapter 8.

Provided most of the subjects in the experiment obtained scores in the range 20%–80% (i.e. 4/20 to 16/20) it would probably be acceptable to analyse the raw scores directly. However, if more than one or two scores lie outside this range, in particular if any scores are smaller than 10% correct or greater than 90% correct, it will not be safe to analyse them by the methods of earlier chapters without first transforming them.

The traditional solution to this problem is to change the scores of the individual subjects into scores on a different scale in such a way that the new scores will be normally distributed and have constant variance. This is done via the **arcsine transformation**.[3] Standard computer packages will usually include a simple instruction to enable the data to be transformed in this way. The usual ANOVA or regression analysis can then be carried out on the W-scores instead of the X-scores.

Other transformations are in common use. It may happen that for some variables the variability over a population, or subpopulation, is related

---

[3] The transformed scores (W) can be obtained from the original scores (X) (where these are in percentages) by the formula: $W = \arcsin \sqrt{X/100}$. Most scientific calculators have a function key which gives the value of arcsine, otherwise written $\sin^{-1}$.

Table 12.13. *The structure of a 'within-subject' ANOVA model*

Nationality		Stimulus			
		1	2	3	. . . . .
1	Subject 1	Y_{111}	Y_{121}	.	. . . . .
	Subject 2	Y_{112}	Y_{122}	.	. . . . .
	. . . . .	. .	. .	.	. . . . .
2	Subject 1	Y_{211}	Y_{221}	.	. . . . .
	Subject 2	Y_{212}	Y_{222}	.	. . . . .
	. . . . .	. .	. .	.	. . . . .

to the mean value. For example, if two groups of individuals have markedly different mean vocabulary sizes the group with the higher mean will usually show more variability in the vocabulary sizes of the individuals comprising the group. If the variance of the values in the different groups seems to be roughly proportional to their means then analysing the *logarithms* of the original values will give more reliable results. If, instead, the standard deviations of the groups are proportional to their means, taking the square root will help. (See also §13.12.)

12.8.2 *'Within-subject' ANOVAs*

The second general point we have not discussed but which may be important in linguistic experiments is the situation where subjects are divided into groups and each subject is measured on several variables. For example, we might consider an experiment where 12 subjects of both of two different nationalities are tested for their reaction times to several different stimuli. The data would have the structure shown in table 12.13.

The observation Y_{ijk} will be the reaction time of the k-th subject of the i-th nationality to the j-th stimulus. The comparison of stimuli can be carried out *within* each subject while the comparison of nationalities can only be carried out between sets of subjects. Variation in the reaction times of a single subject on different applications of the same stimulus is likely to be rather less than variation between subjects reacting to the same stimulus. Stimuli can therefore be compared more accurately than nationalities from such a design. (Standard texts on ANOVA often refer to this as a **split-plot** design since it typically occurs when several large agricultural plots (subjects) are treated with different fertilisers (nationalities) and then several varieties of a cereal (stimuli) are grown in each plot.) Data with this kind of structure cannot be analysed using the models we have presented in this chapter – see, e.g., Winer (1971) for details.

Analysis of variance – ANOVA

SUMMARY

Analysis of variance (ANOVA) was introduced and a number of special cases discussed.

(1) **One-way ANOVA** was explained and it was stated that to compare several means simultaneously it would not be correct to carry out pair-wise t-tests.

(2) **Two-way ANOVA** was introduced, especially the **randomised block** design which is an extension to several groups of the paired t-test.

(3) The concept of a **factorial experiment** was explained together with the terms **factor** and **levels of a factor**; the possibility of **interaction** was discussed and it was explained that when significant interaction was present it did not make much sense to base the analysis on the **main effects** alone.

(4) A convenient rule of thumb was presented for examining the differences between the means corresponding to different experimental conditions.

(5) The difference between a **fixed effect** and a **random effect** was discussed.

(6) The **reliability** of tests was discussed and it was shown, via ANOVA, that reliability measures based on correlations could be misleading.

(7) It was pointed out that linguistic data may not be suitable for ANOVA and **transformation** may be necessary.

(8) It was stated that the data from experiments which involved **repeated measures** from individual subjects may need to be analysed as a **within-subjects** or **split-plot** design, though this type of ANOVA was not explained further.

EXERCISES

(1) Table 12.14 represents scores on a language test by three groups of subjects from different centres. Using the method outlined in §12.1, test the hypothesis that there is no difference between the sample means overall. Use the rule of thumb procedure of §12.4 to test for differences between individual means.

(2) The values that follow are error scores (read from left to right) from a replication of the Hughes-Lascaratou study performed by non-native teachers of English who were of mixed nationalities.

Non-native teacher scores

35	10	26	40	30	24	26	31	44	14	33	15	24	34	22	24
30	20	25	40	30	15	24	35	40	25	35	26	33	30	42	10

(a) Construct a new table (see §12.4) by substituting this column of 32 numbers for the Greek teachers' scores in the original.

(b) Construct an ANOVA table for this data (see §12.2 and table 12.5).

(c) Construct a table with the new data comparable to table 12.8, and again compare the difference between observed and fitted values for $Y_{20.2}$ and $Y_{20.1}$.

(d) Do the non-native teachers behave similarly to the Greek teachers?

Table 12.14. *Scores of students from three different centres on the same language test*

A	B	C
11	42	34
10	36	39
12	40	38
10	34	41
10	38	38
10	38	36
9	32	38
11	41	30
9	35	39
7	35	36
11	35	31
4	32	33
10	29	29
8	35	28
8	32	33
8	28	30
8	37	39
7	30	26
7	29	32
8	30	20
8	26	27
7	31	27
7	22	21
7	29	23
4	19	29

(3) Using the methods outlined in 12.5:
  (a) Estimate the following parameters from table 12.6: the overall mean; the mean for Location 1; the mean for the male subgroup from Location 2; the mean for the female subgroup from Location 4.
  (b) Using the residual variance, compare the difference between observed and fitted values for $Y_{1.1}$; $Y_{4.1}$; $Y_{3.2}$.

13
Linear regression

In chapter 9 we proposed the correlation coefficient as a measure of the degree to which two random variables may be linearly related. In the present chapter we will show how information about one variable which is easily measured or well-understood can be exploited to improve our knowledge about a less easily measured or less familiar variable. To introduce the idea of a linear model, which is crucial for this chapter, we will begin with a simple non-linguistic example.

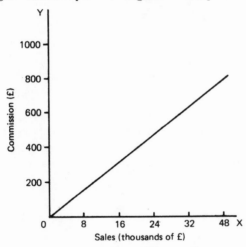

Figure 13.1. Graph of $Y = 0.02X$.

Suppose the manager of a shop is paid entirely on a commission basis and he receives at the end of each month an amount equal to 2% of the total value of sales made in that month. The problem, and the model for its solution, can be expressed mathematically. Let Y be the commission the manager ought to receive for the month just ended. Let X be the total value of the sales in that month. Then:

$$Y = 0.02X \qquad \text{(Remember, } 0.02 = 2\%\text{)}$$

The model can be represented graphically as in figure 13.1 by a straight line passing through the origin of the graph. When the value of X, the month's total sales, is known, then the corresponding value of Y, the commission, can be read off from the graph as shown in the figure. Note that for every £1 increase in X, the commission increases by 2p or £0.02. We would say that the **slope** or **gradient** of the line is 0.02. This tells us simply how much change to expect in the value of Y corresponding to a unit change in X.

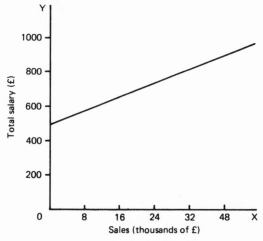

Figure 13.2. Graph of Y = 500 + 0.1X.

Suppose that the shop manager does not like the extreme fluctuations which can take place in his earnings from one month to another and he negotiates a change in the way in which he is paid so that he receives a fixed salary of £500 each month plus a smaller commission of 1% of the value of sales. Can he still find a simple mathematical model to calculate his monthly salary? Clearly he can. With X and Y having the same meanings as before, the formula:

$$Y = 500 + 0.01X$$

will be correct. The corresponding graph is shown in figure 13.2. Again it is a straight line. However, it does not pass through the origin, since even if there are no sales the manager still receives £500; nor does it slope so steeply, since now a unit increase in X corresponds to an increase of only 0.01 in Y. We would say in both cases that there was a **linear relationship** between X and Y, since in both cases the graph takes the form of a straight line. In general, any algebraic relation of the form:

$$Y = \alpha + \beta X$$

225

will have a graph which is a straight line. The quantity β is called the **slope** or **gradient** of the line and α is often referred to as the **intercept** or **intercept on the Y-axis** (figure 13.3). The values α and β remain fixed, irrespective of the values of X and Y.

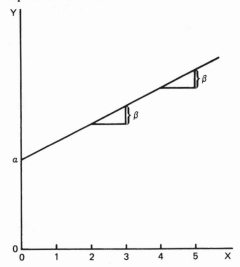

Figure 13.3. Graph of the linear equation $Y = \alpha + \beta X$.

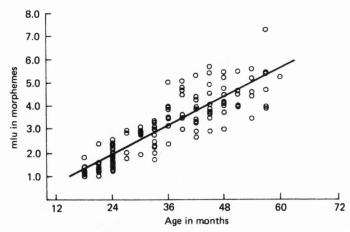

Figure 13.4. Relationship between age (± 1 month) and mean length of utterance (mlu) in morphemes in 123 children: mlu = $-0.548 + 0.103$ (age). Reproduced from Miller & Chapman (1981).

13.1 The simple linear regression model

Is this notion of a linear relationship useful to us in linguistic studies? Consider figure 13.4, which represents data described by Miller

Table 13.1. *Age and mean length of utterance for 12 hypothetical children*

Child	Age in months (X)	mlu (Y)	Predicted mlu ($\hat{Y}$)	Residual
1	24	2.10	1.82	0.28
2	23	2.16	1.73	0.43
3	31	2.25	2.43	−0.18
4	20	1.93	1.47	0.46
5	43	2.64	3.49	−0.85
6	58	5.63	4.80	0.83
7	28	1.96	2.17	−0.21
8	34	2.23	2.70	−0.47
9	53	5.19	4.36	0.83
10	46	3.45	3.75	−0.30
11	49	3.21	4.01	−0.80
12	36	2.84	2.87	−0.03

COV(X,Y) = 13.881
s_X = 12.573 $\bar{X}$ = 37.081
s_Y = 1.243 $\bar{Y}$ = 2.966

& Chapman (1981). They calculated mean length of utterance (mlu) in morphemes for a group of 123 children between 17 months and 5 years of age. In figure 13.4, X, the age of each child, is plotted on the horizontal axis, and Y, the corresponding mlu, on the vertical axis. It is clear that these points do not fit *exactly* on a straight line. It is equally clear that mlu is increasing with age, and that it might be helpful to make some statement such as 'between the ages of a_1 and a_2 mlu increases by about so much for each month'. It will make it simpler to introduce and explain the concepts of the present chapter if we use the same two variables as Miller & Chapman, mlu and age, but with data from a smaller number of children. We have therefore constructed hypothetical data on 12 children and this appears in table 13.1. The values in the table are realistic and commensurate with the real data discussed in Miller & Chapman (1981). The corresponding scattergram appears in figure 13.5. The correlation, r, of mlu with age for the 12 children is 0.8882, obtained as follows:

covariance (mlu, age)　　= 13.881 (see §10.1)
standard deviation of ages = 12.573
standard deviation of mlu =　1.243

Hence r = 13.881 ÷ (1.243 × 12.573) = 0.8882. From table A6, the hypothesis that the true correlation coefficient is zero can be rejected with P < 0.001, i.e. at the 0.1% significance level (cf. §10.3.). We can therefore be quite confident that there is some degree of linear relationship between age and mlu. The next step is to construct a model which will specify that relationship and help us to estimate the expected mlu of a child of a given age who was not observed in our experiment.

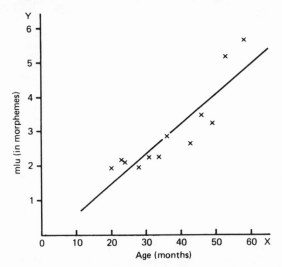

Figure 13.5. Scatter diagram and least squares regression line.
$Y = -0.2897 + 0.0878X$ for the data of table 13.1.

The process begins by defining a model which says that MLU(X), the average mlu of all the children aged X months in the complete target population, will lie on a straight line when plotted against the age, X. Algebraically:

$$MLU(X) = \alpha + \beta X$$

or

$$MLU^1 = \alpha + \beta \times age$$

for some fixed, but as yet unknown, values of the parameters, α and β. The form of the model presupposes that age will be known first and MLU (i.e., mean mlu) calculated afterwards. For this reason we say that age is the **independent variable** and mlu the **dependent variable**. Alternatively, we may call MLU the **predicted variable** and age the **predictor variable**. The next step is to estimate values for α and β using the data. The final stage will be to assess how well the model appears to fit the observed data and the extent to which we can use it to predict the mlu of any child whose age is known.

[1] Note that mlu is the mean length of utterance of a single child while MLU is the average mlu of children of a particular age.

13.2 **Estimating the parameters in a linear regression**

This is entirely a mathematical problem and it is helpful to consider a general formulation of it. We have two variables which we will call X (age) and Y (mlu). We have a number of observations consisting of pairs of values (X$_i$, Y$_i$), a value of X and the corresponding value of Y. We have plotted these points in figure 13.5 and we would now like to draw, on the same graph, the straight line which 'most nearly passes through all the points'. We can attempt to do this 'by eye', which will be subjective and probably inaccurate. Or we can look for an objective method which will ensure that the chosen line is determined automatically by the points we are trying to fit. A mathematician can suggest several ways of doing this, all of which lead to slightly different answers. To choose between the suggestions offered we have to consider the motivation for requiring the model in the first place.

We have implied already that we will want to use the model to estimate the mlu of a child of a given age. This suggests that we require from the mathematician a solution which ensures that the MLUs assigned by the model for the various ages which are represented in our sample will be close to those actually observed. We will adopt the notation that $\hat{Y}_i$ is the MLU predicted by the model corresponding to the age, X$_i$, of the i-th subject while Y$_i$ is the value of the mlu observed for the i-th subject in the sample. The difference:

$$r_i = Y_i - \hat{Y}_i$$

is called the **i-th residual**. If all the residuals were zero, the model line would pass exactly through the observed data points. We would like to achieve this if possible, but in practice it will never occur. In some sense, we could try to make sure that these residuals were as small as possible. However, there will be conflicts. Making the line pass closer to some points will make it move further from others. Again, some of the residuals will be positive, when the line passes below the corresponding point, while others will be negative, when it passes above. Perhaps we can solve the problem by choosing the line for which the algebraic sum of the residuals is zero? Unfortunately, there are many different lines for which this is true. It is rather similar to the problem we encountered when we were looking for a measure of dispersion of sample data about the sample mean in chapter 3 and discovered that the sample deviations always summed to zero. The solution we will adopt here is similar to the one we chose there. We will obtain estimates a and b of α and β, in such a way that the line, $\hat{Y} = a + bX$, will be **the line which minimises $\Sigma(Y_i - \hat{Y}_i)^2$, the**

sum of squared residuals. The resultant line is called the **least squares line of linear regression of Y on X**.[2]

The calculations needed to obtain the a and b are very similar to those required for the calculation of r, the correlation coefficient, which we will usually have carried out anyway with this kind of data. They are:

$$b = \frac{COV(X,Y)}{s_X^2} \text{ and } a = \bar{Y} - b\bar{X}$$

For the data of table 13.1 we have:

$$COV(X,Y) = 13.881, s_X^2 = 158.080, \bar{X} = 37.081, \bar{Y} = 2.966$$

whence

$$b = 0.0878 \qquad a = -0.2897$$

The estimated linear regression is therefore:

$$\hat{Y}_i = -0.2897 + 0.0878\,X_i$$

For example, for the first child in table 13.1 who is aged 24 months, the model predicts an MLU of $\hat{Y}_i = -0.2897 + (0.0878 \times 24) = 1.82$, which should be compared with an observed mlu of 2.10. The residual therefore has a value of $r_1 = Y_1 - \hat{Y}_1 = 0.28$. The full set of fitted values and residuals is given in the final two columns of table 13.1. Note that the sum of the residuals is -0.01, which is effectively zero. The small discrepancy is caused by rounding errors accumulated in the series of calculations needed to produce the residuals.

13.3 The benefits from fitting a linear regression

What do we hope to gain by the use of a simple linear regression such as we have just carried out? The significant correlation tells us that at least part of the variation between the mlus of individuals is due to their different ages, in the sense that MLU tends to increase linearly with age. Fitting the regression line provides us with a tool for taking this

---

[2] Why 'regression'? Yet another instance of confusing terminology. The term was first used by Karl Pearson – cf. Pearson's r. To demonstrate the procedure we are discussing here, Pearson fitted a linear relationship between the heights of sons and the heights of their fathers. Pearson noted that, although there was a good-fitting linear relationship, the sons of small men tended to be taller than their fathers, while the sons of tall men tended to be smaller than their fathers. In other words, in both cases, the sons of fathers of extreme heights, either very small or very tall, would usually be nearer to average height than their fathers had been. Pearson referred to this as 'regression towards the mean'. Although this was a special case unrelated to the general principles of fitting linear relationships the term 'linear regression' was adopted for general use.

into account, as we can demonstrate by pretending that we do not know how old each subject is, though we still know the subject's mlu. We would then be able to say only that, for these 12 subjects, the sample mean mlu was 2.966 morphemes with a standard deviation of 1.243. We might comment further, by calculating a confidence interval (see chapter 7), that 95% of the children in our target population, aged between 15 and 60 months, should have an mlu in the range $2.966 \pm (2.2 \times 1.243)$. (We are assuming here that mlu is normally distributed and are using the sample mean and standard deviation as estimates of the population values.) In other words, we believe 95% of children between 15 and 60 months will have an mlu in the range 0.53–5.40. This information is of little use. In the first place, the interval is too wide to be meaningful. In the second, we know already that expected MLU depends on age and we are not exploiting this knowledge.

It might then have occurred to us to carry out a bigger study, drawing several separate samples of mlus, each provided by subjects of a specified age, say 15 months, 20 months, etc. In this way we might hope to estimate the MLU for each age group and the range into which mlus might be expected to fall for, say, 95% of that age group in the population. We would expect that for each age these 95% confidence intervals would all be narrower than the rather wide one we have just estimated for the whole population when we ignored age differences. This is exactly what fitting a linear regression allows us to do, without the need to carry out different experiments separately for each age group. Of course, it will not be as accurate as carrying out several separate studies, but it will cost a great deal less effort and, under certain assumptions which we make explicit below, it will give results which are almost as good.

Note that the model purports to describe how the average mlu, which we have designated as MLU, alters with age. For example, it predicts that the *average* mlu of *all* children aged 24 months will be 1.82, from the model:

$$MLU = \alpha + (\beta \times age)$$

estimated by $MLU = -0.2897 + 0.0878 \times age$.

Of course, *within* each age group there will still be variation in mlu; individual children of the same age will have different mlus. We will have to assume that this variation can be modelled successfully by a normal distribution with mean MLU(X) and some standard deviation σ. The mean will be different for different age groups, but it will be assumed that the standard deviation is the same for all age groups, as in the ANOVA models for the last chapter. This can be summarised in the model, appropriate to individual subjects:

$$\text{mlu} = \alpha + (\beta \times \text{age}) + e$$

or

$$Y_i = \alpha + \beta X_i + e_i$$

where e is the residual difference between the true value of a subject's mlu and the expected value predicted by the regression line. It will be

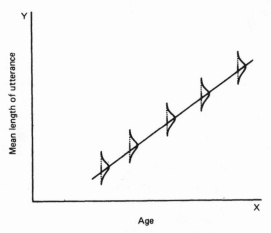

Figure 13.6. A normal distribution of mlus for each age group. All the distributions have the same standard deviation.

assumed that the residual 'error', e, is normally distributed over the population with mean zero and standard deviation σ within a particular age group and that σ has the same value for all age groups. These assumptions are illustrated in figure 13.6.

The last column in table 13.1 gives the observed residuals from the fitted regression line. The sum of these residuals approximates to zero and hence their mean, $\bar{e}$, is also zero. The sample standard deviation of the residuals, s_r, is then estimated:

$$s_r = \sqrt{\frac{\Sigma(e_i - \bar{e})^2}{n - 2}} = \sqrt{\frac{\Sigma e_i^2}{n - 2}} \; (\text{since } \bar{e} = 0) = 0.599$$

This is the familiar formula for the calculation of a sample standard deviation, except that the denominator is $(n - 2)$ instead of the $(n - 1)$ you might have expected. We have used up 2 df in obtaining the two estimates a and b and this leaves only $(n - 2)$ for the residual error. It is common practice to assess the explanatory powers of a regression model in terms of the percentage reduction in the sample *variance* of the dependent variable brought about by fitting the model. The sample variance of the mlus was $1.243^2 = 1.545$. After the model is fitted the residual variance is $0.599^2 = 0.359$. The percentage reduction is:

$$\frac{1.545 - 0.359}{1.545} \times 100 = 76.8\%$$

You may remember that in the previous chapter we suggested that the degree to which two variables might be linearly related could be measured by r^2, the square of the sample correlation coefficient. Here we have $r = 0.8882$ and $r^2 = 0.789 = 78.9\%$, very similar to the percentage reduction in variance. In fact, for larger samples the two values will be virtually identical.

It is not necessary to calculate all the residuals to obtain the value of s_r; it can be calculated more efficiently using the formula:

$$s_r = \sqrt{\frac{n-1}{n-2}\left(s_Y^2 - \frac{\{COV(X,Y)\}^2}{s_X^2}\right)}$$

$$= \sqrt{\frac{11}{10}\left(1.243^2 - \frac{13.881^2}{12.573^2}\right)}$$

$= 0.599$, as before

13.4 Testing the significance of a linear regression

Although a regression line may seem to fit the data points quite well, there is, as always, the possibility that the effect is a property of a particular sample. It may be due simply to a chance selection of a few subjects in which the relation appears to hold, though for the population values as a whole there is no such relationship. We can test the hypothesis $H_0: \beta = 0$ against $H_1: \beta \neq 0$ using the test statistic:

$$t = \frac{bs_X\sqrt{n-1}}{s_r}$$

and compare its value to the critical values of the t-distribution with $(n-2)$ df. Here we have:

$$t = \frac{0.0878 \times 12.573 \times \sqrt{11}}{0.599} = 6.11$$

and this is significant even at the 0.1% level. We can therefore be confident that there is a real gain to be made by fitting the model, a result we had already discovered by considering the correlation coefficient. In fact the test of the null hypothesis H_0: $\beta = 0$ is equivalent to the test of H_0: $\rho = 0$.

We must not forget that the values a and b are estimates of the population values and are therefore subject to sampling error. We have estimated that the slope of the regression line is 0.0878, or, to put it another way, on average we expect a monthly increase of 0.0878 in the MLU of children in the target population. An approximate confidence interval for the true value, β, can be obtained as:

$$b \pm \frac{\text{constant} \times s_r}{\sqrt{(n-1)s_X{}^2}}$$

where the constant is the appropriate critical value from the t-distribution with $(n-2)$ df. Here we have 10 df and the corresponding 95% confidence interval will be:

$$0.0878 \pm \frac{2.23 \times 0.599}{\sqrt{11(12.573)^2}} \quad or \quad 0.0558 \text{ to } 0.1198$$

13.5 Confidence intervals for predicted values

It is important to be clear exactly what we are trying to predict, or estimate, using a regression model. There are two possibilities.

We might wish to estimate the population mean of the mlus for all children of a given age, X – the quantity we have previously designated by MLU(X). This can be done by using the confidence interval:

$$\hat{Y}_X \pm \left\{ \text{constant} \times s_r \times \sqrt{\frac{1}{n} + \frac{(X - \bar{X})^2}{(n-1)s_X{}^2}} \right\}$$

where $\hat{Y}_X$ is the value predicted by the regression equation for age X and the constant is again chosen from the t-tables with $(n-2)$ df. For example, for the MLU of children aged 34 months we would calculate a 95% confidence interval as:

$$2.70 \pm \left\{ 2.23 \times 0.599 \times \sqrt{\frac{1}{12} + \frac{(34 - 37.08)^2}{12.573^2 \times 11}} \right\}$$

or 2.70 ± 0.40

Hence, with 95% confidence, we can estimate that MLU(34) lies between 2.30 and 3.10. The calculation of such confidence intervals is the best way to display how precise, or otherwise, are the estimates. This interval is narrowest when estimating the MLU for children whose age is equal to the average for the sample. Note that both the terms under the square root sign will decrease as the sample size increases.

The second possibility is that we might wish to predict the mlu of an individual child of age X, say 34 months. We should not expect predictions for individuals to be as precise as the estimation of the mean for groups of individuals. The correct formula for a confidence interval for mlu(X), the mlu of an *individual* child of age X, is:

$$\hat{Y}_X \pm \left\{ \text{constant} \times s_r \times \sqrt{1 + \frac{1}{n} + \frac{(X - \bar{X})^2}{(n-1)s_X^2}} \right\}$$

Again the constant is chosen from t-tables with $(n-2)$ df. For $X = 34$ months we have:

$$2.70 \pm \left\{ 2.23 \times 0.599 \times \sqrt{1 + \frac{1}{12} + \frac{(34 - 37.08)^2}{12.573^2 \times 11}} \right\}$$

i.e. 2.70 ± 1.39.

We can interpret this by saying that as a result of our regression study we are 95% confident that a randomly chosen child aged 34 months will have an mlu of between 1.31 and 4.09. Note that in the expression under the square root sign this time there is a term (the first) which *does not* decrease with the sample size.

13.6 Assumptions made when fitting a linear regression

The first assumption is that the value of the independent variable should be known exactly for each element of the sample. In the example this means only that we should be certain of the age of each child. If there is some imprecision in the values of the independent variable, this will cause us to underestimate the slope of the regression line which, in turn, will affect the accuracy of the predicted values of the dependent variable.

Secondly, the distribution of the dependent variable about its mean value, for a *given* value of the independent variable, should be approximately normal. This is equivalent to requiring that the residuals have a normal distribution with mean zero.

Thirdly, the residual variance, or standard deviation, of the dependent variable about the line should be the same at all points of the line. In other words, the **variability** of the dependent variable should not be related to its predicted value. For example, it sometimes happens that the variability of the residuals increases in step with the predicted value. You might notice such an effect if you plot the squared residuals against the predicted values as we have done for the mlu example in figure 13.7, although in this case there is no evidence of any relationship. A special plot of the residual values on **normal probability paper** can give a rough check on the validity of the second assumption. Unfortunately, the special paper is not always readily available and the technique is rather tedious

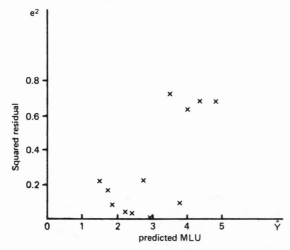

Figure 13.7. Plot of squared residuals against fitted values for the regression of figure 13.5.

so it will not be described here. Some computer packages, such as MINI-TAB (appendix B), will give a normal probability plot as part of the output whenever a regression line is fitted. The points on this plot should lie approximately on a straight line if our second and third assumptions are justified. If you are carrying out important research and use regression as one of your analytical techniques you should consult a statistician about this and other diagnostic tools.

In §10.5, we pointed out that a very few extreme values may have a disproportionate effect on the value of a sample correlation (figure 10.9). Exactly the same will occur with the estimate of the slope of a regression line (see exercise 13.1). As usual, the data should be carefully examined by means of scattergrams to see whether such distortion is a possibility. The program MINITAB draws attention to any individual data points which seem to have an overwhelming influence on the estimation of the regression model.

13.7 **Extrapolating from linear models**

In §13.5 we presented formulae for the calculation of confidence intervals of predicted values. The larger this value is, the less precise will be the predictions. The value of $(X - \bar{X})^2$ is smallest, zero, when the independent variable is equal to $\bar{X}$, the mean of the sample from which we estimated the regression equation. If we try to predict values of the dependent variable corresponding to values of the independent variable

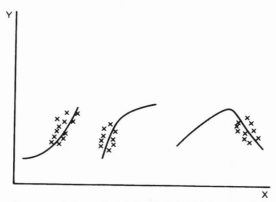

Figure 13.8. Examples of situations in which extrapolation outside the observed data range would be highly misleading.

far from the sample mean, $\bar{X}$, the value of the term $(X - \bar{X})^2$ will become very large and the predictions may be so imprecise as to be worthless. In any case there are special dangers involved in extending the prediction outside the range of values of the independent variable observed in the sample. It may be that the sample coincided with the part of a non-linear graph which can be approximated reasonably well by a straight line: figure 13.8 displays some possible examples. In general it is not wise to extrapolate outside the observed range of the independent variable.

13.8 **Using more than one independent variable: multiple regression**

The simple linear regression model offered an opportunity to increase the precision by which we could make statements about a variable (mlu) by exploiting information about a second variable (age), the variables being observed simultaneously. There is no need to restrict ourselves to just one independent variable. It may very well be possible to improve the prediction of the values of the dependent variable by observing more than one independent variable. We will discuss the possible advantages

Table 13.2. *Hypothetical scores of 30 students on three tests*

Student	Proficiency test (Y)	Cloze (X_1)	Vocabulary (X_2)
1	93	19	29
2	86	16	26
3	69	14	25
4	80	11	25
5	92	19	31
6	53	7	20
7	55	6	19
8	72	13	23
9	79	16	32
10	45	4	15
11	41	7	15
12	51	9	19
13	60	10	16
14	72	11	31
15	42	9	10
16	78	13	28
17	75	15	24
18	70	16	30
19	52	11	16
20	67	14	19
21	45	5	17
22	40	5	16
23	36	4	13
24	49	9	22
25	67	13	21
26	55	8	28
27	36	7	9
28	58	9	20
29	69	14	21
30	58	12	18

of this approach, and the new features that are introduced, by considering a problem involving two independent variables. The extension to a larger number is quite straightforward. Consider the following hypothetical situation.

In the assessment of foreign language learners teachers have available to them several proficiency tests which are often cumbersome and difficult to administer. A teacher with limited time available might prefer to use a simpler test, but only if he could relate the scores on this test to the general proficiency test which has been standardised on a large sample. He has an idea from previous research that a cloze test might be such a predictor. To check on the predictive value of the cloze, he can use the simple linear regression technique above. He also envisages the possibility that another simple test, e.g. of vocabulary, will serve as a predictor of the general proficiency scores. Again the linear regression technique can be used. He chooses 30 students who have recently taken the standard proficiency test, and persuades them to take in addition a cloze test and a simple vocabulary test. The scores of the 30 students in these three tests are given in table 13.2. Figure 13.9 shows the three scattergrams which can be constructed from the data. From the scattergrams it is clear that the scores from both the simpler tests are correlated with the proficiency test score (and that the cloze test scores are somewhat correlated

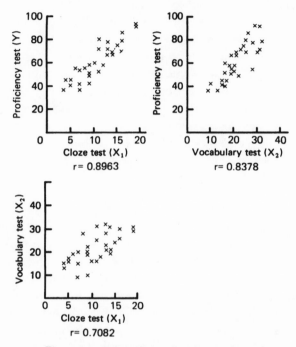

Figure 13.9. Scattergrams of data from table 13.2.

with the vocabulary test scores). However, the cloze test, X_1, has apparently a slightly higher correlation (0.8963) with the proficiency test, Y, than has the vocabulary test, X_2, (0.8378), so that it may be a better predictor of the proficiency test score. Let us begin by fitting the simple linear regression model:

$$Y_i = \alpha + \beta X_{1i} + e_i$$

Using the procedures introduced above, we find the best fitting regression is:

$$\hat{Y} = 24.19 + 3.433 \, X_1$$

with a residual standard deviation, $s_r = 7.372$. The sample mean and standard deviation of the 30 observed cloze scores are $\bar{X}_1 = 10.87$ and $s_1 = 4.26$.

Linear regression

Using the appropriate formula of §13.5 above, he can say that, on the basis of this sample, he is 95% confident that the examination score of a student who scored, say, 8 marks in the cloze test lies in the interval:

$$\hat{Y}(8) \pm \left\{ 2.04 \times s_r \sqrt{1 + \frac{1}{30} + \frac{(8 - 10.87)^2}{29 \times 4.26^2}} \right\}$$

or 51.65 ± 15.40, i.e. between 36 and 67 marks.

This interval is too wide to be useful. It could be reduced by increasing the sample size, but the first term inside the square root sign will always have the same value and eventually the only way to narrow the interval will be to reduce s_r. But this can be done only by fitting a better predicting model. How much more precise might be the prediction if we could take account of the student's vocabulary test score at the same time as his cloze test score? To answer this question we need to extend the regression model to include, as independent variables, the scores on both the cloze test and the vocabulary test. The most obvious way to do this is to add an extra term to the previous model and write:

$$Y_i = \alpha + \beta_1 X_{1i} + \beta_2 X_{2i} + e_i$$

which says that the proficiency examination score of the i-th student in the sample is arrived at as the sum of four terms, a constant, a multiple of his score (X_{1i}) on the cloze test, a multiple of his score (X_{2i}) on the vocabulary test and a random error (e_i) involved in arriving at his proficiency score. There are now three model parameters to estimate: α, β_1 and β_2 (whose estimates we designate by a, b_1, b_2). With more than one independent variable, it is rather tedious to carry out the calculations by hand and we will present the results obtained using the program MINI-TAB.

We find that the least squares regression estimate of the model gives:

$$a = 13.708 \quad b_1 = 2.329 \quad b_2 = 1.057$$

$$\text{i.e. } \hat{Y} = 13.708 + 2.329 \, X_1 + 1.057 \, X_2$$

The residual standard deviation is now $s_r = 5.715$, which should be compared with a value of 7.372 when the model containing only the cloze test score was fitted. As might be expected, including the extra term in the model has allowed it to explain more of the variability in the proficiency scores, thus reducing the level of residual variation left unexplained by the model. In fact, the percentage reduction in the variance of the proficiency scores has been increased from 80% (using cloze test only) to 88% (using the vocabulary test as well).

Table 13.3. *95% confidence intervals for prediction of proficiency test scores of individual students*

Cloze test score (X_1)	Vocabulary test score (X_2)	Independent variables used		
		X_1 alone	X_2 alone	X_1 and X_2
5	15	26–57	29–67	29–54
5	20	26–57	40–78	34–59
5	25	26–57	51–89	39–65
10	15	44–74	29–67	41–65
10	20	44–74	40–78	46–70
10	25	44–74	51–89	51–75
15	15	61–91	29–67	51–77
15	20	61–91	40–78	57–82
15	25	61–91	51–89	63–87

Table 13.3 shows the 95% confidence intervals for the predicted scores of a student who obtains various (arbitrarily chosen) scores in the cloze test and the vocabulary test. It can be seen that the intervals calculated from the model that uses the scores from both preliminary tests are always narrower (i.e. more precise) than those obtained using just one of the scores. They are still rather too wide to be very useful. Can they be made even more precise? There are many possible reasons why the scores in the proficiency test are not predicted very precisely, even using two independent variables, but there are three which have particular importance. First, the model may not be correct. Suppose we write $\hat{Y}(X_1, X_2)$ to mean the average score in the proficiency test of all the students in the population who would score X_1 marks in the cloze test and X_2 marks in the vocabulary test. Then the multiple regression model implies that this average can be calculated exactly by the formula:

$$\hat{Y}(X_1, X_2) = \alpha + \beta_1 X_1 + \beta_2 X_2$$

If this is not true for some values of the independent variables, the predicted proficiency scores for students with those values of X_1 and X_2 will be biassed. This 'lack of fit' will also inflate the value of the residual standard deviation and hence widen all the confidence intervals. The model might be improved by the inclusion of more independent variables but the more complex it becomes, the harder it is to interpret and the more information is needed before it can be used for calculating predicted values. We discuss this possibility further in the following section.

Second, even if the model is correct, so that the *mean* proficiency score is well predicted for given values of the two independent variables, there may still be considerable variation between individual proficiency test scores of students who all have the same scores on the cloze and vocabulary tests; in other words the residual variation may be large. Again the effect of this will be to inflate the residual standard deviation leading to imprecise prediction of proficiency scores for individuals. In this case, too, it may be possible to make improvements by adding another independent variable, if one can be discovered which explains a significant proportion of the residual variance left unexplained by the first two.

The third possibility is that, even if the model is adequate, the sample size is not sufficient to give precise estimates of the parameters. The important quantity here is the number of degrees of freedom available for the estimation of the residual standard deviation, which is obtained by subtracting from the total sample size the number of parameters which have been estimated in the model. In our example, the residual degrees of freedom are $30 - 3 = 27$, which ought to be quite sufficient. Increasing the sample size will always improve the precision of the parameter estimates but the scope for improvement will be limited if either of the first two sources of variability is present.

13.9 Deciding on the number of independent variables

In the example discussed in the previous section there were two possible independent variables which could be used to predict the value of a dependent variable. If we decide to use only one of them, we should clearly use that one which has a higher correlation with the de-

Table 13.4. *ANOVA for the regression analysis of the data of table 13.2*

(a) ANOVA for the model $\hat{Y} = \alpha + \beta_1 X_1$				
Source	df	SS	MSS	F-ratio
Regression	1	6217.87	6217.87	114.4
Residual	28	1521.63	54.34	
Total	29	7739.50		

(b) ANOVA for the model $\hat{Y} = \alpha + \beta_1 X_1 + \beta_2 X_2$				
Source	df	SS	MSS	F-ratio
Regression	2	6857.56	3428.78	105.0
Residual	27	881.94	32.66	
Total	29	7739.50		

SS explained by each variable in order given:			
Source	df	SS	
Regression	2	6857.56	
X_1	1	6217.87	
X_2	1	639.68	

pendent variable, since that ensures that the residual variance will be as small as possible. Although adding in the second will cause some further reduction in the residual variance, it will also complicate the model and it is advisable to increase the complexity of the model in this way only if the extra reduction is statistically significant. In other words, we would like to test whether the second independent variable can explain a significant amount of the variance left unaccounted for by the simple regression model involving only the first variable.

This can be done by exploiting a mathematical link between linear regression and analysis of variance. It is perfectly possible to produce an ANOVA table as part of a regression analysis. We will not explain here how the calculations are carried out, but the principle is important and we will use the ANOVA tables produced by MINITAB as part of the regression analysis of the test scores of the 30 students. In table 13.4(a) is the ANOVA corresponding to the regression of proficiency test scores on the single independent variable, cloze test score. The effect of the regression is highly significant ($F_{1,28} = 114.4$).[3]

The ANOVA for the multiple regression model containing the cloze and vocabulary test scores as independent variables appears in table 13.4(b). It is in two parts. The first simply shows that the multiple regression accounts for a significant proportion of the variance ($F_{2,27} = 105.0$). This is not surprising, since we already know that just one independent variable causes a significant effect. The second part of the ANOVA allows us to test whether the *additional* effect of adding in the second independent variable is significant. The *extra* reduction in the residual sum of squares (639.68) due to adding in X_2 is tested for significance by dividing it by the residual mean square (32.66). The result, $639.68 \div 32.66 = 19.6$, should be compared with critical values of $F_{1,27}$ and is highly significant. We conclude that it is worthwhile to include both X_1 and X_2 in the model.

This whole procedure generalises easily to more than two independent variables. The only new feature is that it will not usually be obvious what is the best order in which to introduce additional independent variables into the regression equation. Many computer packages will include an option for **stepwise regression** in which the 'best' regression model (i.e. the model which leaves the smallest residual variance after it is fitted) with just one independent variable is calculated, then the best model with

---

[3] If we test the significance of the regression using the test suggested in §13.4, we get $t = 10.7 = \sqrt{114.4}$. This relationship between the t-distribution with k degrees of freedom and the F-distribution with (1,k) degrees of freedom holds generally, and ensures that the test of hypothesis $H_0: \beta = 0$ will give the same result whichever test statistic is used.

just two variables, and so on, until the addition of further variables does not cause a significant improvement. If there are many possible independent variables, the simple variable which gives the best fitting model will not necessarily appear as one of the independent variables in the best two-variable model. It is also possible to carry out stepwise regression by first including all the possible independent variables and deleting them one at a time. You should consult a statistician if you are considering fitting models in this way.

13.10   The correlation matrix and partial correlation

The value of adding in a second independent variable, X_2, to a regression model containing one independent variable, X_1, depends on how much information about the dependent variable, Y, is contained in X_2 *which was not already contained in X_1*. This, in turn, depends largely on the correlation between X_1 and X_2. If they are highly correlated, most of the information contained in one of them will also be contained in the other. Because of the importance of these correlations it is usual to present them in special tabular form called the **correlation matrix**. For the example introduced in §13.8, this is the sample correlation matrix:

	Y	X_1	X_2
Y	1		
X_1	0.8963	1	
X_2	0.8378	0.7082	1

Here the number in any position is the correlation between the variables which are used as labels for the corresponding row and column. All the values in the main diagonal are exactly equal to 1, since they represent the correlations between each variable and itself. The values above this diagonal are frequently left out since they already appear in the lower triangle. For example, the value left off in the upper right-hand corner is 0.8378, since $r(Y,X_2) = r(X_2,Y)$.

The two 'independent' variables X_1 and X_2 have a correlation of 0.7082, which means that they are certainly not independent of one another. To some extent the information contained about the dependent variable in either one of them will be duplicated by the other. It would be useful to have a measure of how much one of these variables is correlated with the dependent variable *even after allowing for the information provided by the other*. Such a measure is the **partial correlation coefficient**. We will use the notation $r(Y,X_2 \mid X_1)$ to mean the correlation of X_2 with Y after the information contained in X_1 has been taken into account. Technically, it is said that $r(Y,X_2 | X_1)$ is the correlation between Y and X_2 with X_1 **partialled out**. It is calculated from the formula:

$$r(Y,X_2 | X_1) = \frac{r(Y,X_1)r(X_2,X_1)}{\sqrt{\{1 - r^2(Y,X_1)\} \{1 - r^2(X_2,X_1)\}}}$$

$$= \frac{0.8378 - 0.8963 \times 0.7082}{\sqrt{(1 - 0.8963^2) (1 - 0.7082^2)}}$$

$$= 0.6485$$

To some extent it is possible to interpret **partial correlation** coefficients in a similar way to ordinary correlation coefficients. In particular, $0.6485^2 = 0.42 = 42\%$, and we can say that adding X_2 into the regression model *after X_1* will account for 42% of the residual variance still remaining after X_1 has been fitted in the simple regression model (see exercise 13.3). The concept of partial regression can be particularly useful when investigating the relationship between two variables, both of which are affected by a third variable in which we may not be particularly interested.

13.11   **Linearising relationships by transforming the data**

Sometimes mathematical transformations are used to make the data fit better to simple models. Figure 13.10 shows a hypothetical relationship between two variables X and Y. The curve drawn through the points

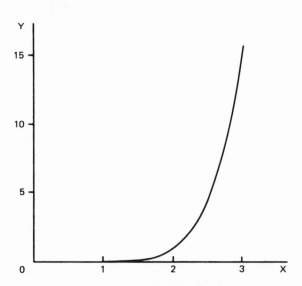

Figure 13.10. Graph of the relationship $Y = 0.1X^{6.7}$.

is clearly not a straight line. It is similar in shape to curves which can be expressed by an equation of the form:

$$Y = AX^b$$

where A and B are constants or parameters. Now, instead of Y consider its logarithm, log Y:

$$\log Y = \log (AX^b)$$
$$= \log A + b \log X$$

(If you do not understand the algebra then clearly you ought to consult a statistician before attempting this procedure.) If we write $W = \log Y$, $Z = \log X$ and $a = \log A$ the equation can be written:

$$W = a + bZ$$

which is exactly the form of the simple linear regression model introduced early in the chapter. Figure 13.11 shows a scatter diagram of W (log Y) against Z (log X) and indicates a much more linear relationship than was apparent in the previous figure. A linear regression could then be fitted safely to the logarithms of the original scores.

Although there are many situations in which data can be transformed to new values which are more suitable (in a technical sense) for statistical analysis, a major disadvantage of this process is that the interpretation of the analysis in terms of the original problem will be more difficult. The results obtained will be in terms of the transformed values, while

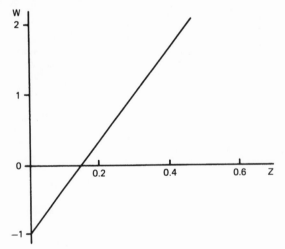

Figure 13.11. Graph of the relation $W = a + bZ$, where $W = \log Y$, $Z = \log X$, $a = \log(0.1)$, $b = 6.7$.

it is likely that the interest of the experimenter will remain with the raw data in the original units. We cannot pursue this further here, but whenever you are advised to transform data it is best to make sure – before going to the trouble of carrying out the analysis – that it will be possible to interpret the results in the way that you require.

13.12 Generalised linear models

We have discussed the traditional transformations of non-normal data in the previous section, and the majority of extant textbooks dealing with ANOVA or regression will state that this is the only option for coping with such data. However, in recent years statisticians have developed tools for analysing directly many types of data without any need for them to be normally distributed. Indeed, these same tools can cope with data which are non-standard in other ways. For example, ANOVA can be carried out even when there are different numbers of subjects in each of the experimental groups, whereas traditional methods allow this only for one-way ANOVA. These new methods fall under the general heading of **generalised linear models** (GLMs). They require specialised computer packages – e.g. GLIM (generalised linear interactive modelling), elaborated at the Rothamsted Experimental Station in England, or the GLM option of SAS, the statistical analysis package usually available on large IBM computers – which may not be widely available. Furthermore, some professional statisticians are not yet familiar with GLMs and their analysis. However, there is no doubt that GLMs will become more widely used in the social sciences, and a recent book by Gilbert (1984) provides an accessible introduction to their applications.

SUMMARY

This chapter dealt with **linear regression models** and how to fit them.

(1) The algebraic equation for a straight line was introduced as $Y = a + bX$ where the parameters a and b were the **intercept** and **slope** respectively. Y was called the **dependent** or **predicted** variable and X the **independent** or **predictor** variable.

(2) The **residuals** were defined as the difference between the observed and predicted values of the dependent variable. The **least squares regression line** was calculated by $b = COV(X,Y)/s^2$ and $a = \bar{Y} - b\bar{X}$.

(3) The **residual standard deviation**, s_r, was calculated by:

$$s_r = \sqrt{\frac{n-1}{n-2}\left(s_Y^2 - \frac{\{COV(X,Y)\}^2}{s_X^2}\right)}$$

Linear regression

(4) The hypothesis H_0: $\beta = 0$ (β being the 'true' slope of the line) *versus* H_1: $\beta \neq 0$ was tested by using the test statistic, $t = bs_X\sqrt{n-1}/s_r$, referring this to tables of the t-distribution with $(n-1)$ degrees of freedom.

(5) Formulae (§13.5) were given for calculating **confidence intervals for predicted values**.

(6) It was shown how to extend the model to incorporate several predictor variables in a **multiple linear regression**.

(7) The concept of **partial correlation** was explained and discussed.

(8) It was noted that when a relationship is apparent between two variables which clearly cannot be represented by a straight line it may be possible to **transform** one or both variables so that the relation between the transformed variables is linear.

(9) It was pointed out that the use of **generalised linear models** allows ANOVA or regression analysis of many sets of data which do not meet the assumptions for the traditional analyses.

EXERCISES

(1) Amend table 13.1 by including these two extra observations:

	Age	mlu
13	24	5.72
14	56	1.90

(a) Recalculate the linear regression for the extended table.

(b) Calculate fitted values and residuals for the new scores.

(c) Test the significance of the new linear regression.

(d) Calculate a 95% confidence interval for the new MLU for children aged 30 months.

(e) Calculate the new 95% confidence interval for a child of 34 months.

(f) Compare all your calculations (a)–(e) with the values derived from the original table.

(2) Using the relevant data of table 13.2, calculate the linear regression for predicting proficiency test score from the vocabulary test score. verify a selection of the confidence intervals in the 'X_2 alone' column of table 13.3.

(3) (a) Calculate $r(Y,X_1 \mid X_2)$, the correlation of Y and X_1 with X_2 partialled out.

(b) Estimate how much of the variability in Y which is not explained by X_2 will then be accounted for by taking X_1 into consideration as well.

(c) (Harder!) Show that the *total* percentage of the variability in Y which is accounted for by X_1 and X_2 together will be the same whether X_1 is fitted first and X_2 afterwards or vice versa.

14
Searching for groups and clusters

To this point in the book the methods introduced and discussed have been appropriate to the presentation and analysis of data consisting of a single variable observed on each of several sample units or subjects. We have discussed situations which involved several experimental conditions, or factors, in the ANOVA chapter, but the data itself consisted of observations of the same variable under each of the experimental conditions. It is true that in chapter 13 examples were introduced where several variables were measured for each subject, but one of these variables was given a special status (the dependent variable) and the others (the independent variables) were used to assist in its analysis via multiple regression.

A rather different situation arises when several variables are observed on each sample unit or subject and we wish to present the data or to extract the information in the complete set of variables without giving *a priori* a special status to any of them. An example of this, which we shall develop in the next chapter, would be the set of scores of a number of subjects on a series of foreign language tests, with no reason for the scores on any one test to be regarded differently from the scores on the remainder of the tests. It is in such cases that **multivariate** statistical analysis is appropriate. Before looking at any technique in particular it may be helpful to make some general remarks about multivariate analysis.

14.1 Multivariate analysis

Multivariate analysis is a term used to cover a considerable variety of techniques for the description, simplification, synopsis and analysis of data sets consisting of several different variables all measured on the same sampling units or subjects. The notation of §13.8 is adapted easily for multivariate data sets by writing X_{ij} for the value or score of the j-th variable observed for the i-th individual. Suppose that we have a total of p different variables all observed on a sample of n individuals. The data can then be written as a matrix:

$$
\begin{matrix}
X_{11} & X_{12} & X_{13} & . & . & . & . & X_{1p} \\
X_{21} & X_{22} & X_{23} & . & . & . & . & X_{2p} \\
X_{31} & X_{32} & X_{33} & . & . & . & . & X_{3p} \\
. & . & . & . & . & . & . & . \\
. & . & . & . & . & . & . & . \\
. & . & . & . & . & . & . & . \\
. & . & . & . & . & . & . & . \\
X_{n1} & X_{n2} & X_{n3} & . & . & . & . & X_{np}
\end{matrix}
$$

The **vector** $(X_{il}, X_{i2}, X_{i3}, \ldots, X_{ip})$ is often called the **i-th observation** or the **observation on the i-th individual**.

Most multivariate methods require extensive calculations and will often be operated on large quantities of data. For these reasons multivariate analysis will usually require a large and powerful computer equipped with special software packages. In this chapter and the next we will consider in detail only a few of the techniques which are, or could be, used in language studies. We will not attempt to describe how any of the calculations are carried out but will restrict the discussion to the motivation and meaning of each technique. Most multivariate methods are *descriptive*; they are used to provide succint means of presenting large volumes of complex data. Few multivariate methods have been developed for fitting models or making precise inferences. Hypothesis testing is relatively rare with multivariate data, partly because the theory is difficult to develop and partly because it is rather hard to believe that a complex set of variables will meet the underlying assumptions required for those tests which have been developed.

Early in this book, in chapter 2, a distinction was made between two different types of data: the categorical, for which each observation was a type, e.g. male or female, and the numerical, for which each observation was a numerical value, e.g. a test score. The same distinction carries over to the multivariate case and the two types of data will often need different treatment. Suppose, for example, that an experiment is carried out to see whether school children with different linguistic backgrounds use English colour words differently. Different languages divide up the colour spectrum in different ways; closely related languages like English and Welsh, or English and French, may have minor differences, while the differences between English and Urdu may be extensive. For children who have already become used, in their home background, to a particular mode of labelling familiar items by colour, the learning of a new set of colour terms which may divide the colour spectrum differently can initially present problems. One way to carry out such an experiment would be to present, say, 12 objects of similar size and shape but of different colours to a number of children from each of several different language backgrounds, and ask every child to name the colour of each object. The resultant observations will consist of a list of 12 colour words for each subject. How can we decide whether, say, children who learned Welsh as a first language tend to use different colour names from those who are English monolinguals? Or if children whose first language is Urdu are different from both groups in the labels they apply? If all the children, irrespective of their first language, use the same 12 colour names to describe the objects, again there is no problem. Of course, it is most unlikely that this will happen. Some Welsh will probably use a set of names which, for at least some objects, agrees with the names used by some English children. On the other hand, there will be variation within the two groups. The question to be considered is whether children of one group seem to make choices which agree more within that group than with the choices made by children from another group.

The problem is to decide what is meant here by 'agree more'. There is no obvious way to give a single score to each child and then compare variability in scores within and between groups (perhaps using ANOVA). There is no 'correct' name for the colour of each object with which we can compare the names given by the individual children. On the other hand, it is not difficult to think of a measure of the extent to which any two children are in agreement. One obvious possibility is to look at the names given by one child and compare these, object by object, with the names given by the other. The number of times that the two children use the same name for the same object could be used as a measure of the extent to which they use colour names in the same way.

It is, in fact, more usual to measure how *dissimilar* the subjects are, and the total number of mismatches would give a measure of that. One problem that frequently arises with this kind of experiment is that some subjects give no colour name, or give an unintelligible response, for one (or more) of the objects. We might then decide to discount the corresponding object when comparing this subject with others. This will tend to reduce, artificially, the number of mismatches. To exaggerate: a subject with no responses could be found to have no mismatches with anybody! Of course, such a subject should be discarded; it is usual to discard subjects with more than a very few missing or unintelligible responses. To cope with the problem of missing values of this type the dissimilarity or **distance** between two subjects would commonly be calculated as the **proportion of mismatches** among the objects for which both subjects give an intelli-

Table 14.1. *Colour names given by three subjects to twelve objects*

						Object							
		1	2	3	4	5	6	7	8	9	10	11	12
Subject	1	C	D	G	H	E	L	J	A	B	F	I	K
	2	C	D	I	H	E	J	K	A	B	F	G	L
	3	C	D	I	L	E	—	J	A	B	G	—	K

Note: Each of the letters represents a different colour name, while a dash stands for a missing response.

Table 14.2. *Dissimilarity matrix of three subjects calculated from their colour descriptions of 12 objects*

	Subject		
	1	2	3
1	0		
2	0.417	0	
3	0.300	0.400	0

$$0.417 = \frac{5}{12}; \ 0.300 = \frac{3}{10}; \ 0.400 = \frac{4}{10}$$

gible response. This type of distance measure is often called a **matching coefficient**. It may be felt that a child's inability to find a colour name for a particular object is important and should be included as part of the assessment of the (dis)similarity between two subjects. In that case a missing value could be treated as the 'colour name' BLANK for the corresponding object and the subjects always compared on their responses (including BLANKs) on the full set of objects. The proportion of mismatched responses would still make a sensible measure of the 'distance' between two subjects.

14.2 The dissimilarity matrix

When all the distances, or dissimilarities, have been calculated for every pair of subjects in a sample they can be presented in the form of a matrix known as the **dissimilarity matrix**. In table 14.1 we have given the responses from three hypothetical subjects presented with 12 different colour stimuli. Note that there are a few missing responses. Table 14.2 gives the corresponding dissimilarity matrix. Only the bottom half of the matrix is given: the missing half can be filled in by symmetry since the dissimilarity between subject i and subject j must be the same as the dissimilarity between subject j and subject i. The main diagonal consists

Table 14.3. *Correlation matrix of ten subjects calculated from their scores on eight tests*

| Subject | Subject | | | | | | | | | |
	1	2	3	4	5	6	7	8	9	10
1	1.000									
2	0.384	1.000								
3	0.729	0.571	1.000							
4	0.088	0.381	0.265	1.000						
5	0.543	0.773	0.510	0.121	1.000					
6	0.409	0.682	0.635	0.358	0.526	1.000				
7	0.239	0.297	0.187	0.211	0.345	0.371	1.000			
8	0.709	0.538	0.700	0.122	0.596	0.468	0.384	1.000		
9	0.714	0.693	0.859	0.356	0.627	0.729	0.416	0.705	1.000	
10	0.639	0.663	0.724	0.415	0.630	0.641	0.249	0.526	0.867	1.000

of zeros, since there can be no mismatches between a subject and himself. These two properties, symmetry and zeros on the main diagonal, are characteristic of a dissimilarity matrix.

Although we introduced the idea of dissimilarity as a means of comparing subjects scored on categorical variables, it is perfectly possible to construct a dissimilarity matrix from numerical variables. For example, suppose that ten students have each taken eight tests. A possible measure of similarity in the pattern of performance of two students across the tests is the correlation, r, between their sets of eight scores. Now, two students with exactly the same scores would have a correlation of 1. If we then choose as a measure of **dissimilarity** $1 - r^2$ (not an uncommon choice), two students scoring exactly the same marks would be found to have zero dissimilarity. Table 14.3 gives the correlation coefficients for pairs of students and table 14.4 gives the corresponding dissimilarity matrix.

Table 14.4. *Matrix of dissimilarities of ten subjects calculated as $(1 - correlation^2)$*

Subject	1	2	3	4	5	6	7	8	9	10
1	0									
2	0.853	0								
3	0.469	0.674	0							
4	0.992	0.855	0.930	0						
5	0.705	0.402	0.740	0.985	0					
6	0.833	0.535	0.597	0.872	0.723	0				
7	0.943	0.912	0.965	0.955	0.881	0.862	0			
8	0.497	0.711	0.510	0.985	0.645	0.781	0.853	0		
9	0.490	0.520	0.262	0.873	0.607	0.469	0.827	0.503	0	
10	0.592	0.560	0.476	0.828	0.603	0.589	0.938	0.723	0.248	0

Looking at the correlation matrix we find that the highest correlation of all is 0.867, between subjects 9 and 10, and we could say that these seem to be the pair that are most alike. Subjects 9 and 3 have a very similar correlation (0.859) and could be linked together. Since subject 9 is linked to both 3 and 10 we could say that these three subjects form a **cluster**. If we require that a correlation be at least, say, 0.80 before a link is formed this would be the only cluster of subjects to be discovered using correlations in this way. If the 'alikeness' criterion is relaxed to allow correlation values down to 0.75 we find that subjects 2 and 5 are linked, so that we now have two clusters of subjects, (3, 9, 10) and (2, 5). If we link all those with correlations down to 0.70, the former group grows to include subjects 1 (linked with 9 and 3), 8 (linked with 3 and 1), while the latter cluster remains with just the same two subjects. By gradually allowing weaker and weaker linkage (smaller correlations) we will eventually arrive at a point where all the subjects form a single cluster (exercise 1). Clearly, instead of using a similarity criterion, linking subjects with the greatest similarity, we could use a dissimilarity criterion, linking subjects with the smallest dissimilarity (exercise 2).

If, in the last example, instead of $1 - r^2$ we used $\sqrt{(1 - r^2)}$, this would still be a sensible measure of dissimilarity. In general, for any set of data it is possible to imagine many different measures of 'distance' which would lead to different similarity matrices. We will return to this point later in the chapter. Note, in passing, that it will not always be the clustering of the *subjects* which is the endpoint of a cluster analysis. It will frequently be the case that interest centres on the different *variables* on which the subjects were scored. If that were the case here we could obtain a measure of the similarity between any two tests by calculating the correlation of the scores on those tests over the ten subjects.

Now that we have a measure of how dissimilar each individual is from all the others in the sample, it ought to be possible to explore questions such as whether Welsh children are less dissimilar to one another, in the main, in their choice of colour names than they are to children of other language backgrounds. There are many ways to continue using the dissimilarity matrix as a starting point. We will describe two widely used techniques: hierarchical cluster analysis and multidimensional scaling.

14.3   Hierarchical cluster analysis

It is difficult to give a good description of this technique in the abstract. We will therefore introduce it via the discussion of a recently published example of its use.

Baker & Derwing (1982), in a study of the acquisition of English plural inflections by 120 children from 2 to 7 years, have developed an analytical technique based on hierarchical cluster analysis to investigate the manner in which the rule system for these inflections is acquired. The data for their study comes from Innes (1974), who employed an improved version of Berko's (1958) technique for eliciting plurals from young children. This technique employs pictures of real or invented objects, with monosyllabic names, which the child is asked to identify. So, for example, the eliciting utterances by the experimenter might be (using Berko's most famous nonsense word) 'Here is a picture of a *wug*. Now there are two of them. There are two ———.' The child's responses constitute the data for analysis. The focus of such studies is the child's acquisition of a *rule* of pluralisation. There are three regular allomorphs of plural in English, and their application is conditioned by features of the final consonant or vowel of the noun to which they are attached. The three forms are /z/, /s/ and /ɪz/. /z/ is the form used after vowels and voiced consonants except /dʒ/, /z/; /s/ appears after voiceless consonants except /t/, /s/; and /ɪz/ is the form used after stems ending in /t/, /dʒ/, /s/, /z/. There are, of course, exceptions to this rule in English – there are various irregular nouns like *foot* or *sheep* which behave differently. But the vast majority of nouns in the language, and any new nouns added, conform to this pluralising rule. In the context of linguistically based approaches to acquisition, a question of interest is how children develop this rule. At what point are they able to treat any new noun appropriately by adding the inflection appropriate to the stem-final item, and what are the stages by which they proceed to this knowledge?

As Baker & Derwing (1982) point out, this is not an easy question to answer from a cross-sectional developmental study. An analysis is required such that stages, or developmental patterns, emerge from the data. The stages of development ought to be identified as a consequence of the analysis. However, the analytical methods adopted with data of this kind have tended to obscure subject-determined patterns of response by using percentage correct scores (generally, the number of children responding correctly to a given item), and then age-blocking the data to try to discern developmental trends. This has the effect of tying the children's performance to adult norms, and of equating 'stage' with 'age'. As Derwing & Baker suggest, it may be that a given data set ought to be arranged by age groups, but this is something that should emerge from the data rather than be imposed on it in advance. A further problem is that the interpretation of group percentage correct scores by age as the basis for the inference of rules in individual children can be quite misleading. Suppose, for example that, in response to a group of final stems requiring /z/ plurals, the pattern emerged as shown in the following table.

Stem-final	Child				
	A	B	C	D	E
Vowel	√	×	×	×	×
l	×	√	×	×	×
b	×	×	√	×	×
d	×	×	×	√	×
g	×	×	×	×	√

We can see that each child has a 20% success rate on /z/-pluralised items, and that if these five stem-finals are the only ones included in the experiment, then the percentage correct rate for children of this age on voiced stem-finals is 20%. Each child, however, contributes to this result quite differently. Baker & Derwing utilise hierarchical clustering to overcome the problems of age-blocking and percentage correct as a measure, and to search out, in the data, groups of children who are treating similar subsets of stem-final segments as classes.

Baker & Derwing had available data consisting of the responses of 94 children to 24 stimuli. Their first problem was to construct a measure of the dissimilarity between each pair of subjects based on the observed responses. Since they wished to leave aside the question of 'correct' or 'incorrect' responses (compared with adult norms) they began by constructing for each child a matrix showing the relationship between the child's responses to the different stimuli. A typical one of these matrices is reproduced here as table 14.5 (Baker & Derwing 1982: fig 1). The 24 stimuli and the child's responses are written across the top and at the left of the table. Wherever two stimuli elicited the same response, that response was entered in the corresponding cell of the matrix, otherwise the entry was zero. (An irrelevant response was marked *Irr*.) Once the 94 'response coincidence' matrices had been constructed (each matrix contains 276 entries) the dissimilarity between each pair of children was then calculated as the proportion of the 276 entries in the coincidence matrices of the two children which were *not* the same. The resulting dissimilarity matrix, made up of the dissimilarities between each pair of children, was then used as input to a standard computer package known as CLUSTAN (see Wishart 1978). Part of the output is shown in figure 14.1 (Baker & Derwing: fig. 2). This graph (often called a **dendrogram**) has subject numbers along the horizontal axis and values of the dissimilarity on the

Table 14.5. *A 'response coincidence' matrix*

Stimulus	Response	/c/ Nul	/ŋ/ /z/	/b/ /z/	/ð/ /z/	/l/ /z/	/v/ /z/	/n/ /z/	/u/ /z/	/d/ /z/	/i/ /z/	/m/ /z/	/r/ /z/	/g/ /z/	/f/ /s/	/p/ Irr	/k/ Nul	/θ/ /s/	/t/ /s/	/s/ Nul	/ʃ/ /ɪz/	/ǰ/ /ɪz/	/č/ /ɪz/	/ž/ Nul	/z/ Nul
/c/	Nul	—																							
/ŋ/	/z/	o	—																						
/b/	/z/	o	z	—																					
/ð/	/z/	o	z	z	—																				
/l/	/z/	o	z	z	z	—																			
/v/	/z/	o	z	z	z	z	—																		
/n/	/z/	o	z	z	z	z	z	—																	
/u/	/z/	o	z	z	z	z	z	z	—																
/d/	/z/	o	z	z	z	z	z	z	z	—															
/i/	/z/	o	z	z	z	z	z	z	z	z	—														
/m/	/z/	o	z	z	z	z	z	z	z	z	z	—													
/r/	/z/	o	z	z	z	z	z	z	z	z	z	z	—												
/g/	/z/	o	o	o	o	o	o	o	o	o	o	o	o	—											
/f/	/s/	o	o	o	o	o	o	o	o	o	o	o	o	o	—										
/p/	Irr	o	o	o	o	o	o	o	o	o	o	o	o	o	o	—									
/k/	Nul	Nul	o	o	o	o	o	o	o	o	o	o	o	o	o	o	—								
/θ/	/s/	o	o	o	o	o	o	o	o	o	o	o	o	s	s	o	o	—							
/t/	/s/	o	o	o	o	o	o	o	o	o	o	o	o	o	o	o	o	o	—						
/s/	Nul	o	o	o	o	o	o	o	o	o	o	o	o	o	o	o	Nul	o	o	—					
/ʃ/	/ɪz/	o	o	o	o	o	o	o	o	o	o	o	o	o	o	o	o	o	o	o	—				
/ǰ/	/ɪz/	o	o	o	o	o	o	o	o	o	o	o	o	o	o	o	o	o	o	o	iz	—			
/č/	/ɪz/	o	o	o	o	o	o	o	o	o	o	o	o	o	o	o	o	o	o	o	iz	iz	—		
/ž/	Nul	Nul	o	o	o	o	o	o	o	o	o	o	o	o	o	o	Nul	o	o	Nul	o	o	o	—	
/z/	Nul	Nul	o	o	o	o	o	o	o	o	o	o	o	o	o	o	Nul	o	o	Nul	o	o	o	—	—

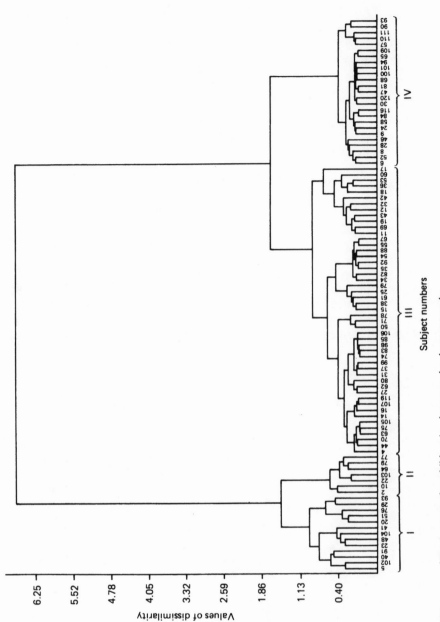

Figure 14.1. Dendrogram of 94 children in a language development study. Reproduced from Baker & Derwing (1982): figure 2.

vertical axis. The diagram can be used to see which children seem to be 'closest together' in the form of their responses (as measured by their response coincidence matrices). For example, subjects 5 and 102 are closer together (dissimilarity = 0.3) than either is to any other subject.[1] The same is true of subjects 107 and 119 (dissimilarity = 0.2), the latter pair being more alike than the former as indicated by the relative values of the dissimilarities. (Note that it is necessary to take care when reading off values of the dissimilarity near the bottom of the diagram – reproduced here as it appears in the original. The horizontal axis has been drawn in at a level which would correspond to a dissimilarity of −0.33, although negative values are meaningless. Presumably this is a peculiarity of the computer package used by Baker & Derwing.)

The dendrogram can be used to look for clusters of children who have become grouped together by the way in which they have responded to the stimuli (according to their individual response coincidence matrices). A cluster is defined by setting a maximum value, d, of the dissimilarity and drawing a line horizontally from that value all the way across the cluster diagram. Every time the horizontal line meets a vertical line a cluster is identified which includes all the subjects who can be reached by moving downwards along the dendrogram from the point of intersection. Each of these clusters had the property that every child in the cluster has at least one 'nearest neighbour' with whom his dissimilarity score is not greater than d. From figure 14.1 we can see that fixing d = 3 defines two clusters, the first containing 20 subjects (from subject 5 to subject 77 on the horizontal axis) and the second containing the remaining 74 subjects. By using d = 1.5 Baker & Derwing found four distinct groups, which they designated I, II, III, IV in their figure. They point out that the links between pairs of subjects in groups I and II are higher up (i.e. correspond to larger dissimilarities) than those in III and IV, suggesting that the latter two groups provide clearer or more consistent results than groups I and II in terms of how they treat the test items. They then go on to argue that the subjects in the four groups demonstrate different levels of evolution of pluralisation rule formation.

14.4 General remarks about hierarchical clustering

Cluster analysis is largely exploratory and descriptive. The number and composition of clusters can depend on several decisions which

[1] Although only 94 children are being compared, the subject numbers go as high as 120. Baker & Derwing eliminated 26 of the original subjects whose response pattern was judged to conform too closely (at least 21 of 24 items agreeing) to adult norms or to be too far from that norm (fewer than 3 of 24 items agreeing).

have to be made by the researcher as well as on the structure of the data. There are essentially three stages in the process, and we will consider them separately. The first stage is the construction of a dissimilarity matrix. For any set of data it will usually be possible to imagine several different ways of measuring the dissimilarity between two subjects, all of which ways give different numerical results. For purely categorical data the matching coefficient is very common, but it is certainly not the only option. Using different similarity measures may give quite different results. The second stage is to adopt a mathematical criterion – the **clustering algorithm** – to convert the dissimilarity matrix to a cluster diagram. Suggestions for suitable criteria abound and the suitability of a particular criterion depends in part on the type of dissimilarity measure used. It is difficult to give general guidelines. The most important feature of this stage is the degree of **linkage** which is required. A subject may be allocated to a group if he is sufficiently like just one member of that group (**single linkage**) – this was the criterion we adopted in the example of §14.2. Or it may be required that the subject be sufficiently close to all pre-existing members of the group (**complete linkage**); or some intermediate level of linkage may be required. (Single linkage is frequently called the 'nearest-neighbour' criterion, since a subject is added to a cluster if he is sufficiently like just one individual already included – the nearest neighbour; complete linkage, on the other hand, is referred to as 'furthest-neighbour' since a new subject has to be sufficiently close to all the current members of the cluster, including the one from whom he differs most.) The third stage is the choice of a value of the dissimilarity at which groups will be defined as in figure 14.1. Different values of d can be chosen to define different numbers of groups.

There are two ways of viewing the high degree of arbitrariness in the cluster analysis technique induced by leaving the investigator the choice of dissimilarity measure, clustering algorithm and cut-off dissimilarity value. It could be considered that this a fatal defect of the procedure, in that too many subjective decisions have to be made; alternatively, it might be felt that the wide variety of possible choices is a positive benefit, allowing the technique to have a useful flexibility. Marriot (1974: 58), discussing methods based on the analysis of dissimilarity measures, says 'The experimenter must choose that which seems to him best for his problem; the mathematician cannot give much guidance. It is precisely this subjective element that gives distance-based methods their particular value.' This viewpoint is justified provided that cluster analysis is used primarily as an exploratory technique to look for plausible structure defined *by the data alone* without the addition of *a priori* assumptions by the investigator. Of course no plausible *theory* can be built on the basis of an exploratory technique. The most that can be hoped for is that clusters will appear whose structure has a plausible linguistic explanation or which suggest a novel linguistic hypothesis. A specific investigation should then be carried out to see whether these tentative hypotheses can be confirmed before any firm conclusions are reached.

14.5   Non-hierarchical clustering

One special problem with hierarchical cluster analysis is that a few very close neighbours can distort the analysis and 'mistakes' made

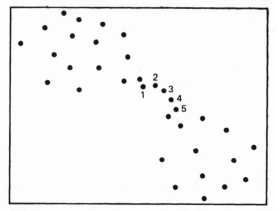

Figure 14.2. An example of two clusters visible to the eye which would be difficult to detect using hierarchical cluster analysis.

early in the clustering process cannot be undone later. Figure 14.2 demonstrates a case where this would happen. The rectangle represents a real pasture in which a wild flower is growing, the dots representing individual plants. It is clear that there are two clusters of plants, possibly the siblings of two different ancestors. However, if the distance between each pair of plants is used as a measure of their dissimilarity and a single linkage cluster algorithm is used, the first 'cluster' to form will consist of plants 1, 2, 3, 4, 5. The other plants will gradually be incorporated into this spurious cluster (which, if hierarchical clustering is used, can never be broken up) and the two clusters which are obvious in the diagram will not be identified in the dendrogram. There are other techniques devised for reducing multivariate data to a two-dimensional graph which do not suffer from this defect, although, on the other hand, they may leave it entirely to the eye of the experimenter to detect 'clusters' in this pictorial representation of the data.

14.6 **Multidimensional scaling**

As with cluster analysis, the starting point for multidimensional scaling is to define a measure of distance or dissimilarity for the objects under study (subjects, variables, etc.). Unlike cluster analysis, multidimensional scaling is not designed explicitly to link the experimental elements in clusters. Instead, its object is to construct a pictorial representation of the relationships between the different elements implied by the values in a dissimilarity matrix. Many of the computer programs commonly used for carrying out multidimensional scaling provide for **nonmetric** scaling, in which the actual magnitude of the dissimilarity between two elements is not preserved but in which the rank order of dissimilarities is reproduced as far as possible. Suppose, for example, A, B and C are three of the subjects being analysed and the dissimilarity between A and B is twice as large as the dissimilarity between B and C. A nonmetric scaling method attempts only to provide a picture in which A, B and C will be represented by points such that A and B are at least as far apart as B and C; no attempt will be made to place the points so that the distance between A and B is still *twice* the distance between B and C. (See Shepard, Romney & Nerlove 1972 for further details.) Again, a full description of a linguistic example seems the best way to describe the process in detail.

Miller & Nicely (1955) carried out a study of the perceptual confusions among 16 English consonants spoken over a voice communications system with frequency distortion and random masking noise. One of the **confusion matrices** resulting from that study (their table v) is reproduced in table 14.6. The spoken stimuli are indicated by the consonants in the first column of the table, while those reported in response by the listener are indicated across the top of the table. Miller & Nicely analysed the data using information theory techniques to investigate the effect of distortion and noise on five articulatory features or 'dimensions': voicing, nasality, affrication, duration and place of articulation. They concluded that perception of any of these features is relatively independent of the perception of the others and that voicing and nasality were least affected by their different experimental conditions. Let us look at a multidimensional scaling analysis of this study.

The first step is to define a measure of the dissimilarity between any two of the 16 phonemes studied in the investigation. The less similar two consonants are, the less frequently should one be confused for the other. Suppose that the i-th phoneme was uttered as a stimulus n_i times in total and that n_{ij} is the number of times the j-th phoneme was perceived

Table 14.6. *Confusion matrix for signal/noise = +6 db and frequency response of 200–6 500 cps*

	p	t	k	f	θ	s	ʃ	b	d	g	v	ð	z	ʒ	m	n
p	162	10	55	5	3											
t	8	270	14													
k	38	6	171	1												
f			2	207	57			3								
θ			2	71	142	3										
s				1	7	232	2									
ʃ						1	239									
b				1	2			214			31	12				
d									206	14		9	1	2		
g								11	64	194		4	2	1		
v				1				14		2	205	39	5			1
ð								2		4	55	179	22	2		
z									3	10	2	20	198	3		
ʒ									3	4		2	2	215		
m															217	3
n									1						2	285

Reproduced from Miller & Nicely (1955: table v)

although the i-th was uttered. Then a possible measure for the *similarity*, s_{ij}, between these two phonemes would be the proportion of times that either one was perceived as the other:

$$s_{ij} = \frac{n_{ij} + n_{ji}}{n_i + n_j}$$

and the dissimilarity can then be defined as $d_{ij} = 1 - s_{ij}$. Shepard (1972) carried out a multidimensional scaling on a dissimilarity matrix derived

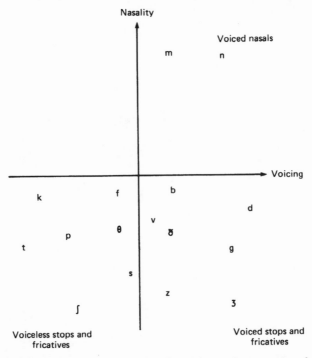

Figure 14.3. Multidimensional scaling of data on the perception of speech sounds (adapted from Shepard 1972).

from the Miller & Nicely data to obtain the two-dimensional scaling solution of figure 14.3. It can be seen that the 16 phonemes are distributed along two dimensions which can be identified as a voicing dimension and a nasality dimension. Furthermore, the 'central' voiced fricatives (alveolar and alveopalatal) [z, 3] appear close together as do the labial and alveolar nasals [m, n]. Among the other voiced consonants we can see relationships between [b] and [v], [v] and [ð] on the one hand, and [b] and [g] on the other. The voiceless phonemes to the left of the vertical axis cluster fairly well into the unvoiced stops (k, p, t), the alveolar and alveolar-palatal voiceless fricatives (s, ʃ) and the 'dental' voiceless fricatives (f, θ). This is a striking demonstration of the way that multidimensional scaling can indicate the structural relationships between individual elements based on dissimilarities between pairs of individuals. Furthermore, one of the important motivations for carrying out multidimensional scaling is to reduce the apparent dimensionality of the data (cf. principal components analysis in the next chapter), and that, too, has occurred here. Although there were initially five articulatory dimensions to describe the 16 consonants, a satisfactory representation has been achieved here in two dimensions.

14.7 **Further comments on multidimensional scaling**

In the example given above, clusters of a particular composition were expected, or hoped for, *a priori*. This will often not be the case: multidimensional scaling is frequently carried out to see whether useful elements of structure will be suggested by the two-dimensional solution. If an experimenter has no prior expectations about clusters which may arise from the analysis, it will frequently be difficult to decide what should constitute a cluster. It may help to carry out both a hierarchical clustering and a multidimensional scaling on the same dissimilarity matrix. Shepard (1972) gives an example of how the results from both can be combined in a single diagram.

As with hierarchical clustering, there are many different mathematical methods and computer algorithms for carrying out multidimensional scaling. However, provided nonmetric scaling is used, the different methods give very similar results. Nevertheless, if there is not a two-dimensional solution which retains the correct ranking for all the dissimilarity values (it may not be possible to find one) it may occasionally happen that different approximate solutions can be obtained from the same data using the same computer program. Discussion of this problem and how to avoid it should appear in the document which explains how to use any computer program for multidimensional scaling, under the heading of 'suboptimal solutions' or 'local maxima'. A full discussion of multidimensional scaling and its use can be found in Shepard, Romney & Nerlove (1972). A suite of computer programs called MDS(X) has been produced to carry out multidimensional scaling (and hierarchical cluster analysis) – see Coxon (1982).

14.8 **Linear discriminant analysis**

Cluster analysis and multidimensional scaling are techniques whose chief purpose is to search for that structure in multivariate data which enables clusters of individuals such as subjects, variables, experimental conditions etc. to be identified. They can be applied to any kind of data, numerical or categorical, providing a measure of dissimilarity can be defined and calculated for each pair of individuals. By contrast, **linear discriminant analysis** is a technique for verifying that apparent clusters are real and for deciding to which cluster a new individual, observed in addition to those used to determine the clusters, should be assigned. The type of linear discriminant analysis to be described here is applicable when all the various scores or measurements observed for each individual are approximately normally distributed. Similar procedures do exist for categorical data, but they are less common and will not be discussed further here. Again we introduce the technique via an example discussed by Fletcher & Peters (1984).

Table 14.7. *Scores on two linguistic variables of 29 subjects*

Subject	X_1	X_2	Y	$\hat{Y}$
1	42	19.00	-1	-0.073
2	63	15.75	-1	-0.992
3	13	19.00	-1	0.730
4	58	16.25	-1	-0.801
5	60	13.75	-1	-1.116
6	26	15.25	-1	-0.018
7	35	15.25	-1	-0.268
8	37	16.25	-1	-0.220
9	28	16.50	-1	0.056
10	28	26.75	1	1.117
11	15	23.25	1	1.115
12	23	22.50	1	0.815
13	45	24.75	1	0.439
14	27	18.75	1	0.316
15	25	20.25	1	0.527
16	23	24.25	1	0.997
17	33	20.25	1	0.305
18	11	20.00	1	0.889
19	36	22.50	1	0.455
20	35	20.00	1	0.224
21	18	14.50	1	0.126
22	29	20.25	1	0.416
23	18	14.50	1	0.126
24	23	22.50	1	0.815
25	30	37.75	1	1.890
26	27	22.75	1	0.731
27	28	23.00	1	0.729
28	28	21.75	1	0.599
29	24	25.25	1	1.072

X_1 is the number of unmarked verb forms (UVF) in 200 utterances
X_2 is the number of verb types (VT) in 200 utterances
$Y = -1$ means that subject was diagnosed as language-impaired

The study explores the grammatical and lexical dimensions which characterise the expressive language of language-impaired children. Spontaneous language data were collected under standard conditions from a group of 20 normal children (henceforth LN) and a group of nine children diagnosed as language-impaired, using standardised test criteria (henceforth LI) and matched for age and intellectual functioning with the LN

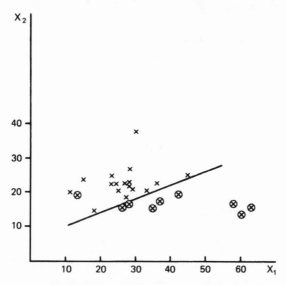

Figure 14.4. Scattergram of data in table 14.7; the circled points originate from language-impaired subjects.

group (mean age for the LN group was 60.86 months, and for the LI group 62.33 months). Samples of 200 utterances from each group were scored on a set of 65 grammatical and lexical categories – largely derived from the LARSP procedure outlined in Crystal, Fletcher & Garman (1976). One of the grammatical variables scored was unmarked verb forms (UVF) – the number of lexical verb stems which had neither a suffix nor any auxiliary premodification. One of the lexical categories used was verb types (VT), referring to the number of different lexical verbs used in the sample by a child. The scores for each subject on these two variables are given in table 14.7, and figure 14.4 shows the scattergram obtained by plotting X_2 (VT) against X_1 (UVF) for each subject. The solid line in the figure divides the graph into two regions, one of which contains only points corresponding to LI subjects; the other contains points corresponding to the 20 LN subjects and to one LI subject. This suggests that it may be possible to formulate a simple rule, based solely on the scores

267

on UVF and VT, for assigning each subject to one of the categories 'language-impaired' or 'normal'. In fact, when there are only two categories (or groups or clusters) as in this case, such a rule can be developed using the multiple regression techniques of chapter 13.

14.9 The linear discriminant function for two groups

Suppose that a number of subjects have been scored on several variables, X_1, X_2, etc., and in addition, each subject in the sample is known or believed to belong to one of two categories. Create a new variable, Y, which takes only two values -1 and $+1$. All the subjects of one category (arbitrarily chosen – the LI groups in the present example) are given a score of $Y = -1$ on the new variable; all the subjects of the other category score $Y = 1$ (the LN group, in our case). Y is then used as the dependent variable for a multiple regression analysis, X_1, X_2, etc. being the independent variables. Such an analysis was carried out on the data of table 14.7 to obtain the multiple regression equation:

$$\hat{Y} = 0.87710 - 0.02770\,X_1 + 0.10354\,X_2$$

Using this equation we find that the 'predicted value of Y' for subject 1 is:

$$\hat{Y}_1 = -0.87710 - 0.02770 \times 42 + 0.10354 \times 19.00 = -0.07324$$

while the 'observed value' of Y is -1, since that subject was in the initial LI group. In the present context the multiple regression equation is referred to as the **discriminant function** and the fitted value $\hat{Y}_1$ is usually called the **discriminant function score** of the i-th subject. The discriminant function scores of the 29 subjects are given in the final column of the table. Seven of the nine language-impaired subjects have negative scores and all the subjects in the LN group have positive scores. Subject 3 has a score more typical of the normal group. If we leave this subject out of consideration for the moment we find that the *maximum* score among the other LI subjects is only $+0.056$ while the *minimum* score for the normal language group is $+0.126$. In other words, if we adopt the rule that any subject whose discriminant function score is less than, say, 0.1 will be assigned to the LI group, while if the score is greater than 0.1 we assume the subject is linguistically normal, only one of the 29 subjects of the sample (subject 3) will be wrongly classified.

However, there is a degree of arbitrariness in this discrimination rule. Why use the value 0.1 as the boundary value for separating discriminant scores into two groups? Any cut-off value between 0.056 and 0.126 will cause all the normal-language subjects to be correctly classified and only one of the LI subjects (subject 3) to be misclassified. Why then choose 0.1 as the cut-off value? Does it matter? If our only object is to see how well we can discriminate between the two types of subject *in the sample*, it does not. However, it does matter which value we choose if we would like to use the discriminant function to classify *new* subjects (i.e. subjects not included in the original sample) into the normal or impaired categories solely on the basis of their UVF and VT scores in 200 utterances. We then need to choose a specific value for the discriminant score which will be the boundary score between the two groups. It might then seem that a reasonable choice would be 0.091, exactly mid-way between 0.056 and 0.126. However, this choice ignores the unfortunate fact that one of the LI subjects had a discriminant score higher than 0.056; subject 3 has been ignored entirely in choosing the cut-off value. We really need some method of choosing the boundary value which takes into account all the discriminant scores in the sample. It is more usual to proceed as follows.

The *mean* discriminant score for the LI group was −0.300 (the mean of the first nine discriminant scores, $\hat{Y}$, in table 14.7). The mean discriminant score for the 20 subjects in the LN group is 0.685. Commonly the cut-off point would be chosen to be mid-way between these two means, i.e. at 0.1925. With this value we find that three subjects of the sample would now be misclassified. Subject 3, as before, with a discriminant score of $\hat{Y}_3 = 0.730$, which is greater than 0.1925, would be wrongly assigned to the normal category. Subjects 21 and 23 with discriminant scores $\hat{Y}_{21} = \hat{Y}_{23} = 0.126$ would be wrongly classified as language-impaired. It may seem perverse to choose a cut-off value which misallocates three subjects when it is possible to choose a value which assigns only one subject to the wrong group. Nevertheless, there are good reasons for doing this which are discussed in the following section.

14.10 Probabilities of misclassification

The classification rule suggested at the end of the previous section can be summed up thus. For any subject, obtain UVF and VT scores as described at the beginning of §14.8. Calculate the discriminant score, $\hat{Y}$, for the subject using the discriminant function:

$$\hat{Y} = -0.8771 - (0.0277 \times UVF) + (0.10354 \times VT)$$

If $\hat{Y}$ is greater than 0.1925 assign the subject to the normal category, otherwise assign him to the language-impaired category. On this basis one of the language-impaired subjects (subject 3) of the nine in the sample would be incorrectly classified, as would two of the 20 subjects with normal language (subjects 21 and 23). The proportion of language-impaired subjects actually misclassified is $1/9$; the proportion of the normal subjects misclassified is $2/20$. This might seem to imply that the probability of misclassifying a subject of either type is about 10%. Unfortunately this is almost certain to be a serious underestimate of the true probability of misclassification. The coefficients of the discriminant function $(-0.8771, -0.0277, 0.10354)$ have been *estimated* using a sample of 29 subjects. A different sample containing subjects of both types would lead to different estimates for these coefficients. The estimation procedure calculates the discriminant function which gives the best discrimination possible *for the subjects in the sample*. (Quite often a discriminant function can be found which makes no classification errors in the sample.) A new subject whose scores were not used to calculate the discriminant function is more likely to be misclassified than a subject of the original sample. This is particularly true when, as here, the discriminant function has been estimated from a small number of subjects. Provided the values of the discriminating variables (UVF and VT) are normally distributed over the target population and the subjects for the exercise are chosen randomly, then it is possible to estimate the probability of misclassification in either direction.

In table 14.7 each subject is given the label -1 or 1 to indicate the group to which he belongs. It is convenient to refer to the subjects of the group labelled with -1 as type 1, the others being type 2. Then we can define the probabilities P_{12} and P_{21} by:

$$P_{ij} = P(\text{subject of type i is misclassified as type j})$$

We will write m_i to stand for the observed mean discriminant score of subjects of the i-th type and c to stand for the cut-off value to divide the discriminant scores into two groups. (Here $m_1 = -0.300$, $m_2 = 0.685$ and $c = 0.1925$.) Then P_{12}, the probability of wrongly identifying as type 2 a new subject who is really type 1, can be estimated, as follows:

$$\text{Calculate } Z_1 = \frac{c - m_1}{\sqrt{(m_2 - m_1)}} = \frac{0.4925}{\sqrt{0.985}} = 0.4962$$

From tables of the standard normal distribution we find that the probability of *exceeding* this value (i.e. getting a discriminant score big enough to misclassify a type 1 subject who should be achieving a small score) is 0.31. This is our estimate of P_{12}. To estimate P_{21} we calculate:

$$Z_2 = \frac{c - m_2}{\sqrt{m_2 - m_1}} = -\frac{0.4925}{\sqrt{0.985}} = -0.4962$$

and the probability of having a smaller Z value than this is 0.31. For this example we have $P_{12} = P_{21} = 0.31$. That the two types of misclassification have equal probabilities is a consequence of the cut-off value being chosen exactly mid-way between the sample discriminant mean scores of the two groups. It is perfectly possible to choose a cut-off value which makes one type of misclassification less likely than the other (exercise 14.3). If the proportions of the two types in the population are known *a priori* then it is possible to choose the cut-off point to minimise $(P_{12} + P_{21})$ the total probability of misclassification (see Overall & Klett 1972: §9.7). The technique of linear discriminant analysis can be extended to the study of several groups (see Overall & Klett 1972; ch. 10; Bennett & Bowers 1976; §7.10). A linguistic study which uses multiple discriminant analysis can be found in Bellinger (1980).

SUMMARY

This chapter has introduced and discussed the notion of **multivariate data** and their analysis.

(1) It was pointed out that most multivariate methods are descriptive.
(2) A **dissimilarity matrix** was defined and the example of a **matching coefficient** was presented. It was shown that when continuous variables are observed on each subject the correlation between subjects can be used as a measure of closeness and **clusters** of subjects identified.
(3) **Hierarchical cluster analysis** was explained and an example was given. The concept of **linkage** was discussed and the terms **nearest neighbour** and **furthest neighbour** defined. It was stressed that cluster analysis is essentially exploratory.
(4) It was stated that a two-dimensional 'map' or picture of a set of multivariate data can be drawn by means of **multidimensional scaling**, and the meaning of **nonmetric scaling** was explained. An example was presented to show that meaningful dimensions can be identified by a multidimensional scaling.
(5) **Linear discriminant analysis** was explained as a special case of multiple regression (chapter 13). It was shown how to use the **discriminant function** and the **discriminant scores** to allocate subjects to one of two possible groups. It was shown how to establish a **cut-off value** and how to estimate **misclassification probabilities**.

EXERCISES

(1) Using the nearest-neighbour approach, continue the clustering process begun in §14.2 until a single cluster is eventually established. If you were told that really there were two types of subject in the sample, each of whom should

belong to a different group, what would be the two groups you would suggest on the basis of the above clustering?

(2) Using the dissimilarity matrix of table 14.4, repeat the clustering process for the ten subjects, but this time putting in the same cluster those subjects who have least dissimilarity to one another.

(3) Using the value of $c = 0.1$ as a cut-off, recalculate the misclassification probabilities for the discrimination example at the end of the chapter.

15
Principal components analysis and factor analysis

In the previous chapter we defined the idea of a multivariate observation and looked at multivariate analysis techniques for discovering and confirming the presence of special groups among the observed individuals. In the present chapter we will look at methods designed specifically to reduce the dimensionality of the data.

15.1 Reducing the dimensionality of multivariate data

Suppose that their scores on p variables, $X_1, X_2, \ldots, X_p$, have been observed for each of n subjects (see §15.3 for a language testing example). Typically, the variables will be intercorrelated, each variable having a higher correlation with some of the other variables than it does with the remainder. It is quite common that the pattern of intercorrelations is rather complex. As is often the case, the major statistical interest will lie in considering the differences between individuals. The special problem to be faced now is that the subjects can be different in a variety of ways. Two subjects may have similar scores for some of the variables and quite dissimilar scores on some of the others. If the number of variables is large, then it may be difficult to decide whether subject A differs more from subject B than from subject C since the *pattern* of differences may be quite dissimilar in the two cases. This prompts the question of whether it is possible to reduce the whole set of scores for each subject to a single score on a new variable in such a way that the variability between the subjects over the original set of variables is somehow expressed by the score on the single new variable. Here we have a situation frequently encountered in economics where, for example, a single variable (the retail price index) is used to indicate changes in the price of a large number of commodities or (the Dow Jones industrial share prices index) to measure movements in the value of shares traded on the New York Stock Exchange.

The advantage of reducing a complex multidimensional data set to a single variable is obvious. Use of the retail prices index allows statements to be made about 'rising prices' or 'inflation' without the need to describe explicitly a confused situation in which prices of some foodstuffs are rising while others are falling, fuel is becoming more expensive while the cost of mortgages is decreasing, and so on. The disadvantage is equally obvious. The changes in any subset of the original variables are more important to some individuals than others. For example, it is of little comfort to a single investor to know that the share price index is rising in value if the few shares that he owns are rapidly becoming worthless.

When it is felt that reduction of a multivariate data set to values of a single variable may be worthwhile there remains the question of how it should be done. For the retail prices index, a 'basket' of commodities such as bread, meat, fuel, rents, mortgages, etc. is monitored, with each commodity given a numerical weight corresponding in some way to its average importance in the community. The price of each commodity is multiplied by the corresponding weight and the weighted prices are added together to create the index. (This is a gross oversimplification which nevertheless describes the essence of the procedure.) Is this type of index relevant to linguistic studies? Are indices ever used in linguistics?

Yes, they are. Two examples have appeared earlier in this book. The numbers in table 2.7 arise as values of an index. The original observation for the i-th subject was a three-dimensional vector (d_{i1}, d_{i2}, d_{i3}) where d_{i1} was the number of tokens expressed by the subject of the first phonological variant, etc. (see §14.1 for notation). The value of the index for the i-th subject was then calculated as:

$$\{(d_{i1} + 2d_{i2} + 3d_{i3}) \div (d_{i1} + d_{i2} + d_{i3}) - 1\} \times 100$$

(see §2.3). Again, we have, at various points in the text, referred to data from the Cambridge Proficiency in English Examination. This examination consists of a number of different sections, or language tasks. The observation for each candidate is the set of marks he obtains on these different tasks which are then combined into a single variable – the candidate's mark for the examination. This is a common procedure in language testing.

It is therefore relevant to ask two questions. When we are faced with a set of multivariate linguistic data, can we reduce them to a single score for each subject and still retain most of the information about differences between subjects which was contained in the original data? If this is not possible, can we at least reduce the original data to a new form of smaller dimensionality (i.e. in which each subject is scored on fewer variables) without significant loss of information? Many of the techniques of multivariate analysis are motivated by the desire to answer these questions.

15.2 **Principal components analysis**

Suppose, again, that we have a set of data consisting of the scores of n subjects on each of p variables, X_{ij} being the score of the i-th subject on the j-th variable, X_j. Usually the scores on some pairs of variables will be highly correlated; other pairs will have only small correlation. The scores of the subjects may have a larger variance on some of the variables than on others or the variances may all be roughly the same.

Principal components analysis (PCA) is a mathematical procedure for converting the p original scores $(X_{i1}, X_{i2}, \ldots, X_{ip})$ for the i-th subject into a new set of p scores $(Y_{i1}, Y_{i2}, \ldots, Y_{ip})$ for that subject in such a way that the new variables thus created will have properties which help to provide answers to the two questions posed at the end of the previous section. The endpoint of a PCA is to calculate a set of numerical weights or **coefficients**. An individual's score on one of the new variables, Y_k say, will be calculated by multiplying his score on each of the original variables by the appropriate coefficient and then summing the weighted scores. If we write Y_{ik} to mean the score of the i-th subject on the new variable, Y_k, this can be written succinctly as:

$$Y_{ik} = a_{k1}X_{i1} + a_{k2}X_{i2} + a_{k3}X_{i3} + \ldots + a_{kp}X_{ip}$$

where a_{ki} is the coefficient by which the score on the i-th original variable is being calculated. Note that the values of the coefficients a_{kj} are the same for every subject. The set of coefficients, $(a_{k1}, a_{k2}, \ldots, a_{kp})$, used to calculate a subject's score on the new variable, Y_k, are called **the coefficients of the k-th principal component**, Y_k is referred to as **the k-th principal component** and the score Y_{ik} as **the score of the i-th subject on the k-th principal component**. There is a danger that the average reader is already becoming lost in what may seem to be a plethora of algebraic notation. A simple biological example may help to clarify the concept.

Jolicoeur & Mosimann (1960) used a PCA to analyse measurements of the length, height and width of the carapaces of painted turtles.[1] The original data is three-dimensional, X_1, X_2 and X_3 being, respectively, the length, height and width of each turtle shell. The set of coefficients, a_{jk},

---

[1] The discussion of this data is adapted from Morrison (1976). Although Morrison's book may be too mathematical in its presentation to suit the taste of most of our readers, it can be recommended for the clear discussion of examples of all the multivariate procedures treated there.

Table 15.1. *Coefficients of principal components from a PCA of measurements of turtle shells*

Original dimension (X)	Component (Y)		
	Y_1	Y_2	Y_3
Length (X_1)	0.81	−0.55	−0.21
Height (X_2)	0.31	0.10	0.95
Width (X_3)	0.50	0.83	−0.25

Adapted from Morrison (1976: 274)

is given in table 15.1, from which it can be seen that the first principal component, Y_1, can be defined as:

$$Y_1 = 0.81X_1 + 0.31X_2 + 0.50X_3$$
i.e. $Y_1 = 0.81 \text{ (length)} + 0.31 \text{ (height)} + 0.50 \text{ (width)}$

In other words, to calculate the score on the first principal component of any turtle shell of the original sample we need only multiply the length, height and width of the shell by the appropriate weights and sum the weighted scores. Note that in table 15.1 some of the coefficients are negative. This is quite usual. The score of the i-th shell on the second component Y_{i2} would be given by:

$$Y_{i2} = -0.55X_{i1} + 0.10X_{i2} + 0.83X_{i3}$$
i.e. $Y_{i2} = -0.55 \text{ (length of i-th shell)} + 0.83 \text{ (height of i-th shell)}$
$+ 0.10 \text{ (width of i-th shell)}$

and could possibly be negative: this point is discussed further below.

Of course, all that has happened so far is that the three scores or measurements (length, height and width) have been changed into three different scores (on the three principal components). To see what has been gained in the process we have to look at the properties of these principal components.

The calculation of the coefficients of the principal components is carried out in such a way that the following statements are true:

(a)   The total variance of the principal component scores of the n subjects in the sample is the same as the variance of their scores on the original variables, i.e.

$$VAR(Y_1) + VAR(Y_2) + \ldots + VAR(Y_p) = VAR(X_1) + VAR(X_2) + \ldots + VAR(X_p)$$

(b)   The coefficients, $a_{11}, a_{12}, a_{13}, \ldots, a_{1p}$, of the first principal component are chosen so that $VAR(Y_1)$ is as large as possible. Colloquially we

Table 15.2. *Variance–covariance matrix of measurements of a sample of carapaces of painted turtles*

	Length (X_1)	Height (X_2)	Width (X_3)
X_1	451.39	168.70	271.17
X_2		66.65	103.29
X_3			171.73

Adapted from Morrison (1976: 274)

say that Y_1 is constructed to explain as much as possible of the total variability in the original scores of the sample subjects.

(c) The coefficients, a_{21}, a_{22}, a_{23}, . . . , a_{2p}, of the second principal component, Y_2, are chosen so that Y_2 is *uncorrelated with* Y_1 and Y_2 is as variable as possible, i.e. explains as much as possible of the total variance remaining after Y_1 has been extracted.

(d) The coefficients, a_{31}, a_{32}, a_{33}, . . . , a_{3p}, of the third principal component, Y_3, are chosen so that Y_3 is *uncorrelated with both* Y_1 and Y_2 and explains as much as possible of the total variance remaining after Y_1 and Y_2 have been extracted. This process continues until the coefficients of all p principal components have been obtained.

Table 15.2 gives the **variance–covariance matrix** for the measurements made by Jolicoeur & Mosimann. The numbers on the main diagonal are the sample variances of the indicated variables. The off-diagonal terms are the sample covariances. (The matrix is, of course, symmetric – see chapter 10 – so that it is sufficient to fill in only the upper triangle.) We see that $VAR(X_1) = 451.39$, $VAR(X_2) = 66.65$ and $VAR(X_3) = 171.73$ so that the total variance is $451.39 + 66.65 + 171.73 = 689.77$.

The corresponding PCA, for which the coefficients are given in table 15.1, gives a first principal component, Y_1, with variance 680.40, i.e. 98.64% of the total variance! In other words, almost all the overall variability in the three dimensions of the turtle carapaces can be expressed in a single dimension defined by the first principal component. The remaining two principal components have variances of 6.50 and 2.86 respectively, both very small proportions of the total variance.

Before leaving this example, two further points should be noted. The first is that the coefficients of the principal components are calculated or **extracted** from the values of the variance–covariance matrix – the actual measurements of the shells are not required; any other sample which gave rise to the same variances and covariances would result in an identical PCA. Second, it may be necessary to consider more than one component.

In the turtle shell example almost 99% of the total variance was explained by the first principal component and there is obviously no need to go further. Frequently, as happens in the language testing example in the following section, several components are needed to explain a reasonably large proportion of the total variance. However many principal components are required, it is customary to attempt to interpret them meaningfully (some authors use the term **to reify**). From table 15.1 it can be seen that the first principal component has coefficients which are all positive, so that Y_1 is a kind of weighted average of the original measurements. The score of any shell of this component is necessarily positive and will increase as any of the three measurements, length, height or width, increases. For this reason it might be considered as a 'size' component: 'large' turtle shells will have a high score on this component. The later components, on the other hand, can be thought of as 'shape' components. For example, the score on the second component of an individual shell can be either positive or negative. Shells which are unusually long for their height and width will have negative scores, while shells which are untypically short compared to their height and width will have positive scores. PCAs of biological measurements often result in the extraction of a first principal component which corresponds to an overall measure of size, which may be relatively uninteresting, and later components corresponding to aspects of shape, which may be more useful or interesting for purposes of classification or comparison.

15.3 A principal components analysis of language test scores

How may PCA be used in language studies? An obvious candidate for such analysis, mentioned earlier, would be the set of scores of a group of subjects on a battery of language tests, not all of which claim to be measuring the same ability. Some of the tests might claim to measure 'vocabulary', others 'grammar', yet others 'reading comprehension', and so on. The purpose of carrying out PCA would be to determine how many distinct abilities (appearing as components) are in fact being measured by these tests, what these abilities are, and what contribution each test makes to the measurement of each ability. This is obviously of interest to researchers in language testing. It can also be seen as possibly providing clues to the nature of language ability in general, which psycholinguists may make use of in developing theories and devising experiments.

Hughes & Woods (1982, 1983) studied the performance on the Cambridge Proficiency Examination (CPE) of candidates at different examination centres in June 1980. In this chapter we will concentrate on just

70 candidates, those who took the examination in Hong Kong. At that time the CPE could be seen as comprising 19 recognisable subtests:

(1) Multiple choice vocabulary (40 items): supply missing word in single-sentence context.

(2,3) Multiple choice reading comprehension (each 10 items): questions on passages of about 600 words in length.

(4) Multiple choice listening comprehension (15 items): 5 questions on each of three passages read twice.

(5,6) Essays: one requires the students to describe or narrate, the other to discuss.

(7) Extended reading: the candidates answer questions of a rather literary nature (e.g. what is the extended metaphor . . . ?) on a passage of English. Scoring is without reference to the quality of expression shown in the answers.

(8) In a conversation based on a photograph the candidates are scored for overall communication.

(9) In the same conversation the candidates are scored for vocabulary.

(10) The candidates speak on a prepared topic for about two minutes. They are scored for overall communication.

(11) They are also scored for 'grammar and structure' for their performance on the prepared topic.

(12) The candidates read one part in a dialogue, the examiner the other. Scoring is for pronunciation.

(Tasks 8–12 are all scored on a ten-point scale)

(13) Situation: the candidates respond verbally to three situations put to them by the examiner. Scoring is out of 3 for each situation.

(14) Cloze (20 items): rational deletion and acceptable response scoring.

(15) Paraphrase (10 items): the first word or two of the paraphrase is given.

(16) Sentence completion (8 items): the mid-point of a sentence is omitted, the candidates having to fill the gaps 'with a suitable word or phrase'.

(17) Paraphrase (9 items): with the requirement that a given lexical item be used in making the paraphrase.

(18) Summarise (14 questions): the candidates answer questions on a passage of about 750 words, a test of their ability to 'understand, interpret and summarise'.

(19) Style: the candidates are required to convey information in a particular form or style.

Correlations between scores on the various subtests, as shown in table 15.3, varied from 0.12 (subtests 16 and 19) to 0.95 (subtests 10 and 11). The fact that two tests correlate as highly as 0.95 (and several pairs had correlations greater than 0.80) suggests strongly that the CPE was not

Table 15.3. *Mean, standard deviation and variance of a sample of 70 candidates for the Cambridge Proficiency Examination*

Subtest	Mean	Standard deviation	Variance
1. M/C vocabulary	22.0	6.7	44.7
2. M/C reading comprehension	5.2	1.6	2.5
3. M/C reading comprehension	6.0	2.1	4.6
4. M/C listening comprehension	9.1	3.1	9.6
5. Essay (describe/narrate)	8.3	2.6	6.9
6. Essay (discuss)	7.8	2.4	5.7
7. Extended reading	6.4	5.2	27.5
8. Conversation (communication)	5.1	2.0	3.9
9. Conversation (vocabulary)	5.1	1.9	3.6
10. Communication (prepared topic)	5.3	2.1	4.5
11. Grammar (prepared topic)	5.2	2.1	4.3
12. Pronunciation	4.7	2.0	4.1
13. Conversation (response to situation)	4.7	2.0	4.0
14. Cloze	8.6	4.3	18.9
15. Paraphrase (free)	5.1	2.7	7.5
16. Sentence completion	4.4	2.5	6.1
17. Paraphrase (constrained)	4.3	3.3	10.8
18. Summarise	13.1	5.8	33.9
19. Style	1.8	2.4	5.8
COMPLETE TEST	132.2	44.0	

measuring 19 distinct abilities. But how many? Hughes and Woods subjected the scores to a PCA. The results of the analysis, as output by the computer program used to carry it out, are shown in table 15.4.

The output begins by reminding the researcher how many variables have been measured (19) and the number of subjects involved (70). Note that the precise statement is NO. OF OBSERVATIONS = 70. As we have already mentioned, it is usual to consider the whole set of scores observed for any subject as a single observation – a **multivariate observation**. This is a useful convention which, apart from its mathematical convenience which we do not discuss here, serves to indicate the real size of sample involved. If an investigator chooses five subjects or five pieces of text, say, it does not matter whether he measures one variable or 60 variables on each, the sample size is still only five, and the data cannot be expected to give a reliable indication of the structure of a complete population based on a sample of five. Of course, looking at more variables may give a much more complete picture of the *sample*, but even this will be true only if the extra variables are not very highly correlated with those already observed. If they are, they will simply repeat information already contained in the earlier variables. It is to be recommended, in general, that the

Table 15.4. *Principal components analysis of subtest scores of 70 subjects*

NO. OF VARIABLES = 19
NO. OF OBSERVATIONS = 70
EIGENVALUES OF COVARIANCE MATRIX

138.39	14.10	13.45	8.51	6.45	5.17	4.17	3.75	3.12	2.66	2.42	1.75	1.34	1.10	1.00	0.65	0.42	0.23	0.14

PRINCIPAL COMPONENTS OF COVARIANCE MATRIX

COMP1	0.51	0.07	0.12	0.21	0.17	0.15	0.38	0.10	0.10	0.12	0.12	0.12	0.10	0.32	0.18	0.15	0.24	0.42	0.09
COMP2	0.56	-0.01	-0.02	0.00	0.05	0.12	-0.35	-0.04	-0.01	0.00	0.04	-0.01	-0.01	0.17	0.12	-0.08	0.09	-0.67	0.18
COMP3	-0.40	0.07	0.07	0.12	0.17	0.08	-0.10	0.36	0.35	0.37	0.33	0.29	0.28	-0.01	0.13	-0.06	0.09	-0.24	0.01

sample size – the number of sample units or subjects – should be several times as large as the number of variables observed. The **dimension** of a multivariate observation is simply the number of different variables it contains.

Look next at the heading PRINCIPAL COMPONENTS OF COVARIANCE MATRIX followed by several rows of numbers, each row headed COMP1, COMP2, etc, COMP simply being an abbreviation of COMPONENT. (In the original output there were 19 such rows of which only the first three are reproduced in the table.) Each of these rows gives the values of the coefficients required to calculate scores on the corresponding principal component. For example, to obtain the score of each student on the first principal component we take:

$$0.51 \times \text{(score on subtest 1)} + 0.07 \times \text{(score on subtest 2)} + 0.12 \\ \times \text{(score on subtest 3)} + \ldots + 0.42 \times \text{(score on subtest 18)} + \\ 0.09 \times \text{(score on subtest 19)}$$

The variances of all the principal components are given, in order, in the row of table 15.4 headed EIGENVALUES OF THE COVARIANCE MATRIX. The variance of COMP1 is 138.39, that of COMP2 is 14.10, and so on, and it can be seen that the variances decrease rapidly, until the last few principal components have very low variances indeed. The first five components (whose coefficients are given in the table) together account for 86% of the total variance – 66%, 7%, 6%, 4% and 3%, respectively. The remaining 14 components together account for only 14% of the total variance. As expected, the sum of the variance of the principal components (208.82) is equal to the total variance of the subtest scores (208.9) – the tiny discrepancy is due to rounding errors in the calculations. The latter total can be obtained by summing the variances in the last column of table 15.3.

15.4 Deciding on the dimensionality of the data

Our first purpose in carrying out this PCA, it will be remembered, was to determine how many distinct abilities were being measured by the Cambridge Proficiency Examination. How do we decide this? Well, if we look again at table 15.4 we see that the 19th (and last) principal component had a variance of only 0.14 (less than 0.1% of the total variance). In effect, this means that when the sums of the subjects on this component are calculated all 70 scores turn out to be almost exactly the same. The small amount of residual variation could very easily be attributed to random measurement variation unrelated to the subjects' language proficiency.

It seems most unlikely that this 19th component measures any real dimension of language proficiency. It certainly does not uncover any differences between the subjects in the sample on this putative dimension, and it is not credible that 70 subjects would achieve *exactly* the same score in a real test of some aspect of proficiency. A similar argument can be used to eliminate more than half the components. They have so little variation that we can readily accept the possibility that it is entirely due to random error and not to real differences in the subjects in some aspects of language proficiency. On the other hand, the first principal component has a large variance which accounts for 66% of the total variance. Does this component already measure all the reliable variability in proficiency among the 70 subjects? Does the second component, with a variance of 7% of the total, measure some genuine aspect of language proficiency? If so, it is measuring something quite distinct from whatever is measured by the first principal component, since the variables defined by the components are completely uncorrelated. An objective method has been developed recently for deciding how many components to accept. Eastment & Krzanowski's (1982) technique determines whether more information than 'random noise' is obtained through the acceptance of more principal components. The procedure begins with the first component and tests whether the second should be accepted too. If it is, the third is tested and so on until the point is reached where the inclusion of any further components would add more noise than information. The remaining components are rejected while the previous ones are all accepted. In the present case, all but the first three components were rejected by the technique. It appears that the CPE subtests were measuring three distinct (presumably language) abilities in the Hong Kong candidates. In the next section we will discuss what these three abilities might be.

The Eastment & Krzanowski method requires a special computer program and a large computing facility. In their absence a rule of thumb is frequently employed in deciding how many components to accept. The rule is: if the original data has p dimensions, assume that components which account for less than a fraction $1/p$ of the total variance should be discarded. There is no theoretical basis for this rule but it has frequently been adopted by users of principal components analysis. In the present example there were 19 subtests, and the rule would imply that any component accounting for less than $1/19$ of the total variance (i.e. less than 5.3%) should be eliminated. On this basis, three components are accepted. The two methods give the same answer on this occasion, but that will frequently not be the case.

15.5 **Interpreting the principal components**

In the example of §15.2, where PCA was carried out on the measurement of turtle shells, the three principal components were interpreted in terms of size and shape. The interpretation was carried out by looking at the coefficients of the principal components to see what weight was to be given to each of the original variables when calculating the scores on a given component. An alternative, and better, method is to look at the correlation between each component and every variable. If a component is very highly correlated with a particular variable then, in some sense, the component contains nearly all the information about differences in the subjects expressed by their scores on that variable (see chapter 10). The correlations of each of the 19 CPE subtests with the first three principal components of the scores of the Hong Kong candidates are given in table 15.5.

As can be seen from the table, the first principal component has a noticeable correlation with all of the subtests, the lowest correlation being 0.44. This happens frequently with the first component. As noted earlier in the chapter, the biologist will frequently interpret the component as a measure of size and may find it relatively uninteresting. Similarly, a researcher investigating 'athletic competence' might give tests of skill in several different sports. The first, general, component will really be a measure of the overall health and fitness of his subjects, not of their *specific* athletic skills: speed, hand–eye co-ordination, etc. Our first principal component would likewise seem to represent the subjects' general level of ability in English (or perhaps something even deeper, like an aptitude for learning new languages or even general intellectual ability). It is hardly surprising that the general level of ability should be correlated with all of the 19 subtests: the better one is in English, the better one is likely to do on each subtest, broadly speaking. This is more likely to be the case when, as here, the subjects have been preparing for the test, presumably practising for its various parts.

Let us for the moment ignore the second component and turn to the third. Here there are six correlations over 0.5, the remainder being less than 0.25. These six correlations are between the component and subtests 8 to 13, all of which are related to what we might call 'speaking ability'. (Note that such a 'speaking' component did not appear in the PCA of every group analysed by Hughes & Woods. Remember that PCA is designed to pick out those components or dimensions on which the subjects had scores which were rather variable. If the subjects of a particular group

Table 15.5. *Correlations of first three principal components of CPE scores of 70 subjects with the 19 subtests*

										Subtest									
	1	2	3	4	5	6	7	8	9	10	11	12	13	14	15	16	17	18	19
COMP1	0.90	0.51	0.67	0.80	0.77	0.74	0.86	0.59	0.61	0.67	0.67	0.71	0.59	0.88	0.78	0.71	0.86	0.85	0.44
COMP2	0.30	−0.02	−0.04	0.00	0.07	0.19	−0.25	−0.08	−0.02	0.00	0.07	−0.02	−0.02	0.15	0.17	−0.12	0.10	−0.43	0.14
COMP3	−0.22	0.16	0.12	0.14	0.24	0.12	−0.15	0.66	0.68	0.65	0.58	0.53	0.51	−0.01	0.18	−0.09	0.10	−0.15	0.02

Note: Some values in this table are slightly different from those in Hughes & Woods (1983: table 6.2). The values here have been calculated from the standard deviations in table 14.3 which are given to one decimal place only.

are relatively homogeneous in their overall speaking ability then no component corresponding to that skill will appear in the analysis.)

The meaning of the second component is less obvious. There are just three correlations with a magnitude of at least 0.25: 0.30 with subtest 1, −0.25 with subtest 7 and −0.43 with subtest 18. A subject who has a large, positive score on this component will be one who scores above average on the multiple choice vocabulary subtest and below average on the other two subtests, which both involve written answers to questions or texts presented (they were the only two subtests involving such a task). What ability does this second component represent? While we might wish to make something of the similarity between subtests 7 and 18, it is hard to see why performance on them should be related in the way it is to performance on subtest 1. All we can be sure of is that an important source of variability in the subjects was that while some did well in subtest 1 and badly in subtests 7 and 18, others showed the reverse pattern. It simply does not seem possible to identify the second principal component with a specific language skill.

Our failure to identify this component, indicated as significant by the Eastment–Krzanowski criterion, makes this an appropriate moment to point out the exploratory nature of PCA, especially in this study. The CPE is a practical language test, not a research instrument, and little is known of the subjects except that they took the examination at a particular centre. Using PCA in this way is best thought of as a preliminary step to more carefully controlled studies in which components indicated by PCA can be investigated in greater detail. Further data from the Hughes & Woods study will be found in the exercises in previous chapters.

Before leaving this topic we should point out that (except in the special case discussed in §15.7) the standard output of a PCA is unlikely to include the correlations between components and variables. However, these correlations can be calculated by the simple formula:

$$r_{ij} = \frac{a_{ij}\sqrt{v_i}}{s_j}$$

where v_i is the variance of the i-th component, s_j is the standard deviation of the j-th variable and r_{ij} is the correlation between the scores of the subjects on the i-th principal component and the j-th variable. For example, r_{15}, the correlation between the first principal component and the fifth subtest, is given as 0.77 in table 15.5. It has been calculated as:

$$r_{15} = \frac{a_{15}\sqrt{v_1}}{s_5} = \frac{0.17\sqrt{138.39}}{2.6} = 0.77$$

15.6 **Principal components of the correlation matrix**

In the examples discussed so far in this chapter the principal components were extracted from the covariance matrix of the subjects' scores. It is perfectly possible to extract components instead from the correlation matrix of the scores. Indeed this latter is the only option for PCA offered by some computer packages (e.g. SPSS). Before discussing why and when one might be preferable to the other, we will show that it can matter which is chosen. The results of the principal components analysis based on the correlation matrix of the 19 subtest scores of the same 70 subjects as before is presented in table 15.6. A cursory comparison with table 15.4 is sufficient to see that the sets of coefficients are quite different. For example, the coefficients of the first component now all lie in a narrow range (0.13 to 0.26) compared to the much wider range (0.07 to 0.51) for the first component based on the covariance matrix. In the solution based on the covariance matrix the second component had much larger coefficients for subtests 7 and 18 than the others. In the new solution this is not true. The Eastment–Krzanowski criterion indicates that only the first two components – accounting for 58% and 10% respectively – are significant, i.e. a different conclusion about the inherent dimensionality of the data is reached depending on which matrix is analysed. The correlations between the two significant new components and the subtests are given in table 15.7, and again we can see that the results look different from those of table 15.5. The first component is still a 'general' component which has a highish correlation with all the subtests (all but one over 0.5). However, the second component is negatively correlated with scores on all the speaking tasks and positively correlated with some of the writing/reading tasks. No component of this structure was isolated from the covariance matrix.

15.7 **Covariance matrix or correlation matrix?**

That this is a question worth addressing has just been demonstrated. The apparent number and the structure of the significant components in a principal components analysis can depend on which matrix is used as a basis for the analysis. It is not difficult to show that the correlation between two variables is just the covariance of the corresponding standardised variables. This means that the question used as a heading for this section can be paraphrased as, 'When a principal components analysis is to be carried out on the scores of several variables measured on a sample of subjects, should the components be extracted from the covariance matrix of the original scores or should the scores be standardised

Table 15.6. *Principal components analysis of subtest scores of 70 subjects*

NO. OF VARIABLES = 19
NO. OF OBSERVATIONS = 70
EIGENVALUES OF COVARIANCE MATRIX
10.98 1.97 1.15 0.85 0.62 0.56 0.43 0.36 0.35 0.32 0.26 0.26 0.22 0.21 0.14 0.12 0.09 0.09 0.04

PRINCIPAL COMPONENTS OF COVARIANCE MATRIX

COMP1	0.24	0.17	0.21	0.25	0.24	0.23	0.24	0.23	0.24	0.26	0.26	0.25	0.21	0.25	0.24	0.20	0.25	0.23	0.13
COMP2	0.26	0.07	0.16	0.10	0.07	0.14	0.22	−0.40	−0.38	−0.32	−0.31	−0.22	−0.28	0.21	0.10	0.23	0.13	0.20	0.16

Table 15.7. *Correlations of first two principal components with the 19 subtests (the principal components were extracted from the correlation matrix, i.e. the covariance matrix of the standardised scores)*

	Subtest																		
	1	2	3	4	5	6	7	8	9	10	11	12	13	14	15	16	17	18	19
COMP1	0.80	0.56	0.70	0.83	0.80	0.76	0.80	0.76	0.80	0.86	0.86	0.83	0.70	0.83	0.80	0.66	0.83	0.76	0.43
COMP2	0.36	0.10	0.22	0.14	0.10	0.20	0.31	−0.56	−0.53	−0.45	−0.43	−0.31	−0.39	0.29	0.14	0.32	0.18	0.28	0.22

first?'[2] Standardising the variables before analysis means that the components will be based on the correlation matrix of the original variables. There is no way to formulate a clear criterion on which to base this decision, though there is some support from theoretical statisticians for the use of unstandardised scores (e.g. Morrison 1976: 268). It is probably best to leave the original scores alone, i.e. to base the analysis on the covariance matrix, unless there is a good reason to standardise. One good reason would be if the data consist of variables which are not commensurable, such as age, income and IQ; in such a case they should almost certainly be standardised. If the variables are all of the same type, for example a set of scores on different language tests, they should be analysed in their original form. In general, the effect of standardising the scores will be to give extra weight to the first, general component. Also, the table of coefficients of the components (table 15.6) will then tell a very similar story to the table of correlations between the components and the original variables. This can be seen from the formula for calculating the correlation, r_{ij}, between the i-th component and the j-th variable:

$$r_{ij} = \frac{a_{ij}\sqrt{v_i}}{s_j}$$

Since, for all standardised variables, the variance (and hence the standard deviation) is unity, i.e. $s_j = 1$, it follows that, for components based on standardised variables (i.e. on the correlation matrix):

$$r_{ij} = a_{ij}\sqrt{v_i}$$

so that the correlation between a component and a variable will be proportional to the coefficient, a_{ij}, which determines how much weight a subject's score on the variable has in determining his score on the component. If we then look at the relative weights given to two variables in calculating a component, it will not matter whether we consider the correlations or the original coefficients. For example, from table 15.6, in the second principal component, subtest 6 (coefficient 0.14) has twice the weight given to subtest 5 (coefficient 0.07); in table 15.7, the correlation of subtest 6 with the second component ($r_{26} = 0.20$) is also exactly twice the correlation of the fifth subtest with that component ($r_{25} = 0.10$). The only difference is that to obtain the correlation all the coefficients of the i-th component have been multiplied by $\sqrt{v_i}$, the standard deviation of the

---

[2] Standardised variables (§6.4) always have variance equal to 1. Since we have 19 variables all with variance 1, the total variance is 19, which is again the sum of the eigenvalues in table 15.6.

component. It is worth noting that this means that the coefficients of earlier components are forced to be quite small. In the example, the variance of the first component extracted from the correlation matrix is 10.98 and its standard deviation is 3.31. Since $r_{1j} = a_{1j} \times 3.31$, and r_{1j} can never be greater than 1, a_{ij} cannot be greater than $1/3.31 = 0.30$. On the other hand, the second component has variance 1.97 and standard deviation 1.40. It is therefore possible that a coefficient of this component could be as high as $1/1.40 = 0.71$. This makes nonsense of any rule for interpreting components which looks only at the size of the coefficients. If we decide to reject coefficients smaller than, say, 0.35, *all* the coefficients in the first principal component are *certain* to be too small to be considered. It is recommended always to construct the table of correlations between components and variables (subtests), whether or not the variables have been standardised, and to base any empirical interpretation of the components on these correlations. However, although it does seem advisable to extract the principal components analysis from the covariance matrix of the unstandardised variables, some widely used statistical analysis computer programs, e.g. some versions of SPSS, do not permit that option and automatically standardise the variables before analysing them. This is unfortunate, to say the least.

You may also find the recommendation that a component should be included as significant or useful if its variance is greater than 1. This is a special case of the ad hoc rule suggested in §15.4. Since all standardised variables have unit variance, the total variance of, say, 19 *standardised* variables will be 19, and $1/19$ of this total is 1. For the example we have been discussing in this chapter the first three principal components of the correlation matrix have variances greater than unity, and the customary empirical rule would suggest that there are three recognisable dimensions in the data. However, according to the Eastment—Krzanowski criterion there are only two.

A discussion of principal components analysis with an extended example of its use in sociolinguistics can be found in Horvath (1985).

15.8 Factor analysis

PCA is certainly not the only technique widely used to determine the inherent dimensionality of a multivariate data set and identify the meaning of the underlying dimensions. An alternative technique with a longer history – the basic mathematical formulation was proposed by Spearman (1904) as a means of investigating the structure of 'intelligence' – is **factor analysis** (FA). FA is widely used in psychometrics and related fields, and there exists an abundance of texts describing the technique and giving examples of its use (e.g. Bennett & Bowers 1976; Maxwell 1977). For reasons explained below we will not attempt a detailed exposition of FA here, but there is often confusion about the difference between PCA and FA – indeed some researchers imply that they are the same thing – and it therefore seems worthwhile to make some attempt to discuss the essential differences between the two. Although testing is not by any means the only area of application for these techniques, they are commonly applied to sets of test scores in an attempt to discover the latent dimensions or constructs actually being measured by the tests, and we will discuss them in that context.

Carroll (1958) reports the results of a study of test batteries to measure the possible aptitude for learning foreign languages using subjects about to undertake a short intensive 'trial course' of Mandarin Chinese. Two independent samples, each of about 80 subjects, were presented with different batteries of tests and their scores analysed via a factor analysis. Our table 15.8 is adapted from Carroll's table 1 and shows the results of the analysis based on one of his samples. The numbers in the table (except for the final column) are the **factor loadings** which, for the moment, we will interpret as though they were coefficients of principal components since that is how they are interpreted by many authors, including Carroll in this paper. We discuss below what is the essential difference between factor loadings in a FA and the coefficients in a PCA.

Table 15.8. *Factor analysis of test scores of students of Mandarin Chinese*

Test	F_1	F_2	F_3	F_4	F_5	F_6	h^2
1. Tem-tem learning I	0.13	−0.07	−0.15	0.37	0.56	0.03	0.69
2. Tem-tem learning II	−0.08	0.05	0.16	0.12	0.69	−0.05	0.68
3. Tem-tem learning III	0.07	0.00	0.19	−0.02	0.46	0.30	0.46
4. Turse spelling	0.40	0.42	−0.06	0.12	0.03	0.33	0.61
5. Turse phonetic association	0.45	0.27	−0.04	0.43	−0.03	0.24	0.77
6. Spelling clues	0.70	0.00	0.11	0.01	0.07	0.26	0.89
7. Disarranged letters	0.38	0.27	0.06	0.36	−0.24	0.25	0.62
8. Rhyming	0.56	0.17	0.04	0.35	−0.07	−0.05	0.69
9. Co-operative vocabulary	0.55	0.26	0.01	0.18	0.01	−0.01	0.56
10. Number learning	−0.06	−0.01	0.57	0.04	0.01	0.07	0.48
11. Words in sentences	−0.07	0.35	0.18	0.22	0.19	0.29	0.46
12. Phonetic discrimination	0.05	−0.45	0.34	0.12	0.01	−0.12	0.47
13. Paired associates	0.32	0.51	0.38	−0.03	−0.07	0.01	0.56
14. Devanagari script	−0.09	0.19	0.30	0.02	0.19	0.39	0.48
15. Perdaseb	−0.10	0.19	0.30	0.02	0.19	0.39	0.48
16. Phonetic script	0.12	0.41	0.08	0.47	0.11	0.04	0.67
17. Criterion	0.05	0.33	0.43	0.18	0.28	0.13	0.77

Adapted from Carroll (1958: table 1)

Carroll points out that factor 1 (F_1) has high loadings for tests 4, 5, 6, 7, 8, 9, 13 and argues that it can therefore be identified as a 'verbal knowledge' factor. Note, in particular, that tests 6 and 9 do not have high loadings on any other factor. In a similar fashion he identifies an 'associative memory' factor (F_3), a 'sound–symbol association ability' factor (F_4), and an 'inductive language learning ability' factor (F_5). He suggests that F_6 might be related to 'syntactical fluency' or 'grammatical sensitivity' but cannot find a simple interpretation for F_2, although he notes that 'whatever the nature of the factor, it is probably one of the most important components of foreign language aptitude'. He argues that this factor may represent 'an increment of test performance ascribable to a specific motivation, interest, or facility with respect to unusual linguistic materials' and tentatively suggests the name 'linguistic interest' factor.

So much then for possible interpretation. However, what exactly is a 'factor'? What does factor analysis 'do'? Full answers to these two questions would require more space than we wish to devote to them here, and interested readers should refer to the texts we have mentioned above. Unfortunately for those who do not have a good grounding in mathematics it is necessary to come to grips with the underlying mathematical concepts in order to have a good understanding of FA in all its detail. However, we can go some way towards an explanation of the process by comparing PCA and FA.

As we have seen, the essential step in a PCA is to convert the scores on the p original variables (X_1, X_2, ..., X_p) into scores on p new variables (Y_1, Y_2, ..., Y_p) by a rule of the form:

Equation 1 (PCA)

$$Y_k = a_{k1}X_1 + a_{k2}X_2 + \ldots + a_{kp}X_p$$

(i.e. the Ys are linear combinations of the Xs), where the coefficients are chosen to give special properties to the new variables. There is only one set of coefficients which will cause the Ys to have the required properties. In other words, the solution to a PCA is unique in the sense that two different researchers analysing the same set of test scores will arrive at exactly the same principal components. There is no underlying model for PCA (as there is, for example, for a discriminant analysis or a multiple regression), nor are any assumptions needed about the distribution of the test scores in some population. PCA reorganises the data *in the sample* without the need to assume anything about its relation to a wider population. FA is more flexible but less objective.

To carry out a factor analysis we must assume that the scores on each of the tests are normally distributed. Indeed, it is assumed that for a given subject each test score is made up of a linear combination of that subject's scores on a set of **latent dimensions** or **factors** plus a component particular to that subtest, i.e.

$$X_{ij} = b_{j1}F_{i1} + b_{j2}F_{i2} + \ldots + b_{jm}F_{im} + \varepsilon_{ij}$$

where X_{ij} is the score of the i-th subject on the j-th subtest and F_{ik} is the 'score' of the same subject on the k-th dimension of, say, language ability, among the m dimensions being measured by the various subtests. The quantity ε_{ij} is the part of the score X_{ij} which is not accounted for by the common dimensions and can be thought of as something particular to the j-th test. The factor equation can be written with simpler notation, thus:

Equation 2 (FA)

$$X_j = b_{j1}F_1 + b_{j2}F_2 + \ldots + b_{jm}F_m + \varepsilon_j$$

and is often expressed in words as 'any score on subtest j is a linear combination of the scores on the **common factors** $F_1, F_2, \ldots, F_m$ plus a contribution from the **specific factors**, ε_j'. The quantity, b_{jk} is the **loading** of the k-th factor in the j-th response (i.e. subtest score).

Although Equations 1 and 2 look very similar, there is a crucial difference. The values of all the Xs in Equation 1 are observed for all the subjects and the coefficients a_{kj} are estimated using the criteria that Y_1 is as variable as possible, Y_2 is uncorrelated with Y_1, etc. These criteria are sufficient to lead to a unique set of values for the a_{kj}. It is these criteria which ensure that every experimenter who carries out a PCA on the variance–covariance matrix of a given set of data will arrive at the same principal components coefficients. FA, however, does *not* lead to a unique solution. The process known as **rotation of factors**, discussed below, allows an experimenter to choose the solution he prefers from an infinite set of possible solutions.

Factors are referred to as 'latent' because they have not been, and possibly will never be, observed directly. Their existence, importance and structure have to be inferred from data via the model described above. The model, described by Equation 2, has many superficial similarities with multiple regression (chapter 13). The model assumes that there is a (small) number of universal latent dimensions or variables, called factors; that any individual has an unobserved 'true score' on each factor; and that the individual's score on any of the observed variables (i.e. the test scores in the language aptitude example) can be 'explained' or predicted to a greater or less extent by his factor scores when these are combined using Equation 2. The final column of table 15.8 gives the values of h^2, the proportion of the variability of the sample scores in each test which is 'explained' by the factor scores. The values of h^2 are usually called the **communalities** while $1 - h^2$ gives the estimated value of the **specific variance** of each test – that part of the variability in the sample scores *not* explained by the factors.

However, the resemblance to multiple regression is only superficial. First, the factors, which here play the role of the independent variables, are not observed. In other words, we are trying to fit a model without knowing the values of the independent variables! Second, there is not just one dependent variable – there are always several. Carroll's test battery contained 17 tests and his FA attempts to explain simultaneously the scores on these 17 'dependent variables'. Not surprisingly, it is a far from trivial exercise to solve this problem and several different methods have been proposed. The most common are the **centroid method**, the **principal-axes method**, and the **maximum likelihood method**. It is impossible to discuss the difference between them in the present book (see e.g. Cureton & D'Agostino 1983 for discussion and further references), but they will give different results, estimating different values for the communalities and perhaps even indicating different numbers of important factors. The maximum likelihood method provides a test of the hypothesis that no further factors are required after the first few have been fitted and is **scale invariant**, which means that the same solution will be reached whether the analysis is carried out on the variance–covariance matrix or on the correlation matrix of the sample. However, whichever method is used, even once the number of factors has been decided upon there are very many (an infinite number!) mathematical solutions, all of which are 'correct' but all of which will give different values to the factor loadings. It is possible to explore these solutions, by a process called **factor rotation**, to look for a set of factor loadings which the experimenter believes to give a meaningful solution. It is not easy to give a short and clear description of this process and interested readers should consult the references.

From the brief discussion above it should be clear that there is a certain amount of indeterminancy in the FA process. The experimenter has a choice of methods of factoring which will give different solutions. For some of those methods it will matter whether the factors are extracted from the covariance or the correlation matrix. A first solution from any of these methods will allow a decision about the number of factors and will give an estimate of the communalities. Without changing the number of factors or the communalities it is possible to alter the factor loadings by rotating the factors to search for loading patterns which offer simple interpretation. In the main this will mean trying to establish factors with very high loadings on just a few tests and almost zero loadings on the others. All of this is a valid process in any case only if the assumptions of the factor model are justified.

Cureton & D'Agostino suggest that if the purpose of analysis is to convert a battery of test scores into a single, composite score the first principal component will give the best weights for doing this. Furthermore, principal components are much more accurately estimated from any sample than factor loadings from the same sample and may give a clearer indication of the underlying dimensionality of the data. On the other hand, factors are usually easier to interpret than principal components and the plausibility of a particular factor solution could be checked by means of further data and a **confirmatory factor analysis** which allows hypotheses to be tested about the original solution. Further discussion of the similarities and differences between PCA and FA in a linguistics context can be found in Woods (1983).

SUMMARY

This chapter has introduced and compared **principal components analysis** (PCA) and **factor analysis** (FA).

(1) PCA produces a set of coefficients which allow the original scores to be converted into scores on new variables, the principal components, each of which is independent of the others and each of which successively accounts for as much as possible of the total variability left after the earlier components have been extracted.

(2) It was recommended that PCA be carried out usually on the **variance–covariance** matrix and the **correlation matrix** be used only where there are good reasons for doing so.

(3) By means of an example, the problems of **reifying** the components and deciding on the **inherent dimensionality** were discussed.

(4) The model for FA was introduced and discussed. The different variables are assumed to be **normally distributed**. The interpretation of **factors** was discussed and exemplified.

(5) It was pointed out that PCA gives a unique solution while FA leaves a great deal of choice to the experimenter through **rotation of factors**. It was pointed out that this flexibility could be used creatively but must be used carefully

Table A1. *Random numbers*

44 59	62 26	82 51	04 19	45 98	03 51	50 14	28 02	12 29	88 87
85 90	22 58	52 90	22 76	95 70	02 84	74 69	06 13	98 86	06 50
44 33	29 88	90 49	07 55	69 50	20 27	59 51	97 53	57 04	22 26
47 57	22 52	75 74	53 11	76 11	21 16	12 44	31 89	16 91	47 75
03 20	54 20	70 56	77 59	95 60	19 75	29 94	11 23	59 30	14 47
40 91	24 41	01 45	51 98	22 54	82 44	43 43	23 29	16 24	15 62
91 14	61 71	03 40	15 69	44 46	54 66	35 01	87 61	23 76	36 80
27 71	29 93	52 89	64 78	32 97	65 28	99 82	41 10	97 52	41 91
12 96	17 70	72 76	17 93	38 26	72 96	28 73	27 64	78 16	72 81
54 30	61 13	60 50	61 56	40 20	19 22	30 61	43 89	60 09	82 39
83 32	99 29	30 06	19 71	11 32	69 17	86 34	50 76	37 41	76 54
27 17	25 61	91 76	19 54	99 73	97 21	44 87	39 63	24 22	74 30
40 89	21 88	56 84	11 75	74 88	23 55	48 98	19 48	79 81	92 62
51 66	17 48	26 96	00 83	81 23	58 09	21 39	39 20	83 46	30 75
95 22	63 34	58 91	78 22	50 22	77 21	14 19	58 66	49 25	03 51
93 83	73 70	80 88	71 85	64 44	57 50	19 82	60 77	38 95	93 33
42 02	33 18	33 55	96 66	88 38	16 80	77 51	17 96	49 76	99 28
42 42	13 33	66 00	18 37	58 80	54 32	00 96	25 16	15 37	34 12
66 71	67 54	79 25	64 34	82 15	28 97	88 84	84 51	62 90	17 71
73 05	53 85	63 18	06 47	71 00	32 31	59 72	34 28	70 83	12 90
02 80	12 24	34 78	22 50	57 02	07 01	13 00	78 80	94 93	14 53
22 89	81 32	32 72	48 92	95 75	88 56	75 73	79 17	53 81	54 17
94 45	64 84	17 28	06 57	71 96	81 36	37 65	42 62	43 84	45 23
10 30	05 07	21 34	59 18	85 95	21 87	73 16	78 37	15 98	16 66
73 39	21 94	01 84	28 20	50 35	57 82	88 13	52 53	76 73	68 22
47 91	87 36	45 69	03 01	24 25	13 64	42 74	36 67	77 67	00 92
39 24	26 77	62 37	82 46	93 96	82 75	75 16	95 05	30 68	83 02
77 29	09 12	41 77	29 57	34 89	94 95	45 70	59 85	38 04	04 80
04 78	20 07	17 15	68 12	38 26	01 90	68 30	83 80	19 89	98 65
83 81	53 08	09 23	22 61	99 41	27 90	35 43	07 09	62 26	45 83
97 67	74 54	96 14	63 28	98 11	18 33	82 60	90 41	33 11	77 59
52 80	26 89	13 38	70 08	73 22	64 70	83 44	49 24	20 93	12 59
80 69	43 27	33 56	39 88	73 31	22 44	87 33	08 21	40 06	77 91
00 48	24 08	73 92	37 19	69 87	91 79	86 27	47 91	31 70	53 52
14 91	97 37	53 40	46 26	29 25	96 42	57 22	94 34	59 71	23 59
50 62	28 51	94 10	15 18	06 02	39 94	13 91	54 50	60 27	28 68
17 59	53 08	58 06	80 00	75 71	95 13	76 91	24 55	34 09	97 12
73 17	99 45	85 28	63 17	99 31	24 62	75 82	78 89	27 59	18 62
37 95	74 96	25 44	95 66	42 02	31 48	82 21	76 87	86 75	07 95
76 95	18 76	76 28	18 60	44 92	76 09	46 96	39 37	27 12	30 44

Table A2. *Standard normal distribution*

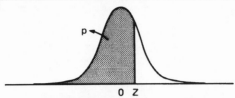

The distribution tabulated is that of the normal distribution with mean zero and standard deviation 1. For each value of Z, the standardised normal deviate, the proportion. P, of the distribution less than Z is given. For a normal distribution with mean μ and variance σ^2, the proportion of the distribution less than some particular value, X, is obtained by calculating $Z = (X - \mu)/\sigma$ and reading the proportion corresponding to this value of Z.

Z	p	Z	p	Z	p	Z	p
−4.00	0.00003	−1.50	0.0668	0.00	0.5000	1.55	0.9394
−3.50	0.00023	−1.45	0.0735	0.05	0.5199	1.60	0.9452
−3.00	0.0014	−1.40	0.0808	0.10	0.5398	1.65	0.9505
−2.95	0.0016	−1.35	0.0885	0.15	0.5596	1.70	0.9554
−2.90	0.0019	−1.30	0.0968	0.20	0.5793	1.75	0.9599
−2.85	0.0022	−1.25	0.1056	0.25	0.5987	1.80	0.9641
−2.80	0.0026	−1.20	0.1151	0.30	0.6179	1.85	0.9678
−2.75	0.0030	−1.15	0.1251	0.35	0.6368	1.90	0.9713
−2.70	0.0035	−1.10	0.1357	0.40	0.6554	1.95	0.9744
−2.65	0.0040	−1.05	0.1469	0.45	0.6736	2.00	0.9772
−2.60	0.0047	−1.00	0.1587	0.50	0.6915	2.05	0.9798
−2.55	0.0054	−0.95	0.1711	0.55	0.7088	2.10	0.9821
−2.50	0.0062	−0.90	0.1841	0.60	0.7257	2.15	0.9842
−2.45	0.0071	−0.85	0.1977	0.65	0.7422	2.20	0.9861
−2.40	0.0082	−0.80	0.2119	0.70	0.7580	2.25	0.9878
−2.35	0.0094	−0.75	0.2266	0.75	0.7734	2.30	0.9893
−2.30	0.0107	−0.70	0.2420	0.80	0.7881	2.35	0.9906
−2.25	0.0122	−0.65	0.2578	0.85	0.8023	2.40	0.9918
−2.20	0.0139	−0.60	0.2743	0.90	0.8159	2.45	0.9929
−2.15	0.0158	−0.55	0.2912	0.95	0.8289	2.50	0.9938
−2.10	0.0179	−0.50	0.3085	1.00	0.8413	2.55	0.9946
−2.05	0.0202	−0.45	0.3264	1.05	0.8531	2.60	0.9953
−2.00	0.0228	−0.40	0.3446	1.10	0.8643	2.65	0.9960
−1.95	0.0256	−0.35	.3032	1.15	0.8749	2.70	0.9965
−1.90	0.0287	−0. ــ	0.3821	1.20	0.8849	2.75	0.9970
−1.85	0.0322	−0.25	0.4013	1.25	0.8944	2.80	0.9974
−1.80	0.0359	−0.20	0.4207	1.30	0.9032	2.85	0.9978
−1.75	0.0401	−0.15	0.4404	1.35	0.9115	2.90	0.9981
−1.70	0.0446	−0.10	0.4602	1.40	0.9192	2.95	0.9984
−1.65	0.0495	−0.05	0.4801	1.45	0.9265	3.00	0.9986
−1.60	0.0548	−0.00	0.5000	1.50	0.9332	3.50	0.99977
−1.55	0.0606					4.00	0.99997

Table A3. *Percentage points of standard normal distribution*

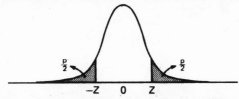

This table gives the values of Z for which a given percentage, p, of the standardised normal distribution lies outside the range $-Z$ to $+Z$.

p	Z
90	0.1257
80	0.2533
70	0.3853
60	0.5244
50	0.6745
40	0.8416
30	1.0364
20	1.2816
10	1.6449
5	1.9600
2	2.3263
1	2.5758
0.2	3.0902
0.1	3.2905

Table A4. *Percentage points of t-distribution*

narrows with increasing degrees of freedom

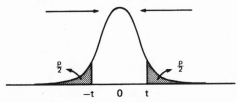

This table gives the values of t for which a particular percentage, p, of the student's t-distribution lies outside the range −t to +t. These values of t are tabulated for various degrees of freedom.

Degrees of freedom	p =							
	50	20	10	5	2	1	0.2	0.1
1	1.00	3.08	6.31	12.7	31.8	63.7	318	637
2	0.82	1.89	2.92	4.30	6.96	9.92	22.3	31.6
3	0.76	1.64	2.35	3.18	4.54	5.84	10.2	12.9
4	0.74	1.53	2.13	2.78	3.75	4.60	7.17	8.61
5	0.73	1.48	2.02	2.57	3.36	4.03	5.89	6.87
6	0.72	1.44	1.94	2.45	3.14	3.71	5.21	5.96
7	0.71	1.42	1.89	2.36	3.00	3.50	4.79	5.41
8	0.71	1.40	1.86	2.31	2.90	3.36	4.50	5.04
9	0.70	1.38	1.83	2.26	2.82	3.25	4.30	4.78
10	0.70	1.37	1.81	2.23	2.76	3.17	4.14	4.59
12	0.70	1.36	1.78	2.18	2.68	3.05	3.93	4.32
15	0.69	1.34	1.75	2.13	2.60	2.95	3.73	4.07
20	0.69	1.32	1.72	2.09	2.53	2.85	3.55	3.85
24	0.68	1.32	1.71	2.06	2.49	2.80	3.47	3.75
30	0.68	1.31	1.70	2.04	2.46	2.75	3.39	3.65
40	0.68	1.30	1.68	2.02	2.42	2.70	3.31	3.55
60	0.68	1.30	1.67	2.00	2.39	2.66	3.23	3.46
∞	0.67	1.28	1.64	1.96	2.33	2.58	3.09	3.29

Table A5. *Percentage points of chi-squared distribution*

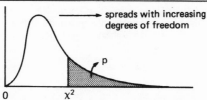

spreads with increasing
degrees of freedom

p

0   χ^2

This table gives the values of χ^2 for which a particular percentage, p, of the chi-squared distribution is greater than χ^2. These values of χ^2 are tabulated for various degrees of freedom.

Degrees of freedom	p=							
	97.5	95	50	10	5	2.5	1	0.1
1	0.000982	0.00393	0.45	2.71	3.84	5.02	6.64	10.8
2	0.0506	0.103	1.39	4.61	5.99	7.38	9.21	13.8
3	0.216	0.352	2.37	6.25	7.82	9.35	11.3	16.3
4	0.484	0.711	3.36	7.78	9.49	11.1	13.3	18.5
5	0.831	1.15	4.35	9.24	11.1	12.8	15.1	20.5
6	1.24	1.64	5.35	10.6	12.6	14.5	16.8	22.5
7	1.69	2.17	6.35	12.0	14.1	16.0	18.5	24.3
8	2.18	2.73	7.34	13.4	15.5	17.5	20.1	26.1
9	2.70	3.33	8.34	14.7	16.9	19.0	21.7	27.9
10	3.25	3.94	9.34	16.0	18.3	20.5	23.2	29.6
12	4.40	5.23	11.3	18.5	21.0	23.3	26.2	32.9
15	6.26	7.26	14.3	22.3	25.0	27.5	30.6	37.7
20	9.59	10.9	19.3	28.4	31.4	34.2	37.6	45.3
24	12.4	13.9	23.3	33.2	36.4	39.4	43.0	51.2
30	16.8	18.5	29.3	40.3	43.8	47.0	50.9	59.7
40	24.4	26.5	39.3	51.8	55.8	59.3	63.7	73.4
60	40.5	43.2	59.3	74.4	79.1	83.3	88.4	99.6

Table A6. *Percentage points of Pearson's correlation coefficient*

This table gives absolute values of the sample correlation coefficient r which would lead to the rejection of the null hypothesis that the population correlation coefficient $\rho = 0$ against the alternative hypothesis that $\rho \neq 0$ at the stated significance levels p.

	Significance levels (p)			
Sample size (n)	0.10	0.05	0.01	0.001
3	0.9877	0.9969	0.9999	0.9999
4	0.900	0.950	0.990	0.999
5	0.805	0.878	0.959	0.991
6	0.729	0.811	0.917	0.974
7	0.669	0.754	0.875	0.951
8	0.621	0.707	0.834	0.925
9	0.582	0.666	0.798	0.898
10	0.549	0.632	0.765	0.872
11	0.521	0.602	0.735	0.847
12	0.497	0.576	0.708	0.823
13	0.476	0.553	0.684	0.801
14	0.457	0.532	0.661	0.780
15	0.441	0.514	0.641	0.760
16	0.426	0.497	0.623	0.742
17	0.412	0.482	0.606	0.725
18	0.400	0.468	0.590	0.708
19	0.389	0.456	0.575	0.693
20	0.378	0.444	0.561	0.679
21	0.369	0.433	0.549	0.665
22	0.360	0.423	0.537	0.652
27	0.323	0.381	0.487	0.597
32	0.296	0.349	0.449	0.554
42	0.257	0.304	0.393	0.490
52	0.231	0.273	0.354	0.443
62	0.211	0.250	0.325	0.408
82	0.183	0.217	0.283	0.357
102	0.164	0.195	0.254	0.321

Table A7. *Percentage points for distribution of the Spearman rank correlation coefficient, r_s, to test the hypothesis $H_0: \rho_s = 0$ versus $H_1: \rho_s \neq 0$*

Sample size (n)	0..10	0.05	0.02	0.01
4	1.000	—	—	—
5	0.900	1.000	1.000	—
6	0.829	0.886	0.943	1.000
7	0.714	0.786	0.893	0.929
8	0.643	0.714	0.833	0.881
9	0.600	0.700	0.783	0.833
10	0.564	0.648	0.745	0.794
11	0.536	0.618	0.709	0.764
12	0.503	0.587	0.678	0.734
13	0.484	0.560	0.648	0.703
14	0.464	0.538	0.626	0.679
15	0.446	0.521	0.604	0.657
16	0.429	0.503	0.584	0.634
17	0.414	0.488	0.566	0.618
18	0.401	0.474	0.550	0.600
19	0.391	0.460	0.535	0.584
20	0.380	0.447	0.522	0.570
21	0.370	0.436	0.510	0.566
22	0.361	0.425	0.497	0.544
23	0.353	0.416	0.486	0.532
24	0.344	0.407	0.476	0.521
25	0.337	0.398	0.466	0.511
26	0.331	0.390	0.457	0.499
27	0.324	0.383	0.449	0.492
28	0.318	0.375	0.441	0.483
29	0.312	0.369	0.433	0.475
30	0.306	0.362	0.426	0.467

Adapted from Glasser & Winter (1961: table 2)

Table A8. *Percentage points of F-distribution*

These tables give the values of F for which a given percentage of the F-distribution is greater than F.

The F-distribution arises when two independent estimates of a variance are divided one by the other. Each of these estimates has its degrees of freedom associated with it, thus to specify which particular F-distribution is to be considered, the degrees of freedom of both the numerator n_1, and the denominator n_2, must be given.

(a) 5 per cent point

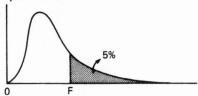

$n_1 = 1$	2	3	4	5	6	7	8	10	12	24
$n_2 = 2$										
18.5	19.0	19.2	19.2	19.3	19.3	19.4	19.4	19.4	19.4	19.5
3 10.1	9.55	9.28	9.12	9.01	8.94	8.89	8.85	8.79	8.74	8.64
4 7.71	6.94	6.59	6.39	6.26	6.16	6.09	6.04	5.96	5.91	5.77
5 6.61	5.79	5.41	5.19	5.05	4.95	4.88	4.82	4.74	4.68	4.53
6 5.99	5.14	4.76	4.53	4.39	4.28	4.21	4.15	4.06	4.00	3.84
7 5.59	4.74	4.35	4.12	3.97	3.87	3.79	3.73	3.64	3.57	3.41
8 5.32	4.46	4.07	3.84	3.69	3.58	3.50	3.44	3.35	3.28	3.12
9 5.12	4.26	3.86	3.63	3.48	3.37	3.29	3.23	3.14	3.07	2.90
10 4.96	4.10	3.71	3.48	3.33	3.22	3.14	3.07	2.98	2.91	2.74
12 4.75	3.89	3.49	3.26	3.11	3.00	2.91	2.85	2.75	2.69	2.51
15 4.54	3.68	3.29	3.06	2.90	2.79	2.71	2.64	2.54	2.48	2.29
20 4.35	3.49	3.10	2.87	2.71	2.60	2.51	2.45	2.35	2.28	2.08
24 4.26	3.40	3.01	2.78	2.62	2.51	2.42	2.36	2.25	2.18	1.98
30 4.17	3.32	2.92	2.69	2.53	2.42	2.33	2.27	2.16	2.09	1.89
40 4.08	3.23	2.84	2.61	2.45	2.34	2.25	2.18	2.08	2.00	1.79
60 4.00	3.15	2.76	2.53	2.37	2.25	2.17	2.10	1.99	1.92	1.70

(b) 1 per cent point

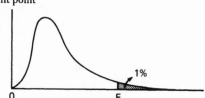

$n_1 = 1$	2	3	4	5	6	7	8	10	12	24
$n_2 = 2$ 98.5	99.0	99.2	99.2	99.3	99.3	99.4	99.4	99.4	99.4	99.5
3 34.1	30.8	29.5	28.7	28.2	27.9	27.7	27.5	27.2	27.1	26.6
4 21.2	18.0	16.7	16.0	15.5	15.2	15.0	14.8	14.5	14.4	13.9
5 16.3	13.3	12.1	11.4	11.0	10.7	10.5	10.3	10.1	9.89	9.47
6 13.7	10.98	9.78	9.15	8.75	8.47	8.26	8.10	7.87	7.72	7.31
7 12.3	9.55	8.45	7.85	7.46	7.19	6.99	6.84	6.62	6.47	6.07
8 11.3	8.65	7.59	7.01	6.63	6.37	6.18	6.03	5.81	5.67	5.28
9 10.6	8.02	6.99	6.42	6.06	5.80	5.61	5.47	5.26	5.11	4.73
10 10.0	7.56	6.55	5.99	5.64	5.39	5.20	5.06	4.85	4.71	4.33
12 9.33	6.93	5.95	5.41	5.06	4.82	4.64	4.50	4.30	4.16	3.78
15 8.68	6.36	5.42	4.89	4.56	4.32	4.14	4.00	3.80	3.67	3.29
20 8.10	5.85	4.94	4.43	4.10	3.87	3.70	3.56	3.37	3.23	2.86
24 7.82	5.61	4.72	4.22	3.90	3.67	3.50	3.36	3.17	3.03	2.66
30 7.56	5.39	4.51	4.02	3.70	3.47	3.30	3.17	2.98	2.84	2.47
40 7.31	5.18	4.31	3.83	3.51	3.29	3.12	2.99	2.80	2.66	2.29
60 7.08	4.98	4.13	3.65	3.34	3.12	2.95	2.82	2.63	2.50	2.12

Table A9. *5% critical values of U for a two-tailed Mann–Whitney test*

	4	5	6	7	8	9	10	11	12	13	14	15	16	17	18	19	20
1	—	—	—	—	—	—	—	—	—	—	—	—	—	—	—	—	—
2	—	—	—	—	0	0	0	0	1	1	1	1	1	2	2	2	2
3	—	0	0	0	2	2	3	3	4	4	5	5	6	6	7	7	8
4	0	1	2	3	4	4	5	6	7	8	9	10	11	11	12	13	13
5		2	3	5	6	7	8	9	11	12	13	14	15	17	18	19	20
6			5	6	8	10	11	13	14	16	17	19	21	22	24	25	27
7				8	10	12	14	16	18	20	22	24	26	28	30	32	34
8					13	15	17	19	22	24	26	29	31	34	36	38	41
9						17	20	23	26	28	31	34	37	39	42	45	48
10							23	26	29	33	36	39	42	45	48	52	55
11								30	33	37	40	44	47	51	55	58	62
12									37	41	45	49	53	57	61	65	69
13										45	50	54	59	63	67	72	76
14											55	59	64	67	74	78	83
15												64	70	75	80	85	90
16													75	81	86	92	98
17														87	93	99	105
18															99	106	112
19																113	119
20																	127

Adapted from Siegel (1956: tables J, K).
Note: Values of U *less than* the tabulated values are significant.

Table A10. *Significance levels for the sign test (the values given are relevant to a two-tailed test)*

T	0	1	2	3	4	5	6	7
5	0.061							
6	0.031							
7	0.015	0.070		greater than 0.1				
8	0.008	0.039						
9	0.002	0.022						
10		0.011						
11		0.006	0.064					
12		0.003	0.037					
13		0.002	0.021	0.092				
14			0.012	0.057				
15			0.007	0.036				
16			0.003	0.023	0.077			
17			0.002	0.013	0.050			
18			0.001	0.008	0.029	0.096		
19				0.005	0.019	0.064		
20	very small			0.002	0.012	0.041		
21				0.001	0.007	0.027	0.078	
22					0.004	0.016	0.053	
23					0.003	0.009	0.034	0.095
24					0.002	0.005	0.021	0.064
25						0.003	0.015	0.043

Statistical computation

1. Calculators

Most of the measures, estimators and test statistics discussed in the first thirteen chapters of the book can be obtained from data by the use of a modest electronic calculator costing less than £20. To be at all useful a calculator must have the following features: (a) an automatic square root function (key usually marked '√'); (b) at least two memories. It is certainly worthwhile to buy a calculator which has some built-in statistical calculations. Most calculators now have a facility to calculate the mean and variance of a single data set. Many will also calculate correlations (look for the letter 'r' – usually to be found in a different colour *beside* one of the keys rather than on it) and simple linear regressions.

2. Using a computer

However, throughout the book it has been assumed that, except where the calculations are simple and straightforward, the analysis will be carried out using a suitable computer package. There are several stages involved in that process. The data have to be put in an appropriate form and possibly stored in advance, the analysis carried out and the results printed on paper so that they can be studied carefully at leisure. It will be assumed in what follows that the analysis is to be carried out on a moderately large computing facility accessed via a terminal (or **remote terminal**) which is not an integral part of the computer. It is possible that you may have access to a microcomputer which has a program for analysing statistical data. As yet there is no comprehensive statistical analysis program widely available for microcomputers so that we can offer no general advice here, although much of what follows below will still be relevant. (Versions of MINITAB, SPSS, BMPD have been written for various microcomputers but the authors have no information about their reliability or availability.)

From a remote terminal it will be necessary to establish communications with the computer and identify yourself to it. Exactly how this is done will depend on local conventions as well as on the type of computer you wish to use and the type of terminal at which you are working. You will probably have to apply to a Computer Centre for a personal identification code (to which you will usually add a private password) and at the same time you should be able to receive copies of the documents which explain the basic procedures. While communications are being established from the terminal the computer may respond to each of your instructions by printing messages on the screen. These messages may be quite long and technical. It is usually worthwhile learning to recognise those phrases or symbols which indicate that connections are being established as expected.

Now, suppose that your terminal has been successfully connected and the computer has accepted you as a valid user. The next stage depends on whether you will be using the statistical analysis package in **batch mode** or **interactively**. In batch mode you will have to prepare all your instructions to the package in a kind of shopping list or **program** and then submit the complete program to the computer. The machine will attempt to carry out all your instructions in sequence and will reply to your terminal only when it has completed *all* the tasks requested in the program or until an erroneous instruction is discovered. In the latter case it will usually carry out all the instructions prior to the error and print out the corresponding results – the **output** – together with information about the error. Whether or not it attempts to carry out the rest of the program will depend on the seriousness of the error, but even if it does continue it is wise to be highly sceptical of any analysis subsequent to an error and to repeat it after making the required modification to the program.

A program is stored in the form of a **file** with a unique **filename**. It will usually be **created**, i.e. typed into the computer, using a **piece of software** (another program) called an **editor** which also allows you to correct any errors you make, either at the moment of typing or after they are discovered when you attempt to run your program. Again, the Computer Centre will supply instructions for the use of the editor and for the submission of your program to the statistical analysis package of your choice.

If the package is **interactive** or **conversational** and facilities are available to use the computer interactively or in **interactive mode** then it will be convenient to take advantage of this. It means that you can submit your instructions one at a time to the analysis package and you will receive an immediate response on the screen. There are at least two advantages in this. First, if you write an instruction incorrectly the computer will refuse to accept it and will respond with a message which will be more or less helpful. You can then try again until you get it right. Second, the results obtained from one step in the analysis may help to suggest new ideas or may indicate that the analysis you have planned is clearly going to be unsuccessful or inappropriate. It will also be possible to experiment and, with an immediate response to each of your attempts, reach a satisfactory analysis without spending hours or even days waiting for paper to reach you from the Computer Centre. It will always be possible to get a **hard copy**, i.e. a version printed on paper, of any part or all of the conversation you carry on with the computer and the results of your analysis. The results, and the record of your conversation, can also be **stored** internally in the computer with known filenames which will enable you to recall them later. From the beginning of your computing career you should endeavour to keep good records of your files, their filenames and a summary of their contents. Note that even when using interactive mode it is usually convenient to prepare your data and store it in a file before attempting to analyse it. Interactive packages will usually allow you to type in the data as it is required but if you make a typing error it may then be more difficult to correct it than if it were stored separately.

3. Using MINITAB

The first two elements in the computing process are to connect the terminal to the main computer and to create data files or program files and store them. The third step will be to use a standard statistical analysis package. There are many of these and most computer installations will offer only one or two of them. However, they have many similarities, at least from the point of view of an unsophisticated user. There should be manuals available at the Computer Centre, though these may be difficult to read – computer manuals are not renowned for their clarity. Most interactive packages have a HELP facility which enables the user to request information from the computer about the instructions required to carry out different types of analysis. For some packages there are simplified, introductory handbooks available, e.g. Ryan, Joiner & Ryan (1985).

We give an example below of the MINITAB program required to carry out the analysis of some of the examples discussed in earlier chapters. We have chosen this package as an illustration since, from our experience, it is easily self-taught. Although it is somewhat limited, it can be used to carry out most of the analyses discussed in the book except for the multivariate examples of chapters 14 and 15.

This is not intended to be an exhaustive guide to MINITAB. Here we simply exemplify some of its features in relation to our data. In addition, it is assumed that the user has determined for himself how to access MINITAB on the particular mainframe he is employing. To exemplify the use of the package we will take the error gravity score data analysed in different ways in chapters 10, 11 and 12, which appear in full in table 12.4 on page 201.

In the examples below you may note small discrepancies between the values given by MINITAB and those quoted in the main text of the book. For example, in the correlation matrix calculated below, MINITAB gives a correlation as 0.769 whereas in chapter 10 (page 158) we obtained a value of 0.770 for this quantity. These values are so close that the difference is unimportant. The MINITAB value is probably more correct. Our value is more likely to have some rounding error because of the sequence of calculations – more suitable for hand calculation – which we used to obtain it.

4. Inputting the data

The first task is to provide MINITAB with the data which is to be statistically analysed. Data can either be typed in direct from the keyboard, or alternatively read in from an already extant file in the user's filestore. Both methods make use of the READ command.

4.1 *Direct input*

Data is defined in terms of columns, and read in rows, For the data of table 12.4, type:

READ C_1–C_3

(since there are three columns in the data). After you hit RETURN, the data is typed in as follows (with a space between each data point):

22 36 22	(type RETURN)
16 9 18	(type RETURN)
42 29 42	(type RETURN)

and so on. After the 32 rows of data have been typed in, type:

END

The machine will respond with the number of rows read; if you need to check the file once it is read, the PRINT command is available:

PRINT C_1–C_3

4.2 *File input*

If the data you wish to analyse is already available in a file, simply use the READ command with the name of the file enclosed in quotes, and the number of columns into which you want it to be read:

READ 'filename' C_1–C_3

After RETURN, the machine will respond with the number of rows read and the first few lines of the file, as follows:

32 ROWS READ

Row	C_1	C_2	C_3
1	22	36	22
2	16	9	18
3	42	29	42
4	25	35	21
. . .			

If you want to see more of the file, the PRINT command can again be used.

5. **Analysing the data**

5.1 *Descriptive statistics*

The MINITAB package will readily provide descriptive statistics, including diagrams. The command HISTOGRAM C2, for example, would provide the following histogram of the scores in the second column of the table:

MIDDLE OF INTERVAL	NUMBER OF OBSERVATIONS	
10	1	*
15	2	**
20	4	****
25	7	*******
30	5	*****
35	10	**********
40	3	***

The commands MEAN and STDEV for individual columns will supply these particular measures of central tendency and dispersion, but a comprehensive set of descriptive statistics for the data in our file can be obtained by using the DESCRIBE command, as follows:

DESCRIBE C1–C3

	C1	C2	C3
N	32	32	32
MEAN	25.03	28.28	23.62
MEDIAN	24.50	28.50	22.00
TMEAN	24.86	28.68	23.04
STDEV	6.25	7.85	8.26
SEMEAN	1.10	1.39	1.46
MAX	42.00	41.00	43.00
MIN	11.00	9.00	12.00
Q3	29.00	34.75	27.50
Q1	21.00	23.25	18.00

In addition to the mean and standard deviation, the median (see p. 27), and standard error of the mean (see p. 98) are supplied, as well as information on minimum and maximum values in the description and the points at which the first (Q1) and third (Q3) quartiles fall. (The one piece of information we have not discussed earlier in the book is the TMEAN. This is a **trimmed mean**, i.e. the mean of the data with the extreme values trimmed off. The MINITAB TMEAN is calculated by excluding the highest 5% and the lowest 5% of the data values. Its use is not recommended.)

5.2 *Correlation*

A scatter diagram for two sets of data you want to correlate can be supplied using the PLOT command. Here we PLOT C1 VS C3 (error gravity scores of native English teachers and native English non-teachers; compare figure

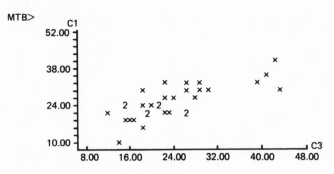

Figure B1. MINITAB plot of C1 vs. C3.

10.1, p. 156). The correlation is provided by the CORR command, and can be used for all possible correlations among our subjects: the command CORR C1–C3 gives the correlation matrix:

	C1	C2
C2	0.321	
C3	0.769	0.000

5.3 *Paired sample t-test*

As a final example, let us see how MINITAB deals with the t-test that we discussed in §11.4. There we were concerned with testing the hypothesis that two groups of teachers (native English teachers and Greek teachers of English) give the same error gravity scores on average, i.e. $H_0: \mu_1 = \mu_2$ against $H_1: \mu_1 \neq \mu_2$. We noted that because judges were addressing the *same* error there was likely to be some correlation between scores awarded by different groups of judges on the *same* error. We were then dealing with 'correlated' samples, and testing the hypothesis was seen to require a paired sample t-test. Within MINITAB this is done as follows: We set up a new column of numbers which corresponds to the differences between C1 and C2 (the $X - Y$ column in table 11.5), as follows:

SUBTRACT C2 FROM C1, PUT DIFFERENCES INTO C4

(The new column, C4, corresponds to the $X - Y$ column in table 11.5; if you want to check, try PRINT C4.)

To test the hypothesis $H_0: \mu_d = 0$ (see p. 185), we proceed as follows:

TTEST MU = 0, FOR DIFFERENCES IN C4

The output we get looks like this:

TEST OF MU = 0 VS MU N.E. 0

	N	MEAN	STDEV	SEMEAN	T	PVALUE
C4	32	−3.25	8.32	1.5	−2.21	0.035

Compare the t-value here with that arrived at in chapter 11.

This is a brief overview of a very few of the capabilities of the MINITAB package, to give you an inkling of what it can do. At the very least it will cut down dramatically on tedious computational time. Also, by doing this it (or a similar package) will enable you eventually to concentrate on interpreting the results of the tests and analyses you apply rather than on the details of their calculation.

Answers to some of the exercises

Chapter 3

(1a) mean = 6.35, median = 6, bimodal with modes at 2 and 7

(1b) mean = 4.13, median = 4, mode = 4

(3) mean = 6.35, standard deviation = 3.32; mean = 4.13, standard deviation = 1.88

(4a) order is: R(1.47), P(1.00), Q(0.33), U(−0.60), T(−1.67), S(−3.25)

(4b) R is class D, T is class F, U is class E

Chapter 5

(3) 0.22, 0.78, 0.64

(4) 0.956, 0.432, 0.954, 0.014

(5) 0.879, 0.758

Chapter 6

(3) standard deviation = 2.035 in both cases

(4) (a) 3.654   (c) 1.0

(5) (a) 0.1587   (b) 0.1587   (c) 0.6915   (d) 0.7734   (e) 0.5328
     (f) 0.1598   (g) 152.9

Chapter 7

(1) (a) 3.74 to 4.52   (b) 3.65 to 4.61

(3a) 0.561 to 0.706 and 0.124 to 0.236

(4) mean = 57.7 and standard deviation = 13.1; confidence interval 28.1 to 87.3.

Chapter 8

(1) t = −1.313

(3) If n = 16 then t = 1.151; if n = 250 then t = 4.548

(4) (i) 33   (ii) 66

Chapter 9

(1) chi-square = 4.62 on 1 df and is significant at 5%, not significant at 1%

(2) chi-square = 3.47 on 2 df and is not significant at 5%

Chapter 10

(2a) cov = 15.8, r = 0.32

(3) $0.05 < p < 0.10$

(4) correlation increases dramatically to r = 0.62

(5) D = 3926 so that rank correlation coefficient = 0.28

Chapter 11

(1) $Z = 1.2427$, cannot reject H_0

(2) paired samples here: t = 2.31 on 31 df, reject H_0 at 5% level

(3) 0.55 to 8.77

(4) $Z = 0.396$, not significant

(5) $F = 1.11$ on (31, 31) df; not significant

(6) $U_1 = 32$ and $U_2 = 11$, hence not significant

REFERENCES

Allen, G. 1985. How the young French child avoids the pre-voicing problem for word-initial voiced stops. *Journal of Child Language*, 12: 37–46.

Baker, W. J. & Derwing, B. 1982. Response coincidence analysis as evidence for language acquisition strategies. *Applied Psycholinguistics* 3: 193–221.

Bellinger, D. 1980. Consistency in the pattern of change in mothers' speech: some discriminant analyses. *Journal of Child Language* 7: 469–87.

Bennett, S. & Bowers, D. 1976. *Multivariate techniques for social and behavioural sciences*. London: Macmillan.

Berko, J. 1958. The child's learning of English morphology. *Word* 14: 150–77.

Brasington, R. 1978. Vowel epenthesis in Rennellese and its general implications. *Work in Progress* 2, Phonetics Laboratory, University of Reading.

Carroll, J. B. 1958. A factor analysis of two foreign language aptitude batteries. *Journal of General Psychology* 59: 3–19.

Clark, H. 1973. The language-as-fixed-effect fallacy: a critique of language statistics in psychological research. *Journal of Verbal Learning and Verbal Behavior* 12: 335–59.

Coxon, A. P. M. 1982. *The user's guide to multidimensional scaling*. London: Heinemann.

Crystal, D., Fletcher, P. & Garman, M. 1976. *The grammatical analysis of language disability: a procedure for assessment and remediation*. London: Edward Arnold.

Cureton, E. E. & D'Agostino, R. B. 1983. *Factor analysis: an applied approach*. London: Lawrence Erlbaum Associates.

Downie, N. M. & Heath, R. W. 1965. *Basic statistical methods*, 2nd edn. New York: Harper & Row.

Eastment, H. T. & Krzanowski, W. J. 1982. Cross-validatory choice of the number of components from a principal components analysis. *Technometrics* 24: 73–7.

Elbert, S. H. 1975. *Dictionary of the language of Rennell and Bellona*. Copenhagen: National Museum of Denmark.

Ferris, M. R. & Politzer, R. L. 1981. Effects of early and delayed second language acquisition: English composition skills of Spanish-speaking junior high school students. *TESOL Quarterly* 15: 253–74.

Fleiss, J. L. 1981. *Statistical methods for rates and proportions*. New York: Wiley.

Fletcher, P. & Peters, J. 1984. Characterising language impairment in children: an exploratory study. *Language Testing* 1: 33–49.

Fry, D. B. 1979. *The physics of speech*. Cambridge: CUP.

Ghiselli, E. E., Campbell, J. P. & Zedeck, S. 1981. *Measurement theory for the behavioural sciences*. Oxford: W. H. Freeman.

Gilbert, G. N. 1984. *Modelling society: an introduction to loglinear analysis for social researchers*. London: George Allen & Unwin.

Glasser, G. J. & Winter, R. F. 1961. Critical values of rank correlation for testing the hypothesis of independence. *Biometrika* 48: 444–8.

Healey, W. C., Ackerman, B. L., Chappell, C. R. Perrin, K. L. & Stormer, J. 1981. *The prevalence of communicative disorders: a review of the literature*. Rockville, Md.: American Speech-Language-Hearing Association.

Hockett, C. 1954. Two models of grammatical description. *Word* 10: 210–31.

Horvath, B. M. 1985. *Variation in Australian English*. Cambridge: CUP.

Hughes, A. 1979. Aspects of a Spanish adult's acquisition of English. *Interlanguage Studies Bulletin* 4: 49–65.

Hughes, A. & Lascaratou, C. 1981. Competing criteria for error gravity. *ELT Journal* 36: 175–82.

Hughes, A. & Woods, A. J. 1982. Unitary competence and Cambridge Proficiency. *Journal of Applied Language Study* 1: 5–15.

Hughes, A. & Woods, A. J. 1983. Interpreting the performance on the Cambridge Proficiency Examination of students of different language backgrounds. In A. Hughes & D. Porter (eds) *Current developments in language testing*. London: Academic Press.

Innes, S. 1974. Developmental aspects of plural formation in English. Unpublished M.Sc. thesis, University of Alberta.

Jolicoeur, P. & Mosimann, J. E. 1960. Size and shape variation in the painted turtle: a principal component analysis. *Growth* 24: 339–54.

Kendall, M. G. 1970. *Rank correlation methods*, 4th edn. London: Griffin.

Khan, F. (forthcoming), Linguistic variation in Indian English: a sociolinguistic study. Unpublished Ph.D. thesis, University of Reading.

Krzanowski, W. J. & Woods, A. J. 1984. Statistical aspects of reliability in language testing. *Language Testing* 1: 1–20.

Labov, W. 1966. *The social stratification of English in New York City*. Washington DC: Center for Applied Linguistics.

Lascaratou, C. 1984. The passive voice in Modern Greek. Unpublished Ph.D. thesis, University of Reading.

Macken, M. & Barton, D. 1980a. The acquisition of the voicing contrast in English: a study of voice onset time in word-initial stop consonants. *Journal of Child Language* 7: 41–74.

Macken, M. & Barton, D. 1980b. The acquisition of the voicing contrast in Spanish: a phonetic and phonological study of word-initial stop consonants. *Journal of Child Language* 7: 433–58.

References

Marriot, F. H. C. 1974. *The interpretation of multiple observations*. New York and London: Academic Press.

Maxwell, A. E. 1977. *Multivariate analysis in behavioural research*. London: Chapman & Hall.

Miller, G. 1951. *Language and communication*. New York: McGraw-Hill.

Miller, G. & Nicely, P. E. 1955. An analysis of perceptual confusion among English consonants. *Journal of Acoustic Society of America* 27: 338–52.

Miller, J. & Chapman, R. 1981. The relation between age and mean length of utterance in morphemes. *Journal of Speech and Hearing Research* 24: 154–61.

Morrison, D. F. 1976. *Multivariate statistical methods*, 2nd edn. New York: McGraw-Hill.

Newport, E., Gleitman, L. & Gleitman, H. 1977. Mother, I'd rather do it myself: some effects and non-effects of maternal speech style. In C. E. Snow & C. A. Ferguson (eds) *Talking to children: language input and acquisition*. Cambridge: CUP.

Overall, J. E. & Klett, C. 1972. *Applied multivariate analysis*. New York: McGraw-Hill.

Quirk Report. 1972. *Speech therapy services*. London: HMSO.

Ryan, B. F., Joiner, B. L. & Ryan, T. A. 1985. *MINITAB student handbook*, 2nd edn. Boston, Mass.: Duxbury Press.

Scherer, G. A. & Wertheimer, M. 1964. *A psychological experiment in further language teaching*. New York: McGraw-Hill.

Shepard, R. N. 1972. Psychological representation of speech sounds. In E. E. David & P. B. Denes (eds) *Human communication: a unified view*. New York: McGraw-Hill.

Shepard, R. N., Romny, A. K. & Nerlove, S. B. (eds) 1972. *Multidimensional scaling: theory and applications in the behavioral sciences*. New York: Seminar Press.

Siegel, S. 1956. *Nonparametric statistics for the behavioral sciences*. New York: McGraw-Hill.

Spearman, C. 1904. The proof and measurement of association between two things. *American Journal of Psychology* 15: 88–103.

Viana, M. 1985. The acquisition of Brazilian Portuguese phonology. Unpublished Ph.D. thesis, University of Reading.

Wells, G. 1985. *Language development in the pre-school years*. Cambridge: CUP.

Wetherill, G. B. 1972. *Elementary statistical methods*. London: Chapman & Hall.

Winer, B. J. 1971. *Statistical principles in experimental design*. New York: McGraw-Hill.

Wishart, D. 1978. *CLUSTAN: user manual*. Program Library Unit, Edinburgh University.

Woods, A. J. 1983. Principal components and factor analysis in the investigation of the structure of language proficiency. In A. Hughes & D. Porter (eds) *Current development in language testing*. London: Academic Press.

INDEX

Allen, 4
alternative hypothesis (H₁), 120ff; *see also* null hypothesis
analysis of variance (ANOVA(R)), 194–223; ANOVA models, 206–15; assumptions for, 195–6; fixed and random effects in, 212–14, 217; for regression analysis, 242–4; multiple comparison of means in, 210–11; one-way, 194–9; split-plot designs in, 221; test score reliability and, 215–19; transforming data in, 220–1; two-way: factorial, 202–6; two-way: randomised blocks, 200–2; 'within-subjects' ANOVA, 221–2
arcsine transformation, 220
audiolingual method, 176ff
average, 3, 29; *see also* mean, median, moving average

Baker, 255ff
bar chart, 11ff
Barton, 4, 5, 50, 58, 178, 188
Bellinger, 271
Bennett, 271, 291
Berko, 255
between-groups variance estimate, 197; *see also* analysis of variance
bias, *see* sampling bias
bilingualism, 61–6, 139–42, 146–7, 149–50, 182
bimodal distribution, 34, 103
BMPD, 307
Bowers, 271–91
Brasington, 58, 142, 143, 144, 145

Cambridge Proficiency Examination (CPE), 16–19, 26–9, 30, 274, 278ff, 284–5
Campbell, 216
Carroll, 291, 292
categorical data, 8–13, 250, 266
central interval, 38–40
Central Limit Theorem, 89, 101, 102, 103, 123, 177
Chapman, 226, 227

chi-squared (χ^2), 132–53; problems and pitfalls of, 144–51; test for goodness of fit, 132–9; test for independence, 139–44; Yate's correction in, 146
Clark, H., 215
class interval, 17
cloze test, 220, 238ff
CLUSTAN, 256
cluster analysis, *see* hierarchical cluster analysis, non-hierarchical clustering
colour words, 250–2
conditional probability, 61–6
confidence interval, 96–8, 101ff; for correlation coefficient, 163–5; for proportions, 184; for regression, 231; for t-ratio, 180, 187
confidence level, 110–11
contingency table, 140, 182
correction factor (CF), 198
correlation, 2, 104, 157–75, 216–19, 287ff; correlation coefficient (r: product–moment), 162–69: confidence interval for, 163–5, comparisons of, 165–7, interpreting, 167–9, significance test for, 163, testing hypotheses about, 162–3, 164; partial correlation, 244–5; rank correlation (rₛ: Spearman's), 169–74: significance test for, 173
correlation matrix, 244, 253, 287
covariance, 155–60, 161, 162, 174, 227, 230; calculation of, 157
covariance matrix, *see* variance–covariance matrix
Coxon, 265
critical value, 126
cross-product, 157
cross-sectional data, 4
Crystal, 267
cumulative frequency, 18
Cureton, 294, 295

D'Agostino, 294, 295
degrees of freedom, 102, 126, 136, 138–9, 141–2

319

Index

linear regression (*contd.*)
  estimating parameters in, 229–30,
  extrapolating from, 237, least squares
  regression line for, 228, testing the
  significance of, 233–4; stepwise
  regression, 243
logarithms, 164, 221, 246
loan words, 142–4
longitudinal data, 4

Macken, 4, 5, 50, 58, 178, 188
Mandarin, 291
Mann–Whitney rank test, 188–9, 306
Marriott, 260
matching coefficient, 252
Maxwell, 291
MDS(X), 265
mean, 2, 29–37, 311; differences between
  two means: independent samples,
  176–81, paired samples, 184–7; multiple
  comparisons among, 210–11; standard
  error of, 97n, 98
mean length of utterance (mlu) and average
  mlu (MLU), 106–7, 227–33
median (score), 19, 27–9, 30–4
Miller, G., 113, 264
Miller, J., 226, 227
MINITAB, 41, 236, 240, 243, 307, 309–13
mode, 33
models, *see* statistical models
Morrison, 275ff, 289
Mosimann, 275, 277
moving average, 22
multidimensional scaling, 262–5
multiple regression, 237–45, 268–93
multivariate analysis, 249–52, 273ff

nasality, 264
Nerlove, 265
Newport, 58
Nicely, 264
non-hierarchical clustering, 261
nonparametric tests, 188–90
normal curve, 87, 88; *see also* normal
  distribution
normal distribution, 86–93; testing fit of to
  data, 132–9
normal probability paper, 236
noun phrase, 147–9
null hypothesis (H$_o$), 120ff; *see also*
  alternative hypothesis
numerical data, 13ff, 250

one-tailed (vs. two-tailed) test, 122ff
oral fluency ability, 169, 176
outliers, 169
Overall, 271
overlapping samples, 21–2

paired samples, 184–7
partial correlation, 244–5
Pascal, 79
passive, 152
past tense, 99–101
Pearson, K., 161, 172, 173, 230
Pearson product–moment correlation
  coefficient, *see* correlation
percentages, 34–7, 150–1, 220
percentile score, 18
Peters, 50, 57, 101, 266
phonology/phonological, 19–20, 142–4; *see
  also* voicing
plural morpheme inflection, 148–9, 255ff
point estimators, 95ff
Politzer, 58, 139, 146, 149, 182
pooled variance estimate, 196
populations, 49ff
power of tests, 191–2
present perfect, 104–5
principal components analysis (PCA), 265,
  275–90; interpreting principal
  components, 284–6; compared with factor
  analysis, 292
probability, 59–75; conditional, 61–6;
  distribution, 67, 84
proficiency tests, 194ff, 238ff
pronoun, 182; agreement, 146–7
proportions, 9, 34, 182, 220; comparing two
  proportions, 182–4; confidence interval
  for, 184; estimating, 99–101; means of,
  34–7

Quirk, 23

random effect model in ANOVA, 212–15,
  217
random error, 79–84; *see also* residual
randomised block design, 202
randomness, 86–7
random number tables, 73–5
random sampling, 52, 54, 72–5
random variable: continuous, 68–72;
  discrete, 66–8
random variation, 86–93
range, 16
rank correlation, *see* correlation
rank order, 170
reaction time, 68–72
regression analysis, *see* linear regression
relative cumulative frequency curve, 18
relative frequencies, 9ff
reliability, 215–19; coefficient of, 216
Rennellese, 142–4
residual, 84ff, 229ff; *see also* error
response coincidence matrix, 256–7
Reynell Developmental Language Scales,
  101

321

Made in the USA
Lexington, KY
07 October 2011